THE TWO CHURCHES

THE TWO CHURCHES

CATHOLICISM & CAPITALISM IN THE WORLD-SYSTEM

Michael L. Budde

DUKE UNIVERSITY PRESS   *Durham and London 1992*

© 1992 Duke University Press
All rights reserved
Printed in the United States of America
on acid-free paper ∞
Library of Congress Cataloging-in-
Publication Data appear on the last
printed page of this book.
Grant support for the
index was provided by
the Humanities Development
Fund at Auburn University.

CONTENTS

ACKNOWLEDGMENTS

Many people gave generously of their time and talents in making this project better than it would have been without them.

Every author should have an editor as good as Lawrence Malley at Duke University Press. His patience, knowledge of the publishing business, and willingness to answer a seemingly endless number of questions all earn him high marks. My journey through the publishing maze was made easier by Larry's sense of perspective and humor, acquired no doubt from years of following the hapless Chicago Cubs and Boston Red Sox.

Also at Duke University Press, Bob Mirandon provided first-rate copyediting and suggestions for improvements. To the anonymous reviewers whose careful evaluations and criticisms challenged me at many points, my debts are many. The many production people at Duke with whom I interacted were unfailingly helpful and efficient.

Among my colleagues, Eric Hanson of the University of Santa Clara provided help above and beyond the call of friendship, much less duty. I owe thanks to Lee Anderson at Northwestern University, who saw the potential in this project before I did and encouraged me to pursue it. Manuscript preparation would have been impossible without the timely technical assistance of John Rogers at the University of Chicago and John Morris at Auburn University.

To my wife Terri Anderson, no expression of gratitude would be sufficient. To my children, Rachel and Sean, thanks for enough sleep—barely—to finish this book. I dedicate this book to my parents, Richard and Marilyn Budde, and my grandmother, Dorothy Meyers.

THE TWO CHURCHES

1

ROMAN CATHOLICISM IN
THE WORLD-SYSTEM

When it finally fell, the Berlin Wall took more than state socialism with it. It also pulled down old certainties about the world, its resistance to change, and its unbridgeable divisions. No sooner had old verities crumbled, however, than new ones rushed to fill the gaps.

These new verities proclaim the final triumph of freedom, the victory of the West, the vindication of capitalism worldwide as the liberator of captives and uplift of the downtrodden. We may not have arrived at the "end of history" (Fukuyama, 1990), but the new wisdom suggests that serious conflicts over political-economic systems seem unlikely in the future. A Nobel laureate economist asserts that "it is now almost universally acknowledged that a private-ownership, free-enterprise economy 'works better' than . . . [a] socialized economy, in which decisions are made by state or cooperative agencies" (Buchanan, 1990).

But even before the bubbles had left the victory champagne, signs of a more ominous reality began to return. Triumphant capitalism, a mighty world edifice, remains built on unstable foundations: on high infant mortality rates in Bolivia, on squatter settlements outside Mexico City, on worldwide debt levels unknown in prior history. Amid the huzzahs for capitalism victorious, there may yet be heard—in the hinterlands, away from the feast—both the rumblings of discontent and an odd silence, acclaim withheld by those to whom capitalism has provided not bread, but stones.

Among the institutions cheering the downfall of communism, surely few cheer more loudly than the Roman Catholic Church. The implacable foe of the Red menace since the latter's inception, the Church kept a steady drumbeat of opposition to communism—on behalf of Catholics in the "captive nations" of Eastern Europe (see Ramet, 1989), in support of the freedoms of liberal democracies, and to preserve its freedom of action worldwide.

But as the world has changed dramatically in recent decades, so has the Catholic Church as an actor within it. In ways unforeseeable a generation ago, developments in world capitalism have provided new challenges and controversies for world Catholicism. In turn, the future of the capitalist world economy may depend, at least in part, on developments within the Catholic Church.

Why should a political economist be concerned with developments within the Catholic Church? The ordinary stuff of political economy— land tenure and labor markets, international trade and tariffs, invest- ment and public policy—seems remote from the world of incense and stained glass, saints and sacraments, popes and prayer. Such a distance, I contend, is more real at the level of academic disciplines—where moats of jargon, theory, and scholarly journals mark the divides—than at the level of lived experience. Real life, fortunately, proceeds in ignorance of scholarly turf and subdisciplines.

A variety of commentators have observed that capitalism, for its on- going reproduction, requires a variety of cultural inputs that it cannot create (see Bell, 1976; Luke, 1989). Religion has long been one such cul- tural system, legitimating capitalist relations of production in diverse times and places. But if such legitimation is instrumental in stabiliz- ing capitalism, the providing of such legitimation cannot be assumed. Those cultural systems built on non- or precapitalist foundations—as are all the major world religions, including Christianity—also have been tapped by groups seeking to delegitimize capitalism in different times and places. So long as religious phenomena retain at least some spark of independence from their surrounding milieus, their capitalist allegiance must be won anew rather than assumed as an eternal constant. What dynamic religious groups legitimize, they can also—under certain cir- cumstances—delegitimize (e.g., Kowalewski and Greil, 1990; Billings, 1990; Gamoran, 1990).

However important in theory religious actors and phenomena are to capitalism (many contemporary scholars suggest, alas, that they are not very important), state actors in their practice attest to the significance of the relationship. Regardless of their legal/constitutional formulations, states in capitalist countries expend significant resources seeking to in- fluence, direct, or inhibit religious activity in ways conducive to state objectives, among which the perpetuation of capitalism ranks at or near the top. While states prefer religious groups to bless and not damn capitalism, most will settle for indifference instead of a considered opinion either way. Tools that include persuasion, legal prosecution, infiltration, subversion, and even assassination have been employed by states in their quest to influence the orientations of religious communities in their midst.

After assessing the complex interactions of economics and religion with reference to the Catholic Church, my main conclusions are these:

(1) The workings of the capitalist world economy and changes within the Catholic Church make it plausible to argue that world Catholicism (led by the Latin American and other Third World churches) will continue to develop in anticapitalist directions.

(2) The churches in core countries (typified by the U.S. Catholic Church) are poorly placed to respond in ecclesial solidarity to the anticapitalist critiques and challenges of their Third World coreligionists, who now compose the majority of members worldwide in the Catholic Church.

FRAMING THIS STUDY

In this book I attempt to apply the insights of world-systems theory (WST) to the study of the Catholic Church. While others have attempted to approach Catholicism within a systems-oriented perspective (notably Vallier, 1970), to my knowledge no one has situated the Catholic Church as an actor within the WST framework explicated by scholars such as Immanuel Wallerstein, Christopher Chase-Dunn, and Albert Bergeson.

The desirability of such an effort reflects two interrelated notions: (1) WST provides important theoretical resources helpful in understanding the changing social environments confronting the universal Church and local churches; and (2) a focus on Catholicism as a transnational cultural and social actor can point toward areas in WST that deserve further development.

Of necessity, an analysis that strives to integrate political economy with religious/theological studies must attempt to cover a broad expanse of literature and research. Fashioning a coherent, consistent, and reasonably compelling explanation of evolving and complex phenomena remains the goal of such transdisciplinary wanderings (Simon, 1982; Wilber and Jameson, 1983) rather than producing some positivistic core of falsifiable or quantifiable generalizations. I am presenting an attempt at explanatory and theoretical development, not original empirical research.

The literature on WST has grown rapidly since 1974. Some of the initial enthusiasm for the framework has faded, replaced by more tempered support (Denemark and Thomas, 1988). Critics have attacked WST both in its particulars and fundamentals (Brenner, 1977; Skocpol, 1977); while I find the fundamentals of WST useful in understanding the world economy, my main disagreements will become apparent (particularly in WST's treatment of cultural phenomena).

The central tenet of WST is the existence of a single world economy, capitalist in nature, originating in the sixteenth century and by the current age encompassing all areas of the world. To Wallerstein, the leader of the WST movement, an "economy" exists when (and only when) "there is an ongoing, extensive and relatively complete social division of labor with an integrated set of production processes which relate to each other through a 'market' which has been 'instituted' or 'created' in some complex way . . ." (Wallerstein, 1984, p. 13).

The structural characteristics of this worldwide division of labor are a concentration of high-productivity, high-wage tasks in a few regions (the *core*), concentration of low-productivity, low-wage tasks in a majority of regions (the *periphery*), and a stratum of midrange regions with both core and periphery characteristics (the *semiperiphery*). This division of labor, significantly, ranges beyond the control of any single political authority. A fragmented system of states exists within the world economy, performing important functions for economic actors in that economy but unable to dominate or control its operations (Wallerstein, 1979, p. 20).

This by now familiar sketch of WST explains the prosperity of some regions (the core) and the immiserization of others (the periphery) as outcomes of the same processes; while purely domestic factors play a role in a region's economic fortunes, WST finds the primary explanatory variables at the level of the system itself, which shapes and situates domestic or national-level factors. WST sees itself as a framework superior in explanatory power to state-centered levels of analysis (and analyses between and among nations), which it regards as reductive (Wallerstein, 1979).

Studies of the Catholic Church up to 1992 have not reflected the WST paradigm. Most of the best recent studies of Catholicism, while attentive to international factors, have been nation-based works (e.g., Mainwaring, 1986; Bruneau, 1982). Most recent studies of the Vatican, the symbolic and administrative center of Catholicism, have been superficial (e.g., Packard, 1985; Wynn, 1988); Hebblethwaite's and Granfield's books and articles remain bright spots in an otherwise dim picture (Hebblethwaite, 1986a, 1986b, 1988a; Granfield, 1987, 1988). And while Hanson's 1987 book on world Catholicism remains the best contemporary work (one important to this study), it primarily concentrates on matters other than specifically political economy concerns.

A competent study of the Catholic Church is further complicated by the nature of religious organizations generally and the Church in particular. The Catholic Church is a large, bureaucratic, administratively complex institution—and much more. To understand it solely in terms that apply to other complex organizations—like states and corporations, for example—is to misperceive what makes religious groups so difficult to study, in particular their self-understanding, their points of ultimate reference, and their specific ideological developments (in the form of various theological traditions). Purely extrinsic studies of religious phenomena (Wiebe, 1985) fail to grasp the distinctively religious qualities they contain and invariably misunderstand the actors, motivations, and ideologies involved. Such failures, evident also in Wallerstein's limited treatment of religion in WST, are all too common.

A more detailed discussion of how WST has understood matters religious is offered in chapter 2. That chapter also reviews some theoretical literature relevant to issues considered here and more extensively considers previously unexplored relationships that hold promise in interrelating political economy and Catholicism more precisely. Before considering such matters, however, we should look at real-world changes in the world economy and in the Catholic Church.

TWENTIETH-CENTURY CHANGES IN THE CHURCH AND THE WORLD

RISE AND DECLINE OF U.S. HEGEMONY SINCE 1945

The United States emerged from World War II with a world economic and political superiority that had few historical precedents. So dominant was this position from 1945 through 1967 that the United States enjoyed a *hegemonic* position in world affairs, understood in the sense offered by Wallerstein:

> When providers located in a given state can undersell producers located in other core states in the latter's "home market," they can transform this productive advantage over time into one in the commercial arena and then into one in the financial arena. The combined advantages may be said to constitute hegemony and are reflected as well in a political-military advantage in the interstate system. (1984, p. 17)

Domestically, the United States enjoyed an era of unprecedented economic prosperity marked by increasing real wage levels and productivity, low unemployment and inflation, and comfortable levels of economic growth. This boom was fueled in no small part by the increasing involvement of U.S. multinational corporations (MNCs) in profitable overseas investment and production. While most of that investment went to Europe and other core areas, it also grew in the peripheral region of Latin America from $400 million in 1945 to $9 billion by 1976 (Evans, 1979, p. 25). Prosperity allowed for years of labor peace, with the 1947 GM-UAW pact inaugurating an era of business-labor cooperation focusing on expanding the pie enjoyed by both. The social strategy of the New Deal—a prosperous business climate with at least the rudiments of a welfare state—worked smoothly, greased as it was by comfortable levels of economic growth.

The U.S. boom lasted for more than two decades before it began to unravel. Wars of national liberation and civil wars throughout the Third World started to threaten U.S. political and military prerogatives. The economies of Western Europe and Japan, which provided profitable and secure havens for U.S. investments and exports after the war, began challenging the U.S. hegemonic position in trade and production. The Johnson administration's decision to finance the Vietnam War without tax increases (Wolfe, 1981, pp. 127–29) helped to inflate the U.S. economy with negative consequences.

By 1973, when the OPEC oil embargo signaled a long-term change in world economic and political relations, the United States had already backed down from its hegemonic perch. The U.S. abandoned the gold standard and important aspects of the Bretton Woods arrangements (in 1971) that had structured much of the postwar prosperity. With hegemony no longer a profitable position, the United States searched throughout the 1970s and 1980s for its place in a posthegemonic arrangement in which it would still enjoy considerable (if not determinative) influence.

Within the United States, life after hegemony has been traumatic for many. With lower levels of economic growth, business interests abandoned their cooperative arrangements with the labor movement, launching a multileveled assault on working-class wage and benefit levels. Unemployment, inflation, a severe recession, and a declining middle-class standard of living characterized these changed conditions. In many ways Americans seemed to "have spent the past thirty years getting used to the benefits of a hegemonic position, and will have to spend the next thirty years getting used to life without them" (Wallerstein, 1984, p. 68).

BOOM AND BUST IN THE PERIPHERY

If the United States enjoyed the benefits of hegemonic power through an important part of the twentieth century, the vagaries of the world economy treated most Third World regions less kindly. Many peripheral areas began the century developing or expanding export economies concentrated on one or two products, leaving the regions vulnerable to cyclical world-economic fluctuations over which they had no control. The Depression collapse of world commodity markets fell hardest on such primary product exporters, some of which responded by starting up import-substitution industrialization. In Brazil, for example, where the Depression killed the coffee-exporting part of the economy, the number of workers employed in industry nearly tripled between 1920 and 1940 (Adriance, 1986, pp. 9–10).

The regions in which some domestic industry had developed by 1945, or those regions that managed some political control over a strategic resource (for example, oil), were in a position to reap more benefits from the postwar economic expansion than were those more completely dependent on foreign centers for their economic dynamism. But in both peripheral and semiperipheral regions, broad similarities in patterns were evident: high levels of GNP growth, increasing levels of inequality, growing involvement with core-based MNCs, and chronic political instabilities and the threat of core political/military intervention. Certain sectors of the local elite in such regions prospered, along with a thinly based labor aristocracy; other beneficiaries included the military and state bureaucracy. According to Illich (1977, p. 69):

> In most Third World countries . . . income, consumption, and the well-being of the middle class are all growing, while the gap between this class and the mass of people widens. Even where per capita consumption is rising[,] the majority [of people] have less food now than in 1945, less actual care in sickness, less meaningful work, less protection. This is partly a consequence of polarized consumption and partly caused by the breakdown of the traditional family and consumption. More people suffer from hunger, pain and exposure in 1969 than did at the end of World War II, not only numerically, but as a percentage of the world population.

Third World regions incorporated into the world economy, designed to transfer surplus to core regions, increasingly came to be described as "dependent." Dependency theory, a still-evolving body of theoretical and empirical literature, began reshaping the picture of the world experienced by some scholars, activists, and politicians. As defined by Caporaso and Zare (1981, p. 46):

> Dependency is a structural condition in which capitalist accumulation does not complete its cycle domestically but relies instead on external factors for its completion. . . . As the local economy opens itself up to the international system, these external factors operate in conjunction with internal (domestic) forces to produce distortions in the domestic system. These distortions (for example, internal inequality, either across economic sectors, between urban and rural areas, and across classes; authoritarian forms of government) are clearly not the product of either external or internal factors, but of both types of factors working together.

While explanations of dependency theory have been attacked from various quarters, they have drawn attention to the ways in which prosperity in core regions has come at the cost of immiserization in peripheral regions. Third World regions, in this perspective, are not undeveloped (waiting to imitate the development paths of core actors), but rather are underdeveloped, distorted, and damaged by their involvements in the world economy (Frank, 1968).

The contradictory paths of economic development in many Third World countries, initiated or exacerbated by the workings of the world economy, proved to be too much for liberal political regimes to contain. In Latin America, for example, a wave of military takeovers, beginning with the overthrow of Arbenz in Guatemala in 1954, touched nearly every country in the region as domestic problems and unrest increasingly threatened established interests.

All of which reflected, within the limits of dependent economic relations,

> the inability of moderate political elites to maintain stability without redistributive and welfare programmes to pacify the poor, and their consequent inability to sustain growth via reinvestment if adequate programmes of this sort [were] established. There is not enough capital to go around. In these circumstances, attempts at compromise tend to satisfy neither end of the political spectrum. As a result, discontent, instability and economic chaos emerge, creating a context that invites a take-over by those social forces (the military and its allies) willing and able to impose "discipline" upon the polity. (Falk, 1984, p. 451)

Increasingly, authoritarian political arrangements have come to be a predictable outcome of Third World marginalization. Despite the failure of authoritarian regimes to resolve the contradictions of the unequal world division of labor (for example, in Peru, Brazil, Chile, the Philippines), military and other authoritarian·strategies are unlikely to disappear in the foreseeable future.

The depth of Third World dependency increased during the 1970s and early 1980s as core financial institutions promoted hitherto unimaginable levels of loan capital to Third World borrowers—part of the petrodollar recycling that led to the "debt crisis" discussed regularly in news reports of recent years. While the benefits of the borrowing were distributed most unevenly because of military expenditures, pork barrel projects, elite consumption, and theft in various forms, the brunt of IMF-enforced "readjustment" plans has fallen on popular sectors in debtor countries, further depressing living standards and increasing discontent. Authoritarian regimes or methods remain necessary in many places to enforce the terms of IMF austerity and contain the civil unrest. Venezuela is only one among many countries to experience "IMF riots," in which hundreds of people were killed by government troops and police. Debt constitutes yet another way in which core regions have siphoned resources—in this case, capital—out of peripheral and semiperipheral regions. More has been paid to core creditors in the form of interest than was borrowed in principal (Dietz, 1989, p. 14).

While core countries have struggled to reach a new accommodation in the posthegemony era, peripheral countries have seen their problems multiply, their options diminish, and the majority of their people suffer even more. This century's boom phases, such as they have been, have been fleeting and narrowly received; the bust times, in contrast, have grown more severe and expansive.

WORLDWIDE CHANGES IN CATHOLICISM

The single most important change now well under way within world Catholicism is its transition from a First World to a Third World entity. The enormity of this transition needs to be underscored; exploring its implications constitutes the substantive focus of this study.

Few institutions have been as closely tied to the European experience as the Roman Catholic Church. From Roman catacombs to imperial favor, as political authority and cultural curator, and as peacemaker and fractious dissolute, the Church has been entwined with the history of the continent and its peoples. As the world economy expanded from Europe, so did the Church. With Ricci to China and Marquette to North America, with imperial powers to Latin America and black Africa, no matter where it arrived, the Church retained much of its European flavor. Wherever it planted seeds, and with whatever modest accommodations to local mores and cultures, it was ever a Roman, European church, catholic (universal) in ideal but undeniably provincial in content.

But the unity between Europe and the Church experienced a series of crises that shook the bases of authority and faith. The Reformation and its aftermath, the Enlightenment and its restless children, capitalism and the Industrial Revolution, all broke the connection between European culture and the Catholic Church. The Church's seeds planted in non-European soil, meanwhile, grew and sometimes thrived in ways unforeseen by their sowers.

The Catholic Church today finds itself in a transition like few in its history. Some, including the eminent theologian Karl Rahner, have called it the movement into the Church's "third age." This third age, that of a truly worldwide religious movement—in fact as well as in theory—succeeds the second age of European Catholicism. The present transition, to Rahner, is comparable in importance only to the original movement of Christianity from a marginal offshoot of Judaism (the short-lived first age) to a Gentile, European religious culture (Rahner, 1979).

Numerically, the shift has become apparent only in the second half of the twentieth century. At the turn of the century 70 percent of the world's Catholics lived in Europe and North America; by the year 2000, 70 percent will live in the poor countries of the south (Buhlmann, 1986, p. 94).

The figures in table 1, which reflect total numbers of baptized Catholics who have not formally repudiated their baptism, are not without problems; nevertheless, the same counting norms are applied by the Church worldwide and provide adequate evidence of aggregate trends. With this in mind, the direction of change is clear. By 1987 Latin America was home to 41 percent of the world's Catholics, Europe to 29 percent, and North America to 10 percent. Africa in 1987 had more Catholics than the United States, even though millions of Catholic immigrants came to the United States during the nineteenth and twentieth centuries. The growth among Third World Catholics is caused in large measure by population increases in Latin America and by population increases and rising numbers of converts in Africa, Asia, and Oceania (Buhlmann, 1986, p. 118). Further, while the populations of Europe and North America are increasing in average age, Catholicism's greatest

Table 1   Shifts in World Catholicism

Catholics (millions)	1960	1970	1980	1987
Europe	220	259	272	259
North America	47	55	61	88
North Total	267	314	333	347
Latin America	192	245	324	367
Africa	23	40	59	99
Asia	33	50	63	82
Oceania	3	4	6	7
South Total	251	339	452	555
Percentages				
North	52	48	42	38
South	48	52	58	62

Source: Buhlmann (1986), p. 119.

Table 2   African and Asian Bishops

Year	African Bishops	Asian Bishops
1951	2	31
1961	38	75
1971	133	126
1981	293	408

Source: Buhlmann (1986), p. 123.

growth is in the Third World, where 42 percent of the population is under fifteen years old (Buhlmann, 1986, pp. 4–5).

The Church's institutional leadership, slower to reflect the changes in its base, has nonetheless begun restructuring itself to mirror the new realities. Bishops are the institutional leaders of the church. The highest episcopal level, the cardinalate, has an electoral college of 120 members (a limit set by Pope Paul VI) that chooses the pope (Suro, 1988, p. 1). Until about 1950 the episcopal and cardinalate levels were overwhelmingly European, with Italians staggeringly overrepresented. The first Indian bishop was not appointed until 1923, the first modern Chinese bishop in 1926, the first Japanese bishop in 1927, and the first indigenous African in 1939 (Buhlmann, 1986, pp. 122–23). Since 1950, however, the growth in the number of Third World bishops has been dramatic.

Leadership of the more than 2,400 dioceses worldwide has gradually reflected the shifts in the base of world Catholicism. Slower to shift, however, has been the electoral group within the College of Cardinals, where in 1988 Europeans maintained membership (54 percent) disproportionate to their numbers, and Third World regions were underrepresented (15 percent from Latin America, for example). Appointments by Pope John Paul II returned the electoral group within the cardinalate to its full 120 members without significantly altering its international composition (Suro, 1988, p. 1).

The demographic shifts discussed above, and the corresponding changes in the nationalities of bishops, only suggest the possibility of significant shifts in the Church's direction. More than any other single factor, the Second Vatican Council (1962–65) was instrumental in transforming those possibilities into actual changes and realignments.

Convoked by Pope John XXIII, Vatican II has become identified with that pope's desire to bring *aggiornamento* ("updating") to the Church. A worldwide gathering of the world's bishops, prelates, leading theologians, and observers, Vatican II sought to reinterpret the Church— its self-perceptions, its mission, and its methods—in the modern age, the same rapprochement with "modernity" so vehemently rejected by Leo XIII in the encyclical *Testem Benevolentiae* in 1899. Meeting in four major sessions, Vatican II issued major documents on almost all facets of the Church: the liturgy (introducing the vernacular mass), religious freedom, the nature and mission of the Church, the clergy, relations with non-Catholic Christians and with non-Christian religions, and more. Throughout, the council documents reflect an openness to the world, a willingness to learn from the secular realm without compromising the fundamentals of faith, and an awareness that the Church itself must adapt to a world radically different from the European one in which it grew.

As the Church at all levels struggled to appropriate the new directions mandated by Vatican II, several of the dynamics it inspired proved especially important for shaping the emerging third age of the Church. The council's ecclesiological focus (its "theory of the church") shifted from a fundamentally hierarchical, clerical picture to a more lay-oriented "People of God" image, and was a significant development. The council's embrace of the material world and history as the arena in which religious duties and the Church's mission manifest themselves vindicated and further encouraged the Church's temporal works of mercy and justice. The council's renewed appreciation of the importance of local (diocesan, regional, and national) churches encouraged greater diversity and innovation among clergy and laity.

CHANGES IN THE PERIPHERY/SEMIPERIPHERY:
LATIN AMERICA AS ARCHETYPE

This study focuses on the Latin American Church—both as a set of national churches and as a larger cultural unit—as archetypal of peripheral/semiperipheral Catholicism in matters of political economy and ecclesiology. The Latin American Church is an appropriate case for several reasons. Its numerical weight in world Catholicism gives it an obvious and growing importance. This strength of numbers is complemented by scores of talented and respected episcopal leaders, whose influence on world affairs is increasing.

Pastoral innovation has been a strong point of the Latin American Church in recent decades, with the base Christian Community (BCC, or CEB for *communidades ecclesial de base*) movement only the most notable and imitated example. The CEBs, the theology of liberation, and a more inductivist approach to theology have been adopted by peripheral churches throughout the Third World. On matters of economic/theological analysis and ecclesiology, the Latin American Church continues to provide leadership and experiences for other poor churches (Wan-Tateh, 1984; Pieris, 1988).

That other peripheral churches should learn from the Latin Americans, while also producing their own innovations and insights, is not surprising. With Latin America more thoroughly proletarianized and penetrated by the world economy, the Latin American Church's reflections on capitalism and pastoral practice provide useful insights for African, Asian, and other Church people whose intensive interactions with capitalism are more recent (Budde, 1987; Friesen, 1988).

By the late 1950s Church leaders in Latin America had grown concerned about the "incomplete evangelization" of the majority of the region's peoples. The methods of the early missionaries, compromised by their complicity with imperial authorities and their elitist prejudices, failed to implant a deep or profound sense of the faith within the poor. Instead, all too often Christian sacramentals and various devotions (for example, to patron saints) were merely grafted onto pre-Columbian belief systems.

What brought the superficiality of earlier evangelization to the fore was the perceived threat to the Catholic Church from Protestant missionaries. Bible-believing Protestants and Pentecostals, especially from North America, began making noticeable inroads among the urban and rural poor, threatening to undermine the hierarchy's dominant position in religious and cultural affairs. While the majority of people continued to identify with the Catholic Church, the region's bishops became concerned enough to attempt to shore up their social position, especially among the marginal classes.

One attempt to "re-evangelize" the region took the form of a "movement to the people" on the part of thousands of priests, nuns, and religious. Inspired in part by the worker-priest movement of 1940s France, these clergy left pastoral work among the upper classes (especially in schools) to live and work among the poor. Many of these Church workers were "converted" to the side of the poor as a result of their new pastoral and living situations (see Adriance, 1986).

While many among the indigenous clergy were being evangelized by the people (to paraphrase Gutierrez), the region as a whole was experiencing a severe shortage of ordained clergy. The Latin American bishops' requests for help were heard by Pope John XXIII, who in 1961 asked U.S. religious superiors to commit 10 percent of their personnel to Latin American mission activities. By 1968, the peak year, the U.S. Church had 3,391 missioners in Latin America, 2,000 more than were there in 1960 (Costello, 1979, p. 210).

While many of these missioners returned home dismayed over their failure to implement a brick-and-mortar U.S. church model in Latin America, many underwent a conversion similar in impact to that experienced by Latin American religious leaders who had been exposed to the ravages of mass poverty. Many of these missionaries would be important in generating support from U.S. bishops for the new directions the Church in Latin America began exploring later in the decade (Costello, 1979, pp. 267–70).

Still another significant influence on the Church was the wave of authoritarian repression initiated by the 1954 coup in Guatemala and the 1964 overthrow of Goulart in Brazil. As regimes in the region moved with vigor against "internal subversives," the Church found itself in the unusual position of opposing the military. The military's policies focused repression on virtually all popular sectors of society—unions, opposition parties, universities, the independent press, peasant organizations—precisely those groups with whom the Church's pastoral agents had become involved. The tortures, disappearances, arrests, and killings of people active in the popular sectors also affected unprecedented numbers of church personnel. Rather than intimidating Church leaders, the military's repression solidified the Church's commitment (even among most of the hierarchy) to the poor and enhanced the Church's image as an ally and advocate of the poor (Adriance, 1986, p. 31; Lernoux, 1989,

p. 129). Indeed, it was the military's murder of a priest working with poor peasants that sparked Oscar Romero's conversion from a timid episcopal conservative to San Salvador's champion of the poor. By the mid-1970s the Church seemed to have changed sides from the elites to the poor majorities in most Latin American countries.

At the episcopal level two regional meetings stand as reference points for the Latin American Church and its changing allegiances. The 1968 meeting of the Latin American Bishops Conference (CELAM) in Medellin, Colombia, was an early ratification and impetus for the "theology of liberation" being developed by grass-roots pastoral agents in the region. The final document of Medellin, in reflecting on the Latin American situation, decried the international economic system as a "sinful situation," an example of "institutional violence." It called on all within the Church to build a just social order that defends the poor and oppressed (O'Brien and Shannon, 1977, pp. 567, 565, 569).

By 1979, when CELAM met in Puebla, Mexico, several new factors had entered the equation: years of authoritarian rule across the region, a conservative counterattack within the Church itself, and the installation of a strong, centralizing pope. While most analysts expected Puebla to be a retreat from the radical analysis and progressive commitments framed by Medellin and afterward, in fact the core of the progressive movement withstood reaction.

> We see the growing gap between rich and poor as a scandal and a contradiction to Christian existence. The luxury of the few becomes an insult to the wretched poverty of the vast masses. . . . In this anxiety and sorrow the Church sees a situation of social sinfulness, all the more serious because it exists in countries that call themselves Catholic and are capable of changing the situation. . . .
>
> This poverty is not a passing phase. Instead it is the product of economic, social, and political situations and miseries, though there are also other causes for our state of misery. In many instances this state of poverty within our countries finds its origin and support in mechanisms which, because they are impregnated with materialism rather than any authentic humanism, create a situation on the international level where the rich get richer at the expense of the poor, who get even poorer. Hence this reality calls for personal conversion and profound structural changes that will meet the legitimate aspirations of the people for authentic social justice. (Final Document, 1979 nos. 28, 30)

CATHOLICISM IN CORE REGIONS: THE U.S. CHURCH AS ARCHETYPE

If numbers, leadership, and experience justify a focus on Latin American Catholicism as archetypal for peripheral/semiperipheral Catholicism, the same factors justify focusing on the U.S. Church among core churches. Despite several signs of internal weakness, the U.S. Catholic Church possesses wealth, a large membership, and increasingly influential episcopal leadership. On many measures it is clearly stronger than the Catholic churches in most European countries (see, for example, S. Berger, 1987; Lernoux, 1989). Like the Latin Americans, the U.S. Church is a leader in matters of political and economic theology and analysis, its pastoral letters on military and economic policy inducing other core churches to pursue similar projects.

Much of the strength of the U.S. Catholic Church in world Catholicism is a by-product of the role played by the United States in the world system. As the largest religious group in the single most powerful core country, the U.S. Church enjoys significant influence in the Vatican and with its sister churches in the core (see Fogarty, 1985). With religious interests, at least superficially, more politically salient in the United States than in most other core countries, the strength and potential influence of the U.S. Church is greater than it would be in the more thoroughly secularized cultural settings faced by other core churches.

The U.S. Catholic Church in many ways enters the 1990s as the strongest and most dynamic of First World churches. It was not always so. From the colonizing of the continent until Vatican II, the U.S. Church was seen as a backwoods cousin by its European elders, its theological and cultural attainments viewed as pedestrian and of little consequence in the worldwide Church's affairs. Waves of poor and working-class Catholic immigrants kept the U.S. church preoccupied with internal matters and nearly overwhelmed by the task of protecting the newcomers materially and spiritually from the depredations of an overwhelmingly Protestant culture. For generations the economic and social status of Catholics compared poorly with that of Protestants and Jews.

But compared with the Europeans, the U.S. Catholic Church had numbers in its favor. (Unlike the Europeans' experience, the U.S. Church never lost the industrial working class because of antilabor positions.) Practical leaders like James Cardinal Gibbons blocked conservative attempts to have the Knights of Labor and other union movements declared off-limits to Catholics (Dolan, 1985, pp. 329–38). While the U.S. Church arguably mishandled its relations with organized labor on many fronts (for example, constructing "religious," anticommunist unions like the Association of Catholic Trade Unionists in the 1930s), it did not present working-class Catholics (the majority before World War II) with an either-or choice between their faith and their class interests.

The postwar economic boom, a consequence of the U.S. hegemonic position in the world economy, benefited Catholics even more than society as a whole. The prosperity reaped by unionized white Americans worked to raise the income and educational and social levels of U.S. Catholics beyond mere parity with non-Catholic citizens. By the 1980s U.S. Catholics, previously far behind most white Protestant and Jewish groups in measures of material welfare and social influence, had become as prosperous and powerful as even elite Protestant denominations and Jews (see Roof and McKinney, 1987, pp. 15–16). The working-class Church had become overwhelmingly middle class as U.S. hegemony crested and began to wane (see Coleman, 1988).

There still remains, to be sure, a working-class and poor presence within U.S. Catholicism, most especially in its Hispanic and Asian populations. Many of these people are new immigrants, largely products of political or economic dislocations in peripheral regions, that remind the U.S. Church of its underclass origins and multinational character. They are unlikely, however, to change the dominant middle-class ethos and worldview of the U.S. Church. While the reasons for this are many, two factors loom larger than others: the lack of indigenous clergy accompanying the migrants (akin to the Italians), and the entrenched nature of the receiving religious community (earlier waves of working-class immigrants entered a working-class church, not a middle-class one).

As the once-dominant Protestant worldview continues its decline, the U.S. Catholic Church has continued to grow in numbers and influence. Beginning in the mid-1960s, mainstream Protestant denominations—Episcopalian, Presbyterian, United Church of Christ, among others—underwent significant decreases in numbers and support (Roof and McKinney, 1987). Social movements of blacks, feminists, and other previously marginal groups helped undermine the false universality of the mainline religious culture that provided the language for public discourse on public and social affairs. Sociologists pointed to the demise of mainline civil religion as a force providing images, values, and cultural resources capable of leading the United States into the future (see Bellah et al., 1985; Bellah, 1975).

Whether or not the once-dominant Protestant worldview is in disarray, many observers have called on U.S. Catholicism to provide a "context for discourse" and cultural resources suitable for public life (e.g., Neuhaus, 1984, 1987). With even some non-Catholics hailing a dawning "Catholic moment" capable of providing generalizable norms for reviving discussion of the common good in a fragmented culture, U.S. Catholic leaders seem more than eager to assume responsibilities (and respectability) commensurate with their numbers and achievements. Projects such as the recent pastoral letters on nuclear weapons and the U.S. economy would have been inconceivable thirty-five years ago, as the country then enjoyed one of its regular anti-Catholic crusades; that such pastoral letters are debated, lobbied, and scrutinized by national elites across the political and religious spectrum attests to the American nature of the U.S. Church, a process discerned, not without some regret, by Will Herberg decades earlier (Herberg, 1955).

EMERGENCE OF CORE/PERIPHERY CONFLICT WITHIN THE CHURCH?

Bitter core/periphery conflict is the everyday stuff of the world's political elites: the debt crisis, armed interventions and counterinsurgency, trade restrictions, and more. There is reason to believe analogous core/periphery divisions will rise to prominence within world Catholicism, despite professions from within the Church of unity and mutual support.

Within Catholicism, the core/periphery split is most pronounced in the realm of social ethics, more specifically in different evaluations of the international economic order. Peripheral Catholicism, led by the Latin American churches, increasingly identifies existing structural arrangements as sinful in their fundamentals; the gospel demands of justice, when viewed from the periphery, require the elimination of the capitalist world economy in favor of a less clearly defined successor. The anticapitalist position has both conservative (organic, integralist) and radical variants (liberation theology), but capitalism finds few outspoken defenders among leaders of the Latin American church (the peripheral region where the processes of proletarianization and peripheralization have been most extensively developed). Core Catholicism, led by the United States, believes the capitalist world economy from which it has benefited so greatly can be reformed. This split is more than an incidental disagreement. It involves broad sections (liberal and conservative) within peripheral and core Catholicism and has potentially momentous consequences for the future of both regions and of world Catholicism.

The role of the Vatican in this core/periphery clash remains ambiguous. The clear trend in papal social teaching of the modern era has been toward increasingly harsh condemnations of the capitalist world order; this trend may have ended, however, with John Paul II's *Centesimus Annus* in 1991. In recent decades much of the anticapitalist thrust of peripheral Catholicism has drawn initial inspiration and encouragement from Vatican sources (Dorr, 1983). Many in the Vatican recognize that the "loss of the masses," which dealt European Catholicism a blow from which it has yet to recover, must not be allowed to happen again among the poor majorities of the Third World, the undeniable future of the Church worldwide (Lernoux, 1989). By the same token, however, the Vatican (and indirectly many peripheral churches) remain financially dependent on the churches of the core. The U.S. Church in particular has grown more influential with the Vatican in recent decades, reflecting the Vatican's cash-flow problems and the increasing influence of the U.S. Church within the United States. The geopolitical strength of the United States makes for a greater role for the U.S. Church in worldwide Catholicism, a relationship particularly visible during World War II (Fogarty, 1985, p. 311).

The Vatican's role is further complicated by the enigmatic personality and agenda of the current pope. John Paul II is clearly a centralizing, power-collecting prelate; his administrative conservatism fits poorly, however, with his economic progressivism, which (perhaps until *Centesimus in 1991*) described world capitalism in many of the same terms used by peripheral anticapitalists (for example, in *Sollicitudo Rei Socialis in 1988*). His appointments to vacant dioceses (especially in Latin America) have been "conservative," more in terms of those bishops' degree of deference to Rome (nearly total) than in the content of their views on political economy. Further complicating matters, the present pope vigorously, almost vehemently, rejects the suggestion that class conflict might exist within the Church itself; raising it as a possibility has brought censure on some theologians (Leonardo Boff). How much of the Vatican's difficult position is endemic to its role, and how much reflects the idiosyncrasies of its present pontiff, will become clear only with time.

SOLIDARITY AS AN EVOLVING ECCLESIAL CONCEPT

Solidarity is a notion that is still being developed in the contemporary Catholic world; although its roots are in the Hebrew Bible and the New Testament eras, its vitalization as a theological term is relatively recent. No one has done more to make solidarity a normative, potentially universal guide for action and judgment than John Paul II. In his major encyclical *Sollicitudo Rei Socialis* (On Social Concerns), a series of addresses during his 1988 Latin American sojourn, and other presentations, he has made solidarity intrinsic to his vision of social justice and peace. To measure the U.S. Church, or any local Roman Catholic Church, by the yardstick of solidarity, then, is not to impose a measure alien or extrinsic to the religious community.

The worldwide context in which the Church is called to practice solidarity is described this way by John Paul:

> Unfortunately, from the economic point of view, the developing countries are much more numerous than the developed ones; the multitudes of human beings who lack the goods and services offered by development are much more numerous than those who possess them. We are therefore faced with a serious problem of unequal distribution of the means of subsistence originally meant for everybody, and thus also an unequal distribution of the benefits deriving from them. And this happens not through the fault of the needy people and even less through a sort of inevitability dependent on natural conditions or circumstances as a whole. (1988d, pp. 644–45)

Given this, the pope defines solidarity as

> a firm and persevering determination to commit oneself to the common good; that is to say, to the good of all and of each individual because we are all really responsible for all. This determination is based on the solid conviction that what is hindering full development is the desire for profit and [the] thirst for power. . . . These attitudes and "structures of sin" are only conquered—presupposing the help of divine grace—by a diametrically opposed attitude: a commitment to the good of one's neighbor with the readiness, in the Gospel sense, to "lose oneself" for the sake of the other instead of exploiting him, and to "serve him" instead of oppressing him for one's own advantage (cf. Mt. 10:40–42, 20–25; Mk. 10:42–45; Lk. 22:25–27). (1988d, p. 654)

John Paul's personalist emphasis permeates his understanding of solidarity.

> Solidarity helps us to see the "other"—whether a person, people or nation—not just as some kind of instrument, with a work capacity and physical strength to be exploited at low cost and then discarded when no longer useful, but as our "neighbor," a "helper" (cf. Gen. 2:18–20), to be made a sharer on a par with ourselves in the banquet of life to which all are equally invited by God. (1988d, pp. 654–55)

Solidarity has special ecclesiological significance; more than being only a duty owed to individuals and groups in need, it is a special obligation between local churches. This ecclesial aspect of solidarity is the basis for the periphery churches' claims on those of the core.

> Solidarity is the expression of the church's life and of her dynamism in Christ. Such solidarity involves a practical awareness of the great network of interdependence that exists among God's people. It consists in a firm and persevering commitment to the good of all. (1988b, p. 240)

> All the particular churches that make up the one Catholic Church are called to live the same universal solidarity with their sister churches in an awareness of the one catholic communion that unites them in the mission of Christ. . . . Each local church perceives its interdependence in the need to be open to others and learn from them as well as by helping them bear their burdens according to the expression of St. Paul: "Help carry one another's burdens; in that way you will fulfill the law of Christ" (Gal. 6:2). Wherever, throughout the universal church, the faithful experience need, there the response of solidarity is called for. (1988b, p. 240)

One can argue with certain specific actions that John Paul derives from his understanding of solidarity. Some of the confusion emerges from his use of the term to cover both economic recommendations (for example, reform of international trade, the development of regional economic cooperation; Sollicitudo nos. 43, 45) and as an ecclesiological concept calling for cross-church unity and support. Similarly, the concept as he develops it is not without its problems (for example, an uncritical sense of the "common good," dubious counsels on class cooperation and accord). Overall, however, the reemergence of a religiously grounded sense of solidarity promises to be a significant development in the Catholic Church.

Several examples of religious solidarity in practice have appeared in recent years. For North American participants the Sanctuary movement has weakened preexisting church-state amity, imposed real costs (imprisonment, legal jeopardy) on individuals and congregations, and has spoken of religious duties toward the vulnerable, persecuted, and fellow Christians as its primary language of discourse. Politically salient religious solidarity—with impacts on power relations, imposition of costs, and a deepening and widening of religious discourse—has been present for more than half a century in the Catholic Worker movement, another example of religious solidarity in action.

If, as this study argues, the world Church is growing increasingly anticapitalist, issues of class will increasingly affect matters of religious solidarity. When the poor churches of the world call upon their wealthy coreligionists for support, solidarity becomes a most controversial religious norm.

As mentioned, chapter 2 considers pertinent theoretical and theological matters that relate political economy, the world economy, and the Catholic Church. In chapter 3 I discuss why the peripheral churches, led by the Latin Americans, will continue developing in an anticapitalist direction. Chapter 4 examines Catholicism in a core state—more specifically, the history and current situation of the U.S. Catholic Church. Chapter 5 surveys several recent U.S. Catholic works in social ethics to assess the theoretical possibilities and limitations before the U.S. Church, should it seek to develop perspectives and actions more sympathetic to the religious and political analyses offered by peripheral churches. Chapter 6 offers concluding reflections on the impact of the decline of state socialism on religious anticapitalism, and implications for the future.

2

WALLERSTEIN, RELIGION, AND ECCLESIOLOGY

Given his centrality to world-systems theory, attention to Immanuel Wallerstein's treatment of religion is in order. While not all world-systems theorists understand religion in the way that Wallerstein does, his approach is typical of much in the field. I hope to offer an alternative integration of political economy and religion that will overcome the weaknesses in Wallerstein's approach, while still being anchored in the strengths of the world-economy framework.

RELIGION IN WORLD-SYSTEMS THEORY (WST)

Religion has received little attention from writers within the world-systems theory tradition. Most major scholars within that tradition have been more concerned with establishing and extending the fundamental concepts of the theory of the capitalist world economy; relatively few have been concerned with religious movements, institutions, or ideas (the exceptions include Wuthnow, 1983 and 1980; Hammond, 1983; Lubeck, 1979; and Bergeson, 1982).

The relative lack of interest in religious and cultural matters, while perhaps understandable given the historical development of the world-systems perspective, points to areas in need of sustained study if WST is to develop further as a credible intellectual framework. Both the historical inquiries and the analytical concepts important to WST—which together chart the past and present of the capitalist world economy—require an adequate understanding of religious phenomena. Lacking such an understanding, world-systems analysts will be unable to grasp the evolution of the capitalist world economy and will almost surely overlook important resources available for its transformation.

While Immanuel Wallerstein's treatment of religious phenomena is not typical of all WST analysts, it nonetheless represents an important and perhaps predominant approach within the tradition. The conclusion offered here is that, to the extent that a coherent approach to dealing with matters religious can be derived from Wallerstein's historical corpus (primarily the first two volumes of *The Modern World-System*), that approach is inadequate for several reasons.

WALLERSTEIN, RELIGION, AND HISTORY

In his major historical work Wallerstein deals with religious phenomena only insofar as they relate to the emergence and development of the European world economy. Given this focus, he discusses religion in two principal contexts.

First, he offers religion as a factor contributing to national homogenization and state-building. The formation of a strong state is abetted, in his view, by the creation of a culturally homogeneous group: core states in the sixteenth and seventeenth centuries tended to greater homogeneity, while peripheral areas underwent greater fragmentation. Religion was useful in binding many diverse groups into a single national group, and it served as both a cultural cement and a way through which elites could appeal to the masses (1974, pp. 147, 207–8).

Internal wars of religion in core areas were tied to nation-building and the drive for cultural homogeneity. Protestantism served nationalist motives in the Netherlands, while Catholicism did the same for sixteenth-century France (1974, pp. 205–6, 296). He discusses the importance of cultural and religious homogeneity to core states by noting:

> The creation of a strong state machinery coupled with a national culture, a phenomenon often referred to as integration, serves both to protect disparities that have arisen within the world-system, and as an ideological mask and justification for the maintenance of those disparities. (p. 349)

Appeals to nationalism and religious fervor enabled elites to generate mass support for capitalist goals. Religious fervor, in this view, was more easily mustered when only a single religious group dominated internally, and when economic/political adversaries in the world system were also religious antagonists.

Wallerstein notes that religion need not always be the defining cultural trait of the major status groups within a state. One can use language, for example, in its stead:

> Language indeed began to play such a role in the sixteenth century, and its importance was to increase as the centuries passed. Religious reinforcement of role-specialization (i.e., core-periphery) in a world-economy has, however, advantages over linguistic reinforcement. It interferes less with the ongoing communications process within the world-economy. And it lends itself less (only less) to isolationist closures, because of the underlying universalist themes of world religions. (p. 354)

This leads to Wallerstein's second discussion of religion: in what ways has it been implicated in core-periphery development and stability in the world economy? He summarizes his general position as follows:

> The central pan-European ideological controversy of the sixteenth and seventeenth centuries—Reformation versus Counter-Reformation—was inextricably intertwined with the creation both of the strong states and of the capitalist system. It is no accident that those parts of Europe which were re-agrarianized in the sixteenth century were also those in which the Counter-Reformation triumphed, while, for the most part, the industrializing countries remained Protestant. Germany, France, and "Belgium" were somewhere "in between," the long-term result being an ideological compromise. Germany divided between Protestant and Catholics. France and "Belgium" came to have few "Protestants" but developed an anticlerical, free-thinking tradition to which certain groups could adhere. (pp. 151–52)

On the one hand, Wallerstein says "it is no accident" that Protestantism came to be the core tradition and Catholicism the peripheral one. Such a development occurred because "those with interests in the new thrust of nation-states operating within a world-economy tended to find cognitive consonance in being Protestants" (p. 266). Further, Catholicism (as a transnational institution) responded with hostility to the emergence of a world economy supported by strong state machineries in core areas. This hostility, which put the Church "wholeheartedly into the opposition of modernity," was successful only in peripheral areas, which, according to Wallerstein, helped ensure the long-run success of the core-periphery division (p. 156).

On the other hand, however, Wallerstein associates the ties of Protestantism to capitalism and Catholicism to its opposition with "intellectually accidental historical developments." The split in positions had little to do with theology, according to Wallerstein; Catholicism could have legitimated capitalism as easily as did Protestantism, and Protestantism could have easily become anticapitalist (1974, p. 152–53).

> We have been skeptical that the tenets of the various theologies had too much to do with it, although they may have facilitated the task. Rather, the tenets of the theologies, as they evolved in practice as opposed to their religious conception, reflected and served to sustain the roles of the various areas in the world-system. (p. 353)

Ideas about property, commerce, and related matters, Wallerstein suggests, were relatively unimportant; elites in core areas mined Protestantism for legitimation, while elites in peripheral areas did the same with Catholicism. He uses Poland as an example of how different classes in a peripheral area grabbed different theological mantles, and how the economic crisis of 1557 weakened the aristocratic Calvinists to the permanent advantage of the Catholic agrarian nobility (pp. 154–56).

WALLERSTEIN'S APPROACH TO RELIGION: A CRITIQUE

The preceding review suggests sufficient consistencies to speak legitimately of a distinctively Wallersteinian approach to religious phenomena. Roland Robertson, in an important article entitled "The Sacred and the World System" (1985), identifies two main shortcomings in Wallerstein's treatment of religion: a view of religion as epiphenomenal, to be explained as directly and entirely derivable for other factors; and adherence to a rigid version of the "secularization thesis," which posits the diminished importance of religion as modernization and the world economy expand (Robertson, 1985, p. 350).

A third deficiency, not identified by Robertson, involves Wallerstein's conception of religion as consistently (and perhaps inherently) pro-systemic in function. Finally, Wallerstein's treatment of religious phenomena—of movements, institutions, and ideologies—is relatively undifferentiated, as his views move freely and without apparent distinctions among them.

These four shortcomings, running throughout his treatment of religion, should be explored further.

Religion as Epiphenomenal. Robertson writes that, although Wallerstein does not claim that economic factors are always the motor of history, he uses economics to consign religious matters to epiphenomenal status (1985, pp. 349–50). Religion is always explained away with reference to other, presumably more fundamental forces, according to Robertson.

That Robertson is correct is evident from a review of Wallerstein's treatment of religion as a means of cultural homogenization. In that context, religious institutions and developments have no dynamic of their own; rather, they are better understood as outcomes of elite manipulations and self-interested maneuvers. To understand religion in the sixteenth and seventeenth centuries, according to Wallerstein, one must look at who uses what religious groups—with the result that religious ideas and institutions appear as having no cohesiveness of their own whatsoever.

Similarly, in his examination of the Protestant ethic thesis and its relationship to core-periphery development, Wallerstein concentrates on the conflict between classes and groups to the complete neglect of the ideologies seemingly at stake. Matters of religious belief pale in importance when compared with the economic interests in conflict: "History has seen [religious] passion turn to cynicism too regularly for one not to be suspicious of invoking such belief systems as primary factors in explaining the genesis and long-term persistence of large-scale social action" (1974, p. 48).

In another context—that of the Japanese withdrawal from its initial contact with the emerging world economy—Wallerstein undercuts explanations that involve a partial recognition of religious factors by stressing more economically oriented possibilities (1974, p. 343). Throughout his writings he seeks to deal with religious beliefs as purely derivative phenomena, and with religious action explained by economic imperatives. That people might act for religious motives, that theologies might merit discussion as independent variables, seems inconceivable to him. Religion is something he seeks to explain; it does not have a dynamic of its own, nor can it explain anything else in a meaningful sense.

Religion and Secularization. Robertson notes that the little attention paid to religion in world-systems literature "has promoted a negative view of religion and, for the most part, has implicitly adhered to a strong version of the secularization thesis" (1985, p. 347). Secularization theory posits the decline in importance of religious and other "traditional" value systems as modernization spreads and strengthens. WST, to Robertson, represents the "absolute high point" of secularization theory because it seems "to see the thorough secularization of the entire world":

The making of the modern world-system has, in that perspective, consisted in a five-hundred-year process of the stripping away of the autonomous significance of cultural ideas in the face of the onward march, on an increasingly worldwide basis, of capitalistic forms of economic organization (1985, p. 347).

It is ironic that Wallerstein and his associates show evidence of a strong secularization presumption, given that secularization theory emerged from an analysis of *societies* (Robertson, 1985, p. 354), the unit of analysis so objectionable to Wallerstein. That secularization is an important facet of his approach is evident in his view of the unlimited malleability of religious concepts, doctrines, and institutions. Phenomena and actors so easily manipulated by capitalist groups must have lost all explanatory power, integrity ("meaning"), and dynamism of their own. The ease with which Christianity—Protestant and Catholic—accommodated capitalism is evidence that Christianity as a source of norms and values must decline in importance as capitalist market norms ascend (Robertson, 1985, p. 349). The worldwide dominance of capitalism must entail the worldwide retreat of religious worldviews not amenable to rationalization.

While the elimination of religion—the culmination of secularization—is not proposed in Wallerstein's historical analysis, its emasculation and vitiation as an independent source of cultural criticism seems a reasonable extension of the processes he describes. Something called religion may well persist in his world-system; but religion as a source of meaning and inspiration independent of capitalist norms, it seems reasonable to predict, becomes increasingly less plausible. The prospect of resacralization appears not at all in his picture.

Religion as Prosystemic. Throughout Wallerstein's historical work, religion is seen as something that contributes to the health of the capitalist world economy. Protestantism strengthens the core, Catholicism makes possible the sustained inferiority of the periphery; even the hostility of Catholicism to capitalism strengthens the system by virtue of its activities in peripheral areas. Everything religious, it would seem, strengthens the world-system.

All of which may reflect Wallerstein's alleged propensity to "read back" into history contributions and support for the world-system that exist "of necessity"—in seeing everything as a factor leading to the *explanandum*. Whether or not such is the case, his analysis gives no evidence that religion—any religion, at any time—has served, or could serve, except as a source of support for the world-system.

In contrast, I believe that religious traditions can take antisystemic forms. Further, religious traditions may not be equal in the degree of accommodation with capitalism they allow. Finally, I would argue that current developments within world Christianity, which are using traditional religious symbols and categories, might legitimately be seen as forces working to delegitimate the capitalist world economy.

Religion as Institutions, Ideas, and Movements. A basic tenet of modern religious scholarship is that "religion" means nothing without specification. Religious institutions are not the same as religious movements, official statements do not always correspond with popular piety, and spiritual traditions do not fully reflect the nature of spiritual experiences (real or imagined) (see, for example, W. C. Smith, 1981; Kselman, 1986; and Hammond, 1985).

In his treatment of religion, Wallerstein seems to disregard most elemental distinctions. He fails to break down terms like "Catholicism" and "Protestantism." Does he refer to ecclesial structures, credal and doctrinal statements, popular religiosity, theological orthodoxies and heresies, political leaders or movements? Without such specification, Wallerstein is left with concepts largely devoid of content, which is fine if all matters religious are infinitely malleable, as he seems to conclude. But are institutions, theologies, and movements equally (much less infinitely) malleable? There is no prima facie reason to believe so, yet so casual is his usage that it leads to such a conclusion. Were one not to dismiss a priori the possibility that religious phenomena possess a dynamic and coherence of their own (not entirely derivable from economic matters), one would pay closer attention to levels and specificity of analysis. Wallerstein does not grant religious matters that kind of attention, for reasons already suggested.

ECCLESIOLOGY AND POLITICAL ECONOMY

In evaluating the rift between poor and rich churches, I wish to explore two axes of alignment/nonalignment. These axes—ecclesiology and political economy—together serve as useful tools with which to draw together the many issues and approaches that cross in a social science-cum-theology inquiry of this sort. As I hope to show, ecclesiology in particular is relatively unexplored in understanding contemporary political/economic phenomena in the world system; the more accepted notion, that political/economic structures and processes limit or shape ecclesiologies (and theology more generally) is no less important for its somewhat greater familiarity to social scientists (see Gill, 1987).

Ecclesiology is that branch of formal theology that concerns itself with theories of the church: the nature of its mission, its understanding of internal and external authority, and its self-understanding as a community with criteria for membership, participation, and inclusivity. While most scholarship on ecclesiology has been primarily theological in nature, a few foundational works have explored the social implications and impacts of competing ecclesiologies. Foremost among these is Ernst Troeltsch's *The Social Teaching of the Christian Churches*, first published in 1913. This work, cited almost universally in the academic literature, identified two primary, distinct ecclesiologies within church history—the "church" type and the "sect" type. Both can trace their roots from the New Testament and early church to the present, according to Troeltsch.

The church type is characterized by few demands upon adherents, a view of itself as universal in scope and open to all, an accommodationist approach to secular institutions and culture, and a reliance on rigid, hierarchical norms of authority. The sect type, by contrast, gives rise to smaller, more communal, and intense groups committed to a more rigorous practice of Christian ideals; sects are frequently indifferent or hostile to secular authorities and culture, and do not accommodate themselves to the state or society. Membership in sects is voluntary (unlike the universal church type, which relies on infant baptism and ascriptive identification), and authority is often democratic and egalitarian. While Troeltsch notes that sects can engage in political activity, such is usually less important to them than to the church type; sects often, to Troeltsch, resist the incursions of secular power and try to insulate themselves from it.

It is this latter emphasis in Troeltsch—the sect as apolitical or disengaged from secular affairs—that receives additional attention from the brothers Niebuhr. In his classic *Christ and Culture*, H. Richard Niebuhr constructs five patterns of Christian interaction with secular culture, which he describes as Christ Against Culture, the Christ of Culture, Christ Above Culture, Christ and Culture in Paradox, and Christ the Transformer of Culture. The church type of Troeltsch has aspects relevant to nearly all of Niebuhr's categories, but the sect type fits neatly into the Christ Against Culture category. Sects, to Niebuhr, attempt to live Christian perfection in the midst of worldly sinfulness; significantly, he sees them as avoiding political life and being privatized in their concerns.

His brother Reinhold, in *Moral Man and Immoral Society*, adopts a more polemical approach. A proper view of human nature, inescapably burdened by original sin, requires an ecclesiology cognizant of the modest gains possible in the present world, an ecclesiology willing to work through existing secular powers and processes. The church type described by Troeltsch is for Reinhold Niebuhr a responsible manifestation of Christian values free of idealistic or heroic naïveté. The ecclesiologies that require a more vigorous manifestation of Christian values Niebuhr castigates as utopian, irresponsible, and irrelevant to the real-world problems of power politics.

Max Weber's *The Protestant Ethic and the Spirit of Capitalism*, written in 1905, remains an important study in religion and politics. The debate over Weber's thesis—that the Calvinist theology of vocation held by the Puritans helped advance the spread of capitalism in North America—continues today (e.g., Oakes, 1988–89). His operating assumption—that theological concepts can act as independent, causal factors in social development—remains valid and stands as an early refutation of reductionist epistemologies that would relegate religion to epiphenomenal status. His study of authority and legitimacy (institutional, charismatic, prophetic), while not directly ecclesiological, has implications for studies concerned with the prospects of radical, long-term change in religious communities (Weber, 1964).

Weber's observations on what he calls "congregational religion" are important in assessing the impact of Base Christian Communities (BCCs) on the institutional Church. To Weber, congregational religion is characterized by groups of small, self-directed believers, involving high levels of commitment and participation. Its ethos is democratic and egalitarian, and it integrates religious concepts with everyday concerns. While Weber did not believe such congregational patterns could develop within Catholicism—the epitome of structure and hierarchy—BCCs do indeed seem congregational in their form and function and thus are disturbing both to political and ecclesial elites (Weber, 1978, p. 591).

Avery Dulles is a prominent Catholic theologian whose highly influential *Models of the Church* explores the theological underpinnings for major historical notions of the church. While Dulles notes his debt to H. Richard Niebuhr, he delves more deeply into the theological implications of various ecclesiologies, highlighting the strengths and weaknesses of each. Dulles's book, both in its methodology and content, has contributed significantly to the work of other religious scholars, Catholic and non-Catholic. Like the Niebuhrs, Dulles has done much to promote ecclesiologies free of "sectarian" elements.

In contrast, Mennonite theologian John Howard Yoder and Methodist Stanley Hauerwas are among the most forceful proponents of the view that several of these ecclesiological frameworks, especially Troeltsch's church/sect dichotomy and its use by the Niebuhrs, are intrinsically biased in favor of accommodationist ecclesiologies and treat "sects" in a pejorative fashion. Such a bias equates sect with otherworldly, a correlation Yoder rejects insofar as many groups identified as sects (especially those emerging from the Radical Reformation of the sixteenth century) do not reject engagement with the world. What such groups do reject, according to Yoder, is the particular form of church-world engagement represented by the accommodation of mainstream Christianity with secular power.

Yoder's critique and those like it are important to this study for several reasons. First, Yoder's view cautions against too easy adoption of traditional models of the church, which arrive with a package of normative judgments smuggled in with them. Second, as I will show, the church-vs.-sect dichotomy is operative among many leaders of mainstream (especially U.S.) Catholicism and is used in an attempt to discredit Catholic critics who suggest existing forms of church-world engagement more accurately reflect theological error than providential development through history. Finally, the ecclesiological picture Yoder and others advance is helpful when understanding alternative Catholic views of the church; Yoder's personal influence, direct and indirect, on Catholic theology is also noteworthy (Clapp, 1988).

Among contemporary social scientists, Daniel H. Levine is among those whose research consistently gives central attention to ecclesiology, what he calls "the church's sense of itself." (1986c, p. 187). As he puts it,

> The models of the church held by Catholic leaders shape the way they see themselves, the institutions they lead, and their proper relation to social and political issues. These visions of the church [ecclesiologies] provide an important mediation through which religious ideas are crystallized in structures or organizational life, patterns of authority, and legitimate goals, commitments, and actions. (1986c, pp. 192–93)

Ecclesiologies, it may be added, are also held by grass-roots believers and local leaders (including pastoral agents), not merely by officially recognized leaders such as bishops. Levine broadly distinguishes two competing ecclesiologies in Latin American Catholicism. One of them, a conservative episcopal model, "stresses control from above, obedience to hierarchical authority, the transmittal of truth and hope from the

Church to the world, and an overall emphasis on the rechristianization of society" (Dodson, 1986, p. 97). The other vision, informed by the "People of God" metaphor adopted at Vatican II, sees instead a "historical community of believers." Michael Dodson summarizes:

> In this view a solidarity among bishops, priests and laity replaces a centralized chain of command from top to bottom. In place of strict obedience to hierarchical dicta, it stresses dialogue and shared experience. And it views the church as a pluralistic body encompassing a broad distribution of authority and power that accords a significant pastoral role to the laity. This model seeks to change society rather than impose a new version of Christendom. (1986, p. 97)

TIGHT AND LOOSE ECCLESIOLOGIES

In simplifying matters of ecclesiology, this study will distinguish between "tight" and "loose" ecclesiologies for typological purposes (derived from Kelley, 1972). These categories in themselves are not meant to imply value judgments; more correctly, they refer to the degree of commitment, participation, and initiative required by each for membership in the church. Tight ecclesiologies have much in common with Weber's congregational religion—demanding for its adherents, much mutual support and initiative, and participatory decision-making. Loose ecclesiologies require minimal commitments for affiliation, require little by way of participation in the life of the community, and generally involve a one-way transmission of religious resources from a minority leadership to a more passive membership.

While similarities with the church/sect typology seem evident, the tight/loose dichotomy differs from the former in several respects. For one, interpenetration of types is recognized as more possible in the tight/loose dichotomy. Tight and loose ecclesiologies can coexist within Catholicism (contra Weber), for example, without one dismissed as a sectarian deviation. The theological judgment that tight ecclesiologies are more Protestant than Catholic is rejected; tight ecclesiologies have played an important, if usually subordinate, role throughout Catholic history. Third, the notion—often implied rather than expressed—that tight ecclesiologies are inherently elitist while loose (or church) models are more open to the poor is rejected as empirically untenable (witness the growth of tight Pentecostal communities among the poor, for instance). Finally, no theological disposition can be inferred from a tight or loose ecclesiology; they need not be either theologically or socially conservative or liberal, although, as will be seen, some theological/social positions are incompatible with some ecclesiological choices.

The tight/loose typology does not involve all that needs to be said about ecclesiology—much more will be said, in fact—but it may provide a useful tool in theoretical considerations of how ecclesiologies and political economy interrelate. An important step in such considerations involves attention to those who generate, act on, and live ecclesiologies. Acting on ecclesiologies is what makes them both living and controversial; no ideas, certainly not religious ones, are self-executing or self-implementing.

Within the Catholic Church, ecclesiologies can be acted on (a) from above, that is, by the pope, bishops, Vatican, and others tied to the canonical hierarchy; (b) from below, by those individuals and communities constituting the faithful, those at the base of the pre-Vatican II pyramidal picture of the Church; and (c) from the middle, that is, by semi-institutional actors and agents (including priests, theologians, pastoral leaders, lay catechists, religious, and intellectuals) who operate at some distance from the hierarchy but who themselves possess specialized resources mobilized in church projects. This last group reflects what sociologist John Coleman calls "para-ecclesial" organizations and persons, who have been crucial actors in developing and implementing Catholic social action (1982, pp. 47–54).

Given these three levels of activity, it remains to suggest typical routes of impact and transmission. While exceptions in the form of bishops who live and act in concert with the local communities do exist, most often little direct contact links levels (a) and (b). Most often, actors at the top affect and direct semi-institutional actors, group (c). Those in level (b), in turn, both affect and are affected by the actions of these intermediate actors. These para-ecclesial actors complete the cycle by serving as the primary conduit for mass opinion and activity to those at the top. The relations in real life are more complex, but heuristically figure 1 illustrates the strategic importance of para-ecclesial actors.

As will be seen, the semi-institutional actors are playing a major role in ecclesiological conflict and change. Locating them in the typical routes of church activity is an important theoretical requisite.

ECCLESIOLOGY AND POLITICAL ECONOMY

This study considers political economy on two levels. First, it is viewed on an empirical, intra-ecclesial level concerned, for example, with the class composition, economic status, and social position of church mem-

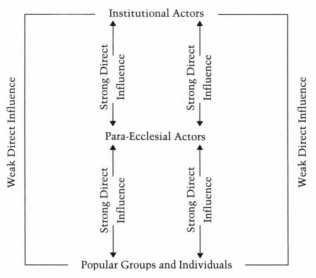

Figure 1.   Intra-Ecclesial Linkages

bers (hereinafter Level One PE). The second level of consideration is ideological: those ideas on wealth and poverty, relationships and networks, and normative judgments on the world (hereinafter Level Two PE, or the PE Critique). Level One PE might ask how many poor people are within a national church; Level Two PE might explain why they are poor and what normative significance such an explanation involves.

The two PE levels are closely interrelated. For example, implementing a given ecclesiology can select the social composition of a church (Level One PE), the problems of which can help suggest the adequacy or inadequacy of previous explanations of wealth and poverty (Level Two PE). Similarly, changes in the social composition of the church's base and the problems encountered by people there (due to demographic change, economic dislocations, or acting on a given explanation of wealth and poverty) can point out inadequacies in the existing ecclesiology, which may then be modified or abandoned with resulting changes in the church's base (Level One PE) and/or critique (Level Two PE).

A more specific example might better illustrate these interactions and focus, at the theoretical level, on the real-world problem that interests this study. Doing so involves a cursory comparison of the Latin American and U.S. churches in their historical origins and development.

In both Latin America and the United States, Catholic clergy brought a loose, sacramental ecclesiology to lands new to the Church. The Latin churches brought this loose ecclesiology to indigenous peoples, the evangelization of whom was both superficial and incomplete. In the North the Catholic clergy dealt with comparatively few indigenous peoples and concentrated primarily on the well-off Catholic enclaves of the mid-Atlantic region, especially Maryland (Dolan, 1985, pp. 69–97). Only later did the people arrive in North America to swell the Catholic ranks; before the mass immigrations of the nineteenth century, Catholicism was a multiclass, tending-toward-comfortable community.

The expansion and deepening of capitalism differently affected the Latin American and U.S. churches. In Latin America the "weak" political-economy critique (Level Two PE) offered by the Church (explaining poverty individualistically as a result of personal sin, or as natural) proved untenable, even to many Church leaders, as the Church's base among the poor experienced severe dislocations and hardships caused by capitalist development. In the United States, by contrast, the other side of a weak political-economy critique (that prosperity comes from individual virtue, hard work, and attention to religious duties) was strengthened and stabilized by the prosperity immigrant Catholics came to enjoy under twentieth-century capitalism.

In Latin American, instability at the Church's base caused by the secular expansion of capitalism showed up the limits of both the Church's incomplete evangelization of the poor and its weak PE critique. Many churches in Latin America opted for tighter ecclesiological positions, typified by the BCC movement, to deal with evangelization more effectively. The practices of Catholics mobilized into the tight ecclesiology of the BCCs, in turn, led to a stronger PE critique (more structural and anti-capitalist in nature), adopted to some degree at all levels of the Church.

Table 3   Ecclesiology and Social Class

	Middle-Class or Upper-Class Base	Predominantly Poor Base
Tight Ecclesiology	Can have strong critique; those who stay and participate do so for reasons of strong religious conviction. Can have weak PE critique, esp. if spirituality is privatized and inward-oriented.	Can have strong critique, aided by capacity for group action, identity-formation, legitimacy.
Loose Ecclesiology	Strong PE critique unlikely because of strength of well-off members threatened by it; influence of affluent enhanced in weak-ecclesiology church.	Strong critique unlikely, few opportunities for popular mobilization, group discernment.

Table 4   Ecclesiology and Political-Economic Critique

	Weak PE Critique	Strong PE Critique
Loose Ecclesiology	Compatible	Incompatible
Tight Ecclesiology	Compatible	Compatible

In the United States, the stable loose ecclesiology/weak PE critique balance has been shaken in recent years by both declining U.S. economic hegemony and theological and ideological challenges from Catholics in poor countries. The present activities of the U.S. church—and its dilemma—might be described as trying to strengthen its PE critique of the capitalist world economy without changing either its base in the middle class (Level One PE) or its loose ecclesiology. If such efforts are doomed to frustration, as I suspect, then it may well be that some types of PE critique require compatible ecclesiological positions. The presence of a compatible political-economic base (Level One PE) also seems important, but less so; a church, unlike some other institutions, can change its Level One PE (that is, social classes in membership) by redefining its ecclesiology and living with the consequences, pro and con. Whereas in the past such redefinition often resulted in formal schism, a trait that seems to be characteristic of contemporary Catholicism is a determination to fight such battles within the walls of the existing structure. A matrix, as shown in table 3, may summarize the theological alignments suggested here. Another matrix (table 4) suggests that the likelihood of a strong PE critique (Level Two) will vary with the dominant ecclesiological position.

Chapters 3 through 5 discuss these interactions of ecclesiology and political economy in peripheral and core contexts. Such a discussion should provide new insights into the past, present, and possible futures of the Catholic Church as a transnational phenomenon.

3

ANTICAPITALISM AND
THE LATIN AMERICAN CHURCH

The position defended in this chapter—that the Latin American Church, taken as a whole, is likely to continue developing its opposition to the capitalist world economy—is one advanced by few scholars. Entire volumes (e.g., Mainwaring and Wilde, 1989) seem to herald the demise of "progressive" Catholicism in the region. Other scholars are impressed by the conservative counteroffensive within the Latin American Church (Levine, 1987a), while some popular accounts sound alarms over the conservative "Restoration" movement led by Pope John Paul II and Cardinal Joseph Ratzinger (Lernoux, 1989).

Surely any analysis must come to terms with changes within "progressive" national churches (and the endurance of reactionary ones such as Argentina and Colombia) in Latin America and with variations among national churches. Similarly, the conservative maneuvers from within and without are important in assessing the possibilities of future development. For my argument to be compelling, it must, of necessity, give full weight to such contrary evidence while offering a plausible account of more important factors moving the Church against the present capitalist order and ideology. If such an argument is made well, it stands more strongly for having answered foreseeable objections from within its overall framework (Kuhn, 1970; Wilber and Jameson, 1983).

The anticapitalism thesis stands or falls on the strength of the following assertion: the factors (religious and political/economic, internal and external to the Church) pushing the Latin American Church against capitalism are more deeply structural, entrenched, and enduring than are opposing, more contingent procapitalist trends. This chapter offers a framework that separates these important factors into three categories: structural, nonstructural but deeply entrenched, and contingent. Such a separation, of course, is schematic and heuristic; nonetheless, it should make it possible to distinguish between developments of greater and lesser significance in the macro-level movements of the Latin American Church. That other observers might consider particular phenomena to be structural rather than contingent does not in itself undermine this approach; the general evidence and the quality of substantiating arguments need to be weighed in judging the framework's value.

At the outset it also is important to recognize that the impacts of religious and political/economic factors are neither necessarily distinct nor additive. Rather, a more dynamic, synergistic process must be considered a possibility when assessing the evidence and experiences at issue. Such a synergistic process may be difficult to quantify or falsify in standard positivistic fashion (e.g., Hempel, 1965), but some such process must be allowed for in a study that aspires to a more systemic, nonreductive explanation.

At this point it is important to be specific about what is being claimed. To assert that the Latin American Church will continue developing an anticapitalist orientation is not saying (a) that this anticapitalism will be manifest to the same degree in all times and places; (b) that the Church is making an affirmative choice for a specific brand of socialism, or even for socialism programatically; (c) that elements favorably disposed to capitalism will not continue to have some influence in the Church; or (d) that an anticapitalist orientation requires a particular political, pastoral, or economic "project" to prove its validity. What I do claim is that opposition to capitalism will (a) increase at the ideological level; (b) affect pastoral practice in a variety of ways; and (c) become an increasingly salient part of the Church's ethos, its atmosphere, even if it is at times more latent than manifest.

Important here is the distinction between "latent" and "manifest" attitudes and orientations, one offered by Alberto Melucci (1980, 1985), among others. That conditions for overt action may be absent does not by itself prove the absence of oppositional attitudes and beliefs (see Scott, 1985); inasmuch as most Latin American Catholics are very poor, the barriers to open political action are significant (Olson, 1965). It is possible for anticapitalist sentiment and positions to increase without their becoming immediately discernible in political action. Further, care must be exercised in evaluating what is manifest; few movements fight the capitalist world economy directly, but rather they take on more proximate and identifiable symbols, actors, and activities. All of which does not render judgment on my argument impossible; it merely specifies what is being claimed and what is not.

STRUCTURAL FACTORS SUPPORTING THE ANTICAPITALIST TREND

For our purposes, structural factors are those that emerge from the fundamental, constitutive features of both the capitalist world economy and the Catholic Church as an actor in that economy. Such factors are unlikely to disappear unless there are basic changes in the world-system or in the Church's institutional design.

POLITICAL-ECONOMIC

The Endurance of Core-Periphery Relations. Fundamental to the capitalist world economy is the division of the world into core and periphery regions, with the prosperity of the former dependent on the exploitation of the latter. The core-periphery division (with an intermediate semiperiphery stratum) is a constitutive feature of the world economy; it has endured from the sixteenth century to the present and will disappear only with the demise of the capitalist world-system (see, for example, Wallerstein, 1979, pp. 1–36, 95–118).

By its nature, the capitalist world economy cannot benefit all people equally; reformist state-level action cannot compensate for the structural imbalances that reserve prosperity for a minority (Wallerstein, 1979, pp. 66–94). While there may be some mobility in the world economy (peripheral countries become semiperipheral, semiperipheral ones enter the core, core countries fall into the semiperiphery or periphery), such movement is within the overarching, unchanged core-periphery structure.

Why should such a structural feature be relevant to discussions of the Latin American Church and capitalism? It indicates that, however distasteful the realization, the future life-prospects for the people of Latin America remain grim. No new development scheme, no amount of debt relief, no set of entrepreneurial innovations are likely to raise the majority of Latin Americans from their status as peripheral members of peripheral countries. There may be some positional changes—Brazil may someday become a core power, although offering a plausible scenario for that seems difficult at present—but the regional reality will be played out within the rigidities of the core-periphery structure.

Further, the core-periphery relationship renders problematic reform or radical efforts aimed at achieving state power. As Wallerstein observes, the international state system is indispensable to the capitalist world economy. Radical movements aiming to achieve control of nation-states also reinforce the world economy by strengthening the state system (Wallerstein 1984, pp. 140–41). The relationship between the state system and the world economy suggests that a country-by-country movement against capitalism (for example, Cuba, Nicaragua) is unlikely to lead to the elimination of capitalism as a systemic force; with the possibilities for transformative praxis severely circumscribed, the endurance of the capitalist world economy seems assured into at least the immediately foreseeable future. Thus, the capitalist world economy, with its exploitation of peripheral and semiperipheral regions and peoples, will continue to confront the Church for years to come.

Secular Trends in the World Economy. Wallerstein identifies several secular trends in the world economy that are relevant to my argument. Increasing proletarianization, incorporation, marginalization, and immiserization are among these trends, which together suggest that the dislocations and suffering visited on the majority of Latin Americans in the postwar era (Levine, 1987a) will spread and intensify. The political-economic changes that affected the Latin American poor, which in part spurred the Church's changing of sides before and after Medellin, are ongoing and may be expected to increase as capitalist relations broaden and deepen their reach into Latin American life.

These trends also reflect the importance of Latin American Catholic thought on economic issues to other Third World churches. More than in Africa or Asia, capitalism has penetrated Latin America broadly and deeply; this largely stems from the absence of direct colonial rule in recent years, early development of export enclaves in the nineteenth century, and the aggressiveness of hegemonic activity—first British, then North American—in the region. Proletarianization, incorporation, marginalization, and immiserization are well under way—and will continue—in sub-Saharan Africa and Asia. Church people there are looking to the Latin American Church as one that already has been confronted with such developments, and many acknowledge the impact of Latin American theological and pastoral developments in shaping their own emerging perspectives and responses (see for example, Boesak, 1978; Wan-Tateh, 1984; Balasuriya, 1984, 1988; Pieris, 1988).

Antisystemic Movements. Another secular trend identified by Wallerstein is the regular emergence of antisystemic movements challenging one or another of the bases of the capitalist world economy. Such movements may take a variety of forms (for example, nationalist or social movements), but all emerge as phenomena related to the ongoing operation, reproduction, and contradictions of the capitalist world economy (Wallerstein 1984, pp. 97–146).

Secular antisystemic movements have been important in encouraging an anticapitalist orientation within the Latin American Church. Many pastoral innovations, policy shifts, and theological changes concerning the victims of market forces and poverty arose from the Church hierarchy's desire to dilute the appeal of communist movements and ideologies, especially the Cuban Revolution. As the Church has found itself competing with Marxist-Leninist movements, it has developed its own rationales for opposing capitalism and has shifted the terms of debate leftward, even among church conservatives (Levine, 1988).

In addition, the presence of antisystemic movements has stimulated the Church's anticapitalist movement in more cooperative ways. Some of that cooperation has been at the level of theory, as liberation theologians have employed frameworks and insights developed by secular thinkers (for example, dependency theory) (Novak, 1982; Hyett, 1987). While this development has had its problems, including at times a too simplistic economic analysis in theological works, on the whole religious groups and individuals have learned much from nonreligious scholars.

At the level of practice, the cooperative efforts between Christians and secular opponents of capitalism have been important in stimulating new innovations and insights (see, for example, Mainwaring, 1986). With antisystemic movements enduring and recurring, the prospects for encouraging anticapitalism within the Church—from competitive or cooperative situations—seems strong well into the future. While not all antisystemic movements should be expected to prompt anticapitalist development within the Church, their impact in combination with other factors seems to point toward less receptivity to capitalism rather than more.

ECCLESIAL

Religious Competition. Denominational pluralism—and competition—is a fact of life within Christianity, one not likely to disappear absent radical, sustained changes within religious communities and the secular cultures within which they operate. When placed in context with a number of nonstructural but entrenched factors in recent Latin American religious experience, religious competition appears likely to push the Catholic Church further from capitalist sympathies.

By itself, of course, religious competition cannot be offered as an anti-capitalist dynamic; the claim here is that competition has encouraged certain pastoral practices, innovations, and lessons (discussed more in a later section of this chapter) likely to endure into the foreseeable future. These innovations and lessons can be expected to reinforce the anticapitalist movement in the Church. Such a dynamic has been noticeable in the postwar era, and current circumstances make it reasonable to predict its recurrence.

Religious competition is not new in Latin America, but a major wave of Protestant mission activity developed after World War II, especially after missionaries were evicted from China. Small, close-knit Protestant communities, sponsored largely by mainline denominations and some Evangelicals in the United States, found support in areas where traditional community and religious (read Catholic) ties had weakened, as in the favelas of Brazil (Adriance, 1986, p. 15). By the end of the 1950s the number of people joining Protestant churches, while still low in overall terms, was sufficient to concern official Catholic leaders. Compared with pre-Vatican II Catholic parishes, Protestant congregations enjoyed many advantages, including ample numbers of clergy, married and living with the community, rather than unmarried priests who received their training in far-away Catholic seminaries; smaller, more personal faith communities; and more emotionally satisfying styles of worship, conducted in the local language.

As mentioned in chapter 2, the challenge of Protestant mission programs helped push the Catholic hierarchy toward a variety of pastoral experiments, most notably the base communities, intended to stop the rising number of defections. These experiments, taken together, have been important in creating new dynamics among hierarchy, priests and religious, and the majority of Catholics that have increased awareness throughout the Church of the impact of market forces. While some of these experiments were initiated with conservative, status quo ends in view, several developed in ways unforeseen by their originators (Adriance, 1986).

The phenomenon of religious competition remains, although the nature of challenges to the Catholic position has changed since the 1950s. According to data summarized by Lernoux, current estimates are that one-eighth of Latin Americans now belong to one or another Protestant group; in some countries, like Guatemala, Church analysts predict that half the population will switch churches by the end of the century. Recent Protestant mission programs in Brazil, primarily Pentecostal in nature, have flourished especially where Catholic parishes are understaffed or where few CEBS exist; research by Catholic scholars there suggest that Pentecostal growth correlates with deteriorating social and economic conditions (Lernoux, 1989, p. 154). As Lernoux notes, religious competition has made CEBS indispensable to many Catholic leaders, whatever their reservations, since many of them see CEBS as

> the best hope to counter the spread of generally anti-Catholic, born-again churches. Although the socially activist communities are the political opposites of the fundamentalists, they offer many of the same things that attract the poor to the latter, including a more personalized religious environment, solidarity, and a sense of equality. Surveys by Catholic institutions showed that wherever base communities flourished, fundamentalist churches were unlikely to gain recruits. (1989, p. 153)

Clergy Shortage. Another impetus pushing the Catholic Church to change is the shortage of ordained Catholic clergy and the central role assigned to them. The shortage presents itself not as inevitable but as the product of longstanding Catholic juridical norms, changes in which would require major structural alterations in the Church's institutional framework.

The clergy shortage assumes a causal role in the matters under consideration by limiting the range of options open to hierarchical leaders; no matter what they might want to do in response to competition from Evangelical and Pentecostal Protestants, they cannot build a strategy around Catholic priests. In one way or another, any response presupposes a significant and meaningful role for the laity and religious congregations. Just as the first postwar response to Protestant mission activities prompted Catholic leaders in Brazil to rely heavily on popular catechists and women religious (Adriance, 1986, pp. 53–54), it is likely that any response to current conditions will of necessity do the same. And as I argue in a subsequent section on pastoral experiences, important sectors of the laity, having experienced real responsibility and collegiality in pastoral activities, are unlikely to submit to a top-down, hierarchically dominated style of pastoral action. The clergy shortage ensures that para-ecclesial actors and the laity more generally will play important roles in Latin American Catholicism. When the nature of those actors' experiences and roles in the recent past are taken into account, the overall movement in opposition to capitalism is likely to continue.

Diversity of Ecclesial and Para-Ecclesial Actors. Religious pluralism within world Christianity, which gives rise both to cooperation and competition among faith communities and institutions, has its parallel within world Catholicism. Within the Catholic Church a variety of actors and institutions coexist in ways relevant to discerning the likely futures of the Latin American Church.

The existence of many types of actors (diocesan vs. religious, for example), of institutions with varying degrees of autonomy from episcopal control (for example, research institutes, universities, lay movements), and of complex and often cumbersome bureaucracies and chains of command, all ensure that hierarchical leaders require broad support and cooperation if their priorities are to be implemented effectively. This is important as a structural concern insofar as overall institutional complexity reduces the short-term impact of sudden top-down reversals of direction. The priorities, values, and programs associated with Vatican II, Medellin, and Puebla have been diffused throughout the structures and animators of the Latin American Church—indeed, of the Church worldwide. This complexity is both an institutional constant and a backdrop for more specific forces pushing the Latin American Church further against capitalism. These nonstructural but entrenched factors, especially relating to religious orders and pastoral resistance to conservative hierarchical edicts, are discussed later in this chapter.

Class Composition of the Latin American Church. This issue, discussed in chapter 2, points to the underlying reality of who makes up the Latin American Church. As a group, these Catholics are extremely poor, and they are growing both in numbers and significance to the Church. The class composition of the Church constitutes a structural fact that, given other developments, plays an important role as the Church at various levels redefines its primary constituency, membership, and target populations. Being a church of poor and relatively powerless people places limits on what Church leaders, activists, and members will ordinarily propose or do; conversely, possibilities exist for a church of poor people that are unavailable to an upper-class or middle-class community. The sheer number of poor people in the Latin American Church has had profound effects on the Church's theology and pastoral practice; as the majority group within the Church, a group suffering most from the workings of the world economy, the poor will continue to confront other Christians regularly and most acutely with questions of economic justice. Being a church of poor people means that decisions about the capitalist economy must be constantly reevaluated; as other developments continue to mobilize and create greater awareness among poor Catholics (as I will argue), their foundational importance in Latin American Catholicism will grow.

STRUCTURAL FACTORS TENDING TO REFUTE THE THESIS

POLITICAL-ECONOMIC FACTORS

The willingness of capitalist elites and state actors to defend the present world-system constitutes a structural feature working in opposition to the trends I discern. The movement of the Catholic Church in an antisystemic direction has provoked a vigorous reaction and numerous strategies designed to undermine the anticapitalist sectors of the Church while building a procapitalist constituency.

A few examples will suffice. As early as 1969, an extensive fact-finding report to President Nixon from Nelson Rockefeller cautioned that the Catholic Church, formerly a reliable ally of the U.S. government, was now vulnerable to "subversive penetration" (quoted in Lernoux, 1980, p. 59; see also Aguirre, 1989, p. 5). In 1980 key members of the incoming Reagan foreign policy team issued *A New Inter-American Policy for the Eighties*. This so-called Santa Fe Document, written by Roger Fontaine (later Reagan's Central America adviser on the National Security Council) and Lewis Tambs (Reagan's ambassador to Costa Rica), suggested that opposition to liberation theology be an important part of U.S. policy in the region. The document charges that liberation theologians "use the church as a political arm against private property and productive capitalism," and it recommends countermeasures (quoted in Aguirre, 1989, p. 5).

In 1984 the second Santa Fe document, also from the private Inter-American Security Council, was published. This piece, *The Pursuit of the Conservative Revolution*, urged the president to establish links with conservative sectors of the Catholic Church and continue efforts against liberation theology (Aguirre, 1989, p. 5).

The U.S. government's strategy in this arena has taken many forms: making common cause with Catholic conservatives to pressure Pope John Paul II into an anti-Sandinista line; using conservative Evangelicals such as Jimmy Swaggart, Pat Robertson, and José Efraín Ríos Montt to advance U.S. interests in Latin America; and equating Church progressives with the international communist movement (Lernoux 1989, pp. 59, 66, 157–58; Aguirre, 1989). On this last point the 17th Conference of American Armies, a gathering of all American military chiefs of staff (except Cuba and Nicaragua) from November 14–17, 1987, in Argentina, studied two themes in detail: the connection between subversion and drug trafficking, and the subversive quality of liberation theology. A confidential conference document on liberation theology, leaked nearly two years later, asserts:

Without doubt, the international communist movement, conscious of the possibility of getting at the power factor at the source of values that is the church, has accentuated the contradiction in what it calls "the religious front." The debates provoked by the new theological reflection, encouraged by the media, intentionally or by negligence, have created a favorable climate and the auspicious tone for Marxist penetration of theology in Catholic and, in general, Christian practice. The contradictions have been accentuated both in strictly doctrinal matters and by the permanent encouragement of the confrontation between the "hierarchy" and the "bases." (quoted in Aguirre, 1989, p. 17)

This structural opposition between the increasingly anticapitalist Church and state/military elites has had a profound effect on the region. The conflict has taken on an exterminatory quality in places where military dictatorships have sought to tame the Church (for example, Guatemala, El Salvador, Paraguay, Brazil). While the conflict has not reached such a state in most of the region, nevertheless the anti-systemic movement of the Church is not going unchallenged by political and economic institutions and actors.

ECCLESIAL FACTORS

Scholars disagree on useful markers of origin, but the Gregorian reforms that strengthened the papal and curial offices in relation to state authority seem a good place from which to date the Vatican's most recent centralizing, controlling tendencies (see Pizzorno, 1987, pp. 27–62). The Vatican bureaucracy, which runs a small city-state and coordinates a worldwide religious organization, has been overestimated by some in its efficiency and size, but it remains a force unique to Roman Catholicism as a religious movement. Curial reforms, some of a potentially drastic nature, were outlined by Pope Paul VI but left incomplete and abandoned by his successors. As one analyst observes: "It must, however, be admitted that the trend over the last 200 years has been toward greater centralization, with the years 1962–66 standing out as the timid and doomed exception" (Hebblethwaite, 1988a, p. 50).

The hostility expressed by many Vatican offices and bureaus to the new directions in the Church are only partly ideological; indeed, statements and programs by Vatican agencies have done much to encourage the critical spirit of the Church in matters of economic justice. It is true, however, that bureaucracies—religious ones being no exception—

usually prefer stable, predictable relations with other power centers, especially with civil authorities. Such relations are threatened by the anticapitalist orientation of many local churches. Further, the organizational complexity of the Vatican provides procapitalist Catholics with many points of entry and influence in Curial politics; the disproportionate leverage of right-wing U.S. Catholic media like the Wanderer is due in no small measure to some skill at manipulating the Vatican bureaucracy.

What puts the Curia as an institution most at odds with the trends discussed here is a profound difference in ecclesiology. The Curia remains the institutional focus for hierarchical, centralized, and universalistic ecclesiologies. More antagonistic than the content of the new directions—hostility to capitalism is not ultimately decisive—are their institutional and methodological qualities. Vatican II's emphasis on collegiality among bishops and local churches has been important in the development of cross-national religious ideas; it is precisely this collegiality that was resisted by the Curia in the 1960s and which it attempted to undermine by attacking national episcopal conferences in the 1980s. Even more dangerous to Curial power, and subject to even more calumny, are the base communities through which grass-roots experience of capitalist dislocation has worked its way through the Church.

According to Leonardo Boff, the distribution of power in CEBS is more participatory, decentralized, and democratic than in traditional Church structures (L. Boff, 1985, p. 9). To another observer, CEBS introduce a congregational element into Catholicism (Levine, 1986a, p. 15); to yet another, they "represent both a theological and organizational revolution for they reflect a democratization of the religious institution" (Dodson, 1986, p. 81). Some scholars continue to debate how great the democratizing effect of the CEBS on the Church has been (Mainwaring and Wilde, 1989, chap. 1). Lernoux (1989, p. 133) captures most of the ecclesiological conflict by noting, in the Brazilian context,

> The Curia did not like the base communities because they were agents of democratization within the church and challenged Brazil's political and economic authorities. According to some in the Vatican, the Brazilian church's concern with the poor made it "sectarian" because it paid insufficient attention to the needs of the middle and upper classes.

Elsewhere, the Curia rejected some proposed constitutions for religious orders because of the more democratic internal governance procedures and strong social priorities sought by the orders (Lernoux, 1989, p. 245).

Unless there are radical changes in the Curia itself, the central structure of the Catholic Church is likely to resist any changes that promise conflict with political elites and greater democratization (see L. Boff, 1985). When this structural factor coincides with a contingent one— the selection of a centralizing, authority-seeking pope—its impact is increased and its reach enlarged. As shown in the case of world episcopal synods, John Paul II and the Curia together have taken a vehicle envisioned at Vatican II as one of ongoing collegiality and are transforming it "into a body that rallies round the primate against perceived troublemakers out there" (Hebblethwaite, 1988a, p. 45).

NONSTRUCTURAL (BUT DEEPLY ENTRENCHED) FACTORS SUPPORTING THE ANTICAPITALIST TREND

POLITICAL-ECONOMIC FACTORS

Factors under this heading are episodic, in the sense of not being of necessity regular, repeating, or easily predictable from structural factors; nevertheless, they are traceable post hoc from such structural phenomena, and thus they are more rooted than are more purely contingent or happenstance events.

Perhaps the clearest example of a nonstructural but entrenched factor pushing the Church toward an anticapitalist position is the Third World debt issue. Given that the deleterious consequences of the external debt—declining public services, rising food and energy prices, rising unemployment—have fallen hardest on the poor in Latin America (see, for example, Guillen, 1989), the Church once again finds itself enmeshed in a controversy. As states push for increased foreign exchange, ecological pressures (for example, in the Amazon) mount, and repression in public and private forms increases (see "War in the Amazon," 1989).

All of this has served to increase Church hostility to capitalism, not only because of increased suffering, but because the role of institutional actors (like the IMF), political machinations, and the exclusionary decision procedures typical of capitalism are unusually visible to all. At all levels, from the hierarchy to the base, the debt is affecting how Catholics view their economic system. Nor is this relevant only to progressive Church elements. Few bodies are more conservative than the Mexican bishops' conference, but even that group has been critical of many fundamentals of capitalism as a result of the debt (see "The External Debt," 1988). Similarly, the Bolivian bishops, by no definition a radical group, unanimously condemned laissez-faire government policies, the IMF, and other capitalist actors; two Bolivian ordinaries said it was immoral for Bolivia to pay its external debt (McCoy, 1987, p. 264).

What makes the debt episode so significant is the extent to which church people—across the ideological spectrum—have begun to link it to other processes and problems tied to the world economy. Given the importance of the issue in the domestic politics of many Latin American countries, it is probably not surprising that Church documents—from base community congresses to episcopal pronouncements (for example, by Samuel Carter of Jamaica, Paulo Arns of São Paulo)—should demonstrate a high level of analytic sophistication. Ironically, the Church document that least effectively analyzes the debt crisis may well be that of the U.S. Catholic bishops, who seek its resolution within the framework of largely unchanged capitalist relations.

ECCLESIAL FACTORS

Papal Encyclicals and Official Documents. Too much can be made of official statements that come from Church leaders. Whether from popes, bishops' conferences, or Church agencies, such statements may only occasionally reflect or affect life at other levels of the Church.

Still, official statements and documents do have some role to play, particularly in a tradition-conscious institution like the Catholic Church. If for no other reason than that it is rare for past statements to be repudiated outright (de facto change is more common), position statements of institutional leaders should be carefully weighed when matters of continuity, change, and struggles over interpretation are considered. Overall, the statements of the official Church—popes and bishops' groups, among others—support the thesis of increasing anticapitalism. This is so despite the generally conservative nature of such statements: their concern for cooperation and aversion to conflict, their often extreme generality and abstraction, and their incrementalist view of acceptable change.

Papal and conciliar statements are discussed in more detail elsewhere (Dorr, 1983; O'Brien and Shannon, 1977). For now, several qualities of such statements are relevant to my thesis.

Considering papal encyclicals, for example, several trends are apparent in economics, from Leo XIII's *Rerum Novarum* (1891) to John Paul II's *Sollicitudo Rei Socialis* (1988). One trend is an increasingly harsh tone critical of capitalism; while Leo XIII criticized what he saw as an extreme form of capitalism, subsequent papal documents focused on capitalism in its fundamentals. Pius XI attacked liberal capitalism as "the international imperialism of money" (*Quadragesimo Anno*, 1931). Among the harshest critics of the international economic order was Paul VI, whose *Progressio Populorum* (1967) pushed developmentalist political economy to its limits with his demands for economic justice. As noted by O'Brien and Shannon (1977, p. 308):

> The Pope rejects quite unequivocally many of the basic precepts of capitalism, including unrestrained private property, the profit motive, and reliance on free trade in the world economy. . . . While overall the call is for the wealthy to fulfill their moral duty, there is at least a suggestion that in the extreme situation, the poor retain the right to a violent solution to their problems.

John Paul II in *Sollicitudo Rei Socialis*, extending Paul VI's themes, writes of the world economy:

> One must denounce the existence of economic, financial and social mechanisms which, although they are manipulated by people, often function almost automatically, thus accentuating the situation of wealth for some and poverty for the rest. These mechanisms, which are maneuvered directly or more indirectly by the more developed countries, by their very functioning favor the interests of the people manipulating them. (Pope John Paul II, 1988d, pp. 646–47)

In a section that infuriated North American conservatives, John Paul II writes:

> In the West, there exists a system which is historically inspired by the principles of liberal capitalism which developed with industrialization in the last century. In the East there exists a system inspired by the Marxist collectivism which sprang from an interpretation of the conditions of the proletarian classes made in the light of a particular reading of history. Each of the two ideologies, on the basis of two very different visions of man and of his freedom and social role, has proposed and still promotes on the economic level antithetical forms of the organization of labor and of the structure of ownership, especially with regard to the so-called means of production. (1988d, p. 647)

> Each of the two blocs harbors in its own way a tendency toward imperialism, as it is usually called, or toward forms of neo-colonialism: an easy temptation to which they frequently succumb, as history, including recent history, teaches (1988d, p. 648).

Elsewhere, this pope has spoken of the judgment of the poor South against the rich North (Lernoux, 1989, p. 195) and has often adopted much of a dependency perspective in his North-South messages.

John Paul's most recent social encyclical, *Centesimus Annus* (1991), may represent an end to the anticapitalist trend in papal documents. Although caution should be used in reading *Centesimus* as an endorsement of capitalism (Windsor, 1991, p. 3; Wilber, 1991, p. 8), I agree with neoconservatives who draw that conclusion (Neuhaus, 1991). While I find *Centesimus* to verge on economic incoherence (see Budde, 1991), its affirmation of what the pope understands capitalism to be is far stronger than anything written by his predecessors. Whether *Centesimus* should be seen as a momentary departure from a more enduring trend, or whether it should be viewed as the first step in a dramatic reversal of that trend, depends on future events. The encyclical's impact on the Church will largely hinge on how effectively procapitalist groups employ it as a theological cudgel, and by whether its intellectual and ecclesial positions are adopted by John Paul's successors.

Two other matters concerning high-level social ethics merit mention. First, while procapitalist groups in the Church may employ *Centesimus* for their own ends, overall the "official" teachings of popes and the universal Church (for example, Vatican II), despite their basic conservatism, have been used to anchor, justify, and encourage more radical moves by Church people. Just as the Medellin documents were validated at Puebla, so did the Medellin authors draw on *Progressio Populorum* and the Vatican II documents to legitimate their new directions. Many activities and viewpoints relevant to increasing anticapitalism, including those of the CEBS, have gained legitimacy from official documents at several levels.

This process is likely to continue because of the second matter of interest here: namely, the perseverance of a distinctly Catholic notion of private property preserved in encyclicals and conciliar documents. The development of this theory of property has been explored elsewhere (Budde, 1985); for now, it is enough to say that this theory, which combines the right to property with a heavy "social mortgage" on right use, widespread distribution, and availability for the needs of the poor, conflicts with liberal and collectivist ideas. This "official" Catholic view provides the basis for a conservative critique of capitalism distinct from neocorporatist arrangements and maintains a critical distance from state-oriented alternatives, including state socialism. This theory may be used more fully in years ahead as another base for critiques of capitalism. (Some developments, for example, journals such as *New Oxford Review*, suggest such a trend already may be under way.) This notion of property is preserved even in *Centesimus*; the lack of fit between that notion and the pope's affirmation of capitalism is among the encyclical's many intellectual weaknesses.

Pastoral Experiences. The postwar era has seen substantial pastoral innovation, giving rise to enriching religious experiences for much of the Latin American Church. Likewise, pastoral innovation and adaptations in response to social challenges and shifts in theological thinking have strongly influenced people throughout the region. Several of these experiences support the thesis of increased opposition to capitalism insofar as they complement the structural factors already discussed; in themselves, such innovations and experiences will not soon be forgotten or eradicated.

Two of them—CEBs and the development of pastoral agents—will be examined. Levine (1987a) is impressed by

> the continued impact of innovations set in motion over the last fifteen years. A new discourse about justice and equality, rooted in biblical and religious themes, is now very widespread and should remain vital to religious life. There will, of course, be continuing struggle to control the specific texts and images used and discussed, but the center of gravity has shifted. (p. 104)

As the Church's experiences of the 1950s suggest, even conservative religious leaders, when pressed, can choose innovative pastoral strategies. This happened with regard to urban and rural co-ops and unions, which were assisted by priests given considerable latitude by conservative bishops concerned about communism (Adriance, 1986, p. 31). One analyst suggests that the impact of pastoral and theological innovations may be more significant in Latin America than elsewhere.

> Chronological and social time are not identical in Latin America. The Second Vatican Council came earlier in the social development of Latin America than in that of Europe. Latin America presents both a past almost lost elsewhere and a future that may be ahead of its time. (Martin, 1988, p. 14)

Finally, as Lernoux suggests (1989, p. 116), to a certain degree the impact of innovative practices are not easily reversed.

> After two decades of church-supported grass-roots organizing, the Latin American poor are too "liberated" in the practice of their faith to return to the old ways. . . . As San Salvador's Archbishop Rivera y Damas observed, the church of the poor will continue on its own path regardless of ecclesiastical power struggles.

CEBs. The base community movement has become perhaps the most closely studied new development within the Catholic Church since Vatican II (see, e.g., Azvedo, 1987; Mainwaring, 1986; Barreiro, 1977). Much early literature on the CEBS reflects a degree of enthusiasm verging on gross naïveté; by contrast, more recent literature highlights problems of CEBS (Mainwaring, 1986) and confusion over basic definitions and qualities (Levine, 1986c).

As usually described, CEBS are small gatherings of people (ten to twenty families) who engage in religious and practical mutual support—from prayer groups and Bible studies, mundane material assistance and self-help projects, to political and social activism on some occasions. CEBS in most countries have begun with the support of local bishops, although Bruneau (1979, p. 231) may overestimate the degree to which CEBS require episcopal support (e.g., Dodson and Montgomery, 1982; Lernoux 1989, p. 120). Almost all CEBS emphasize egalitarian and democratic internal values and seek to apply the Gospel to their everyday reality.

The CEB movement, while not enlisting a majority of Latin American Catholics, has shown itself to be a valuable innovation to Church leaders at all levels and in contexts far removed from Latin America (e.g., Quevedo, 1982, p. 11). Fights for control over the direction and tenor of the CEBS will undoubtedly continue (Levine 1986b; *Latinamerica Press*, March 9, 1989), but they do too many things too well for their elimination from the ecclesial scene to be a serious proposal.

Three qualities of CEBS suggest their importance in increasing the anticapitalist movement within the Church. First is the class composition of most CEBS; almost all are made up of poor people, with little or no involvement of the middle and upper classes (Mainwaring and Wilde, 1989, chap. 1). Surveys of CEBS in Brazil (summarized in Barreiro, 1977, p. 8) attest to the overwhelming presence of extremely poor people; after several years of experience with CEBS, the archdiocese of São Paulo reported:

> the creation of CEBS has taken place among the lower socio-economic classes. And, in the poorer areas, it has been noted that the most underprivileged have been the ones most receptive to this ecclesial notion. The difficulties among the other classes are considerable, and when ecclesial groups come into existence, they often become closed and introspective. (in Barreiro, 1977, p. 13)

In 1989 Lernoux noted that "although the Peruvian church has attempted to attract members of the middle and upper classes to such communities, few have joined the movement because of class prejudices and the indifference of affluent Peruvians to social injustice" (p. 117).

This quality—their compatibility with the poor—has been maintained as CEBS have been instituted outside Latin America. In the Philippines, CEBs have been based primarily among the poor (Butalid, 1982; Friesen, 1988), and similar developments are reported in Africa and Asia (e.g., Height, 1982; Bottar, 1982; Healey, 1987; Quevedo, 1982).

This first consideration—CEBs as intermediate institutions (or "public space") for poor people—takes on greater importance when combined with two other relevant factors. One of them relates to practices within the CEBs; the other to the development of critical thinking skills.

The CEBs often, but not always, offer poor people experiences of democratic decision-making, egalitarianism, and frequently a sense of empowerment. Such opportunities for interaction make it possible for poor people, many displaced by instabilities and changes in economic conditions, to build solidarity and overcome isolation and self-blame. And as Levine (1986d) and others have pointed out, participation in one aspect of life often has increased the desire for participation in others. The spillover into political and religious decision-making is particularly significant. It is precisely the collision between economic development plans premised on popular exclusion (see Evans, 1979) and demands for popular inclusion (Hinchberger, 1989) from which future anticapitalism is likely to emerge. As has been true in the past (Bruneau, 1979, p. 326; B. Smith, 1982, pp. 261–62), the CEBs' social importance may increase if future authoritarian regimes outlaw other forms of opposition or participation.

This participatory style also has implications for internal Church affairs. Episcopal leaders concerned with reining in activist or critical CEBs will find that easier said than done, hence providing some protection against such winds of ecclesial caprice (e.g., Molineaux, 1988, p. 3; Latinamerica Press, March 9, 1989).

The third aspect of CEBs likely to continue moving them in anticapitalist directions is the pedagogical theory of conscientization (growing political and social awareness) that has infused much of the movement since its earliest days. Developed by Brazilian educator Paulo Freire, conscientization is an educational philosophy centered on "learning to perceive social, political, and economic contradictions, and to take action against the oppressive elements of reality" (1970, p. 19). This approach to learning and praxis has formed the centerpiece of countless training programs for CEB leaders and pastoral agents and has influenced religious education materials in fundamentally radical ways (Pastoral Team of Bambamarca, 1985).

These three qualities—class composition, internal relations and dynamics, and conscientization—interact to give the CEBs their radical, anticapitalist character. Individual CEBs may not be socially or theologically radical—indeed, Levine suggests that some conservative bishops have simply renamed conservative, traditional parish groups as CEBs to steal the movement's thunder—but on the whole the movement's direction as an anticapitalist force seems set.

Pastoral Agents. The significance of pastoral agents (the "semi-institutional" actors between hierarchy and base, discussed in chapter 2) cannot be underestimated in assessing the future of the Latin American Church. Throughout the region pastoral agents of many types—lower diocesan and religious clergy, women religious, trained lay persons including Delegates of the Word, and catechists—have sparked many new directions in the Church. Whether organizing CEBs and teaching approaches to the Bible that will raise political consciousness, or reporting on the praxis of poor Christians to episcopal and outside audiences, pastoral agents have been a crucial group in the Latin American religious scene. As Levine notes (1988, p. 256): "Liberation theology's most enduring impacts are likely to come through the development of new structures, mediating agents, and new styles of leaders drawn from hitherto oppressed and quiescent social strata. Pastoral agents play a key role carrying ideas and getting the new groups going."

In Brazil in the 1950s and 1960s, with five times more nuns than priests in the field, it was these religious women who spearheaded early CEB organizing, parish administration, and a general opening of roles to the laity and nonordained. Other factors contributing to the more radical type of pastoral agent were the Catholic Action experience (and shift in methods), innovations in seminary training, and the influx of new missionaries (Adriance, 1986, pp. 57–58, 111).

In Nicaragua, pastoral agents trained by the Jesuits and Capuchins in the early 1970s were instrumental in organizing and assisting the rural poor, and they were outside local episcopal control. The agents' efforts in literacy education, conscientization, and liturgical change eventually became explicitly political, initially "without telling the priests" (Dodson and Montgomery, 1982, p. 171).

Training for pastoral agents has come from many sources—local bishops, independent religious orders, and independent associations—but pastoral agents have done more than carry new organizational and theological ideas to the grass roots. Equally important in some respects is the extent to which they have conveyed the experiences of the base— the suffering, persecution, poverty, and spirituality there—to Church leaders. Adriance's study kept encountering the "conversion of bishops" in Brazil; there, many original supporters of the coup (and conservatives in ideology more generally) changed their views when confronted with the military's impact on the poor. So often did this happen, in fact, that Adriance suggests a general pattern of military repression plus increased impoverishment plus the emergence of conscientized poor people leading to changes in a bishop. She offers Cardinal Ivo Lorscheiter as a prime, but not unusual, example (1986, pp. 142–44).

The interaction between pastoral agents and the poor has been crucial to this process. In one example from the 1950s Adriance notes:

> When the priests began to question the rural situation, the people began to trust them and to tell them more—accounts of abusive treatment by the landowners, imprisonment, torture, death. . . . At the grassroots level, there was the beginning of an intense process of mutual education between the priests and the lay people. (1986, p. 31)

In 1989 Lernoux (p. 129) observed that killings of pastoral agents and others advocating land reform prompted the 11 bishops of Maranhão (Brazil) to excommunicate the state governor, the secretary of justice and public security, and the local head of the landowners' association.

This in-between position of pastoral agents gives them an important role in pushing the Church further into an anticapitalist position. They will be important in transmitting the real-life impact of economic pressures on the Church's base to higher levels; they are crucial to the formation and operation of CEBs and other measures of evangelization and Church presence in an era with a shortage of priests; and the mobility and flexibility of many (especially those affiliated with religious communities) give them some degree of independence from episcopal backlash or timidity.

Religious Orders and Congregations. The structural diversity within the Catholic Church makes unilateral policy implementation no easy task. If it is true that some Church leaders prefer a more congenial relationship with capitalism, such is not the case with many of the most important religious orders and congregations. With notable exceptions, the religious orders—the Jesuits, Franciscans, Dominicans, and Benedictines—in Third World countries and worldwide have maintained a progressive orientation on social ethics and pastoral practice despite hostility from the Vatican. Lernoux suggests why such pressures are less effectively applied to religious orders and congregations:

> An individual bishop can be monitored and isolated, since he is physically stationary in a diocese. A bishops' conference, though more unwieldy, can also be kept under observation by the papal nun-

cio. And of course Rome holds the ultimate weapon in its power to appoint bishops. In contrast, the religious orders are scattered all over the world and are not subject to the same controls as diocesan priests, who work under the bishops in the hierarchical chain of command. The religious have their own constitutions and elect their own leaders, and are self-financed and to a large extent self-motivated. While Rome can cause the religious orders a good deal of distress—and did so—it has not been able to get a hold on them because their memberships are too numerous and diffuse, and their leaders too intelligent. (1989, p. 354)

With their own permanent staff in Rome defending their interests and autonomy, the orders in recent years have proved skilled at playing Curial politics. Effective use of a variety of tactics, including false compliance, foot-dragging, and logrolling have been generally successful in keeping conservative bureaucrats at bay (Lernoux, 1989, p. 360).

In general, the Jesuits, Franciscans, and Dominicans have been receptive to liberation theology and Vatican II and have acted to continue the directions of both. After papal intervention into Jesuit affairs removed progressive leader Pedro Arrupe in the early 1980s, the order elected a low-profile Dutch linguist, Peter-Hans Kolvenbach, who turned out to be "just as committed to liberation theology and an option for the poor as Arruppe had been." With the heads of the Dominicans and Franciscans, Kolvenbach defended religious progressives from Vatican reprisals and oversaw an upsurge in Jesuit vocations from Third World countries. The Dominicans, even more radical on religious and economic affairs, also contributed to Third World progressivism (Lernoux, 1989, pp. 357–58).

While tensions exist within the orders, their Third World members have continued to move ahead in a pro-Vatican II direction and in support of liberation theology (Lernoux, 1989, p. 358). Perhaps most important in the Latin American context, it was the religious orders that mitigated the effects of a conservative takeover of the Latin American Bishops Conference (CELAM) soon after Medellin. Lernoux says most Latin American bishops, despite the change in orientation at CELAM, did not abandon liberation theology and the option for the poor. One reason

was that the religious orders remained steadfast to Medellin, many of their members dying for its commitment to the poor. When CELAM would no longer carry the banner, the Latin American Confederation of Religious (CLAR) took up the cause despite dire threats from CELAM's then secretary general, the Colombian López Trujillo. (1989, p. 354)

In 1988 CLAR reaffirmed that the preferential option for the poor should be the central task of clergy and religious (*Latinamerica Press*, July 7, 1988, p. 2). Given that many leading liberation theologians, pastoral training institutes, and publications are affiliated with religious orders and congregations, such a commitment has great significance. The orders provide institutional support and protection for the anticapitalist elements within the Latin American Church regardless of changes in individual dioceses or bishops' conferences. As an example of such a commitment in practice, a coalition of religious orders decided to establish a human rights monitoring agency after the Guatemala City archdiocese dropped the office ("Religious Take Rights Office Diocese Drops," *National Catholic Reporter*, May 19, 1989).

The Freedom to Fight Back. Another significant factor, less easily classified, is the willingness of lay persons and lower clergy to defend liberation theology and similar movements from ecclesial attacks. This was not always true, to be sure. While compliance with hierarchical decrees has never been complete (witness the vitality of "popular religion," in Reilly, 1986), principled and vocal disagreement with Church leaders is a new experience for poor Latin American Catholics. It suggests that those committed to the option for the poor and alternatives to capitalism will not easily be silenced.

While several Latin American countries have predominantly conservative bishops, all of them have seen "the emergence of a group of radical Catholics, among priests and among laity" (Martin, 1988, p. 20). For example, the top-down CEBs, instituted by the Colombian hierarchy and bearing no resemblance to more participatory CEBs, have prompted a thriving parallel movement of independent base communities (Lernoux, 1989, p. 120). In October 1988, three thousand representatives of Catholic and Protestant CEBs met in Bogotá over the hierarchy's objections. The meeting, composed of 97 percent lay people, rejected payment of the nation's $15 billion foreign debt and denounced land concentration in Colombia. The movement reportedly has grown considerably from a base of 500 CEBs in 1985, although exact numbers do not exist (*Latinamerica Press*, March 23, 1989).

Throughout the region, it remains true that CEBs are unwilling to surrender their autonomy and critical thinking. Leaders of CEBs in the northern zone of Santiago asked Auxiliary Bishop Antonio Moreno to resign, claiming he was an obstacle to the Church's well-being, not open to the CEBS, and a pro-coup sympathizer (*Latinamerica Press*, March 9, 1989).

In Peru, where the hierarchy has moved rightward since a 1971 document rejected capitalism and called for Church support for socialist alternatives, the CEBs remain widespread, vibrant, and committed to liberation theology perspectives (Molineaux, 1988). The enduring nature of previous radical commitments is similarly visible in the diocese of São Luís in Brazil, where progressive Dom José Delgado presided in the 1950s and 1960s; his successors have not been progressives, but in the mid-1980s the diocese was still influenced by lay leadership encouraged and developed under Delgado (Adriance, 1986, pp. 54–56).

Support from Other Churches and Coreligionists. While difficult to assess or measure, the anticapitalist movement within the Latin American Church draws support from like-minded groups and individuals in other countries. This transnational support, possible within the Catholic Church in ways unique to its structures and linkages, has meant that liberation theology, the CEBs, and the option for the poor have become worldwide phenomena. The anticapitalist thrust of liberation theology, for example, cannot be ghettoized as a regional aberration, given its emergence in Africa (Wan-Tateh, 1984; Boesak 1978, 1987), Asia (Pieris, 1988; Balasuriya, 1984, 1988; Song, 1986), the Philippines (Friesen, 1988), and in numerous Northern variations.

At the theological level, the Ecumenical Association of Third World Theologians (EATWOT) has facilitated the exchange of ideas and contacts for more than a decade. Institutional support from Orbis Press, the publishing arm of the Maryknoll congregation, has communicated the EATWOT proceedings (and liberation theology from all parts of the Third World) through much of the English-speaking world.

Missionary congregations such as Maryknoll play an important role in sensitizing First World Catholics to political and religious developments in other parts of the world. Mission linkages also are likely to build Third World support for Latin American efforts, as larger numbers of missionaries are drawn from peripheral countries (the Jesuits in India, for example, are now reputed to be net exporters of mission personnel). Important in both First and Third World contexts is the practice of "reverse mission," a practice Lernoux describes in the United States:

> On average, 1,000 Catholic missionaries return to the United States each year, for leave or reassignment. They form the core for a new type of work, known as "reverse mission," that developed in the early 1980s. Although traditional missionary appeals for prayers and money continued, the emphasis shifted from good works to reforming public opinion about the U.S. role in the Third World. Reverse mission was a way to get Americans to hear what the poor were saying, particularly in Central America. It was also a way to stimu-

late Americans to ask tough questions about what it meant to be a Christian in one of the world's wealthiest, most powerful nations. (1989, pp. 179–80)

The anticapitalist direction within Latin American Catholicism has attracted some support and financial assistance from Catholics, primarily activist groups and individuals, in the United States and other wealthy nations. Such support is yet another factor strengthening and encouraging the trends of interest here.

Quality of Theologians. Yet another element that is hard to evaluate is the superior quality of liberation theologians and others opposed to capitalism compared with the handful attempting theological justifications of the capitalist world order. The latter, far fewer in number, are often either Northerners (for example, Michael Novak) or tied to Northern institutions (like the American Enterprise Institute with which Novak is associated, or the Institute for Religion and Democracy, founded by Richard John Neuhaus). Many religious supporters of capitalism use research provided by the Instituto Libertad y Democracia in Lima, directed by Hernando de Soto, author of *The Other Path.* This institute enjoys close ties with Novak, Neuhaus, and other U.S. neoconservatives.

I do not assume that anticapitalist and liberation theologians as a group are intellectually superior to their procapitalist counterparts. More significant, in my view, is that newer generations of the former have benefited from seminary training based more in life with the poor and separated less from secular affairs (Adriance, 1986, p. 113). This change in training reflects lessons learned by the first generation of liberation theologians, many of whom trained in Europe and returned ill-prepared for life in slums and villages. This early generation faced many adjustments as they and their work were often (but not always) challenged by "the hunger, smells, noises, and sickness that constitute the daily struggle for survival in an overcrowded Third World slum" (Lernoux, 1989, pp. 92–93).

In addition, an increasing number of liberation theology journals, centers, and organizations exist to provide a forum and support for various activities (Richard, 1988). While procapitalist theologians in principle have access to vastly more resources, such support has not yet been institutionalized to a comparable degree. Insofar as theologians are an important contributing force for change within the Church (one of the peculiarly religious qualities of churches), the presence of numerous, diverse, and talented groups of theologians unsympathetic to capitalism cannot be discounted in overall assessments.

OPPOSITION TO THE ANTICAPITALIST TREND

POLITICAL-ECONOMIC OPPOSITION

Concomitant with the backlash of capitalist actors discussed earlier has been the upsurge in influence of the neoconservative movement in the industrialized countries. This movement, more activist, aggressive, and ambitious than the more genteel brands of conservatism that preceded it, has exercised considerable influence in the United States, Great Britain, and other European countries on a variety of fronts. Typical of the neoconservative movement has been an emphasis on cultural factors as crucial to their political agenda; reclaiming the legitimating cloak of religion for market systems has been among their major goals (for example, Novak, 1982).

Numerous organizations—think tanks, research institutes, foundations, and lobby groups—operate under the general mantle of neoconservatism. Without exception, neoconservatives have identified the "Marxist-Leninist" quality of liberation theology as among their major targets; with deep pockets of money, made possible in the United States by new conservative money (especially in oil and gas; see Dolbeare and Medcalf, 1985), the neoconservatives have developed an impressive cottage industry of procapitalist and antiliberation theological publications. The quality of such efforts varies from sophisticated (for example, some of George Weigel's work) to snarling (other parts of Weigel's work).

Two institutions act as centers for the neoconservative assault on liberation theology; their spokesmen have achieved considerable visibility and status among governmental leaders and some mainstream media. First among these is the American Enterprise Institute, whose activities under the rubric of religion and politics are directed by Michael Novak. A former self-described "radical Catholic," Novak has written several books and has organized symposia dedicated to attacking liberation theology and its practitioners. Novak also has organized countermoves to the pastoral letters on nuclear weapons and on the U.S. economy issued by the U.S. Catholic bishops. He criticized the bishops for insufficient patriotism, ignorance of economics, a rosy view of socialism, and an inadequate degree of revulsion toward communism. In recent years he has attempted to identify and showcase procapitalist Church people from Latin America as superior alternatives to liberation theologians; his theological work has focused on developing a Catholic apologia for capitalism, at one point identifying the modern corporation with the "suffering servant" metaphor in the book of Isaiah (usually reserved as a description of Christ) (Novak, 1981, p. 33).

The second organization, the Institute for Religion and Democracy, was founded by Richard John Neuhaus, a longtime Lutheran clergyman (before his conversion to Catholicism in 1990) and cofounder of Clergy and Laity Concerned in the 1960s. Neuhaus's IRD has sought to do with mainline Protestant denominations what Novak attempts with Catholics: to attack liberation theology as heterodox and Marxist-inspired, while promoting a new integration of Christian theology with national values and patriotism. The IRD has enjoyed much attention as the result of its attacks on the National Council of Churches for its "leftist" biases. Recently, Neuhaus has sought common cause with pro-U.S. Catholics in forging a new "language of public discourse" for American political life (see chapter 4). Through an arrangement with Eerdmans, a Grand Rapids, Mich., publishing house, the Rockford Institute, another Neuhaus group, has published a series of monographs attacking liberation theology and promoting a more patriotic alternative. Neuhaus and the Rockford Institute parted company in 1989.

Although the neoconservative offensive is aimed at religious ideas and institutions, it also should be considered as a political/economic force opposing the anticapitalist thrust within the Latin American Church. Much of the funding for groups such as AEI and IRD comes from nonreligious foundations and corporations; the theological quality of their case is uneven at best (e.g., Schaar, 1982; Steinfels, 1983), and overall they operate more as an arm of the neoconservative political movement than as primarily religious organizations. It is more difficult to identify points of disagreement based on theological principles between the secular neoconservative movement and its religious groups, for example, than it would between the secular left and liberation theology, where several disagreements have arisen (for example, over armed struggle and support for revolutionary or Marxist regimes).

ECCLESIAL OPPOSITION

Within Third World Churches. Some significant institutions and groups within Third World Catholicism are actively opposed to the anticapitalist direction charted by Latin American Catholics. Some oppose it because of a positive choice in favor of capitalism, although this is probably a minority view. A majority oppose it based on a variety of motives: anticommunism, a distaste for any conflict with civil authorities, a view of the Church that stresses internal unity at all costs, and dependence on the Vatican and conservatives in the Northern churches.

One of the most noteworthy institutions in this regard has been

CELAM, which now bears the strong stamp of Cardinal López Trujillo of Colombia. López Trujillo wrested control of CELAM from Church progressives after Medellin and attempted to root out any vestiges of liberation theology from its institutions. He attempted to orchestrate the Puebla conference toward a repudiation of Medellin's agenda, only to be thwarted by the Brazilian bishops and his own ineptitude (Eagleson and Scharper, 1979).

López Trujillo's influence has been considerable, although he is not an easily understood person. Known to have close relations with Pope John Paul II, the cardinal is hostile to liberation theology. Yet his hostility comes not from a love of capitalism; on the contrary, he generally finds little good to say about it. More threatening in his view is the ecclesiology of the liberation theologians. His own ecclesiology combines strong hierarchical control with a rejection of pastoral "options" for one group or another; he prefers a minimalist, sacramental universality, a picture of the Church as home to all, rich or poor, saints and sinners (Day, 1988, p. 4).

Two other examples of opposition to the anticapitalist movement reflect the dependence of Third World churches on the Vatican and on their national states. Many African Catholic hierarchies illustrate the former, while the Venezuelan hierarchy typifies the latter.

The Catholic Church in most of sub-Saharan Africa remains institutionally weak twenty-five years after Vatican II. For many, the Vatican remains a major source of funds (along with money from the churches of their former colonizers), with financial dependence exacerbated by the European, nonindigenized nature of the Church in many countries (Budde, 1987a). What progressive reforms did begin after Vatican II were led by white foreigners and bishops (a majority of African bishops were white as late as 1968); the move toward an indigenous clergy coincided with a Vatican retreat from progressivism, resulting in conservative, pro-Vatican hierarchical appointments (Hastings, 1988, p. 314). The Vatican increased its control through nuncios sent to almost all African countries; they kept local bishops in line, removed some, and manipulated financial ties to their advantage (Hastings, 1988, p. 315). Many African priests continue to receive seminary training in Rome, producing clerics "more Roman than the Romans," in one well-worn phrase. Still, while many local African seminaries remain committed to the neo-Thomism of the pre-Vatican II era, liberation theology is being allowed to enter slowly, if grudgingly (some theologians out of favor with the Vatican, including Hans Küng and Edward Schillebeeckx, are not taught in some places) (Hegba, 1988 p. 327). Some African bishops have followed the Vatican line in expressing reservations about the social justice direction of the Latin Church; at other levels, however, liberation theology and dependency theory are having a significant impact on African theology (e.g., Mveng, 1988).

Venezuela presents another example of a hierarchy less than enthusiastic about some of the Latin American Church's directions. Institutionally weak since its inception, the Venezuelan Church has been engaged in struggles with political elites and the state almost continuously since 1870—and has lost miserably on almost every count. The state appointed Venezuela's bishops from 1870 to 1964; most of the twentieth century for the Church has been spent recovering from the damage done by President Gozman Blanco late in the nineteenth century, who almost eradicated Catholicism entirely (Nararro, 1988, pp. 298–99).

What eventually emerged was a Church hierarchy that bought peace for itself via accommodation to state prerogatives and priorities, while receiving in turn the state's financial support. The hierarchy lent support to the state against Marxist movements in the 1960s and has concentrated its resources on attending to the needs and wishes of the upper and middle classes (Nararro, 1988, p. 299, 302, 304). While internal challenges to the Church's accommodationism emerged in the late 1960s and early '70s, the overall tenor of episcopal leadership remains tied to government policies. The protesters did not leave the Church, however. The continued reliance of the Venezuelan Church on foreign mission groups has given Church dissidents a haven of sorts; such groups concentrate on poorer groups, while the hierarchy continues to focus pastorally on privileged social groups (Nararro, 1988, pp. 304–5).

Opposition Efforts of First World Churches. Reinforcing some of the Third World religious opposition to liberation theology and related trends, several First World hierarchies have intervened in Third World religious affairs to protect national secular interests. A prime example is provided by Lernoux's reporting on the West German bishops. Dependent on state subsidies for the bulk of its revenue, the West German hierarchy has intervened on many occasions to protect German corporate interests; in one instance, acting on misleading information provided by German multinationals, the bishops complained about the Brazilian bishops' conference to the Vatican (1989, p. 68). Unlike the U.S. hierarchy, the West German bishops keep tight control on their financial levers, using them effectively in Rome and in the Third World, where their aid organizations (Adventiat and Miserior) are both well-funded and conservative (1989, pp. 41–43). The West German bishops have supported Latin American church groups opposed to liberation theology and similar anticapitalist trends.

CONTINGENT FACTORS OPPOSING THE
ANTICAPITALIST TREND

The most important contingent factor affecting the anticapitalist trend is one opposing it—namely, the papacy of John Paul II. Contingent factors moving that trend forward will not be addressed separately here; some secondary factors will be apparent, however, as mitigations of the "John Paul effect."

THE PAPACY OF POPE JOHN PAUL II

Without a doubt, John Paul II's papacy is the most important contingent factor working against the anticapitalist direction of the Third World Church. What makes this factor a contingent one, rather than a more deeply rooted force, however, is the question of mortality; all popes die sooner or later, and successors have broad discretion in adopting, modifying, or abandoning substantial portions of their predecessors' agendas. John Paul II may convert some parts of his influence into more lasting forces (for example, via appointment of bishops); but such long-term effects are neither assured nor simple.

In assessing present Vatican policy toward the anticapitalist movement within the Church, three sets of consideration need to be explored: John Paul's goals, his leadership style, and his methods of intervention (and their ambiguous impact).

Goals. The pope's overall goals for the Church rest together uneasily; some may justly be seen as contradictory. Among the most important are reasserting Vatican authority and episcopal sovereignty (with the latter subordinated to the former); opposition to "Marxism"; strengthening personal morality, especially with regard to sexual ethics; economic justice within and among nations; and preserving the formal unity of the Church.

The first of John Paul's objectives, concerned with strengthening hierarchical authority and chains of command, was at issue in the year-long silencing of liberation theologian Leonardo Boff, a Franciscan friar. More troubling than Boff's social ethics was his insistence on rights within the Church; his *Church: Charism and Power* (1985) earned him opposition for his ecclesiological, not economic or political, views (Cox,

1988). Toward this same authoritarian end, Vatican offices have sought to undermine the legitimacy of national bishops' conferences, to bring Catholic colleges and universities under episcopal control, and to silence theologians the Vatican finds objectionable.

Concerning Marxism, John Paul remains strongly anticommunist and, unlike Paul VI, is highly skeptical of treating Marxism as an analytic tool separate from a materialistic, atheistic worldview. Some observers have suggested that John Paul's worldview is of Poland writ large (Lernoux, 1989, pp. 28–33), with a fundamental East-West tilt to much of his thinking.

John Paul's concerns with economic justice are deep and important. He seeks to put the Church on the side of the have-nots of the world economy, and he says the rich North will be judged by the poor South for its "imperialistic monopoly of economic and political supremacy [gained] at the expense of others" (quoted in Lernoux, 1989, p. 195). His insistence on sexual ethics is no less substantial, as he speaks forcefully and frequently on maintaining Church teachings on contraception, divorce, premarital sex, and abortion (the latter not treated primarily as a matter of sexual ethics).

Finally, he is concerned with maintaining formal Church unity. Despite his almost implacable firmness on doctrinal issues, John Paul considers formal schism a failure to be avoided at almost all costs. The lengths to which he sought compromise with the ultraconservative Lefebvre movement illustrates the pontiff's willingness to negotiate to preserve "unity," however thin (see, generally, Reese, 1988, p. 573–74; Dinges, 1988, p. 420–21).

Leadership Style. John Paul expresses a leadership style that is cautious and pragmatic, mixed with a stubborn and even parochial streak. His is a carrot-and-stick approach, often employing Cardinal Joseph Ratzinger, prefect for the Sacred Congregation for the Doctrine of the Faith (the former Holy Office), as the heavy in challenging other Church leaders and groups.

The pope's approach is clearest in his dealings with the Brazilian hierarchy, among the world's largest, best organized, and most progressive. Seeing that the Boff sanctions and official attacks on liberation theology only stiffened the resolve of the Brazilian bishops, John Paul relented, offering a supportive message on liberation theology and its role in the worldwide Church. A similar course of events followed Ratzinger's unsuccessful attempts to force the Peruvian bishops to censure Gustavo Gutiérrez; John Paul said liberation theology had been the means to a new commitment to the poor, a resurgence of religious vocations, and a "spiritual deepening." He also noted the need for structural approaches to understanding poverty and privation (quoted in Lernoux, 1989, pp. 100–101).

In Lernoux's view:

> Whereas Ratzinger did not care how much havoc he caused among local churches so long as order was restored, John Paul worried about the loss of large numbers of dissident Catholics. . . . So he used a carrot nearly as often as a stick in confrontations with the Latin Americans, perhaps sensing that a direct attack on liberation theology would alienate the tens of thousands of base communities that formed the most vibrant part of the Latin American church. While Ratzinger played the policeman, the pope attempted a more subtle approach, by appropriating the language of liberation theology in his own social teachings. (1989, p. 97)

Methods and Mixed Results. The appropriation of liberation theology themes by John Paul is apparent in his many encyclicals on economic issues. The biggest difference between the liberation theologians and the pope is not on capitalism, dependency, or exploitation—they agree more often than not, at least up to *Centesimus Annus*—but on John Paul's insistence that "integral" liberation theology is what he and the Vatican say it is. Papal social teaching is the standard, in his view, to which liberation theology must conform; issues of authority permeate John Paul's work on the topic.

Vatican statements critical of liberation theology, one method employed, have been generally unsuccessful in redirecting its course. The first *Instruction Concerning Certain Aspects of Liberation Theology* (Sacred Congregation, 1984), written by Ratzinger, was a caricature of liberation theology that met with criticism from across the theological spectrum. So bad was it that John Paul issued a second document, supposedly on liberation theology's "positive" aspects, but in fact it was another assertion of the Vatican's right to judge the movement. While consoling to conservatives, the documents have had virtually no impact on theologians, seminaries, or most episcopal bodies.

Similarly ambiguous, if not counterproductive, have been disciplinary measures like those aimed at Boff and others. The most immediate impact of Boff's silencing was to increase his popularity and the reach of his ideas. After the silencing, *Church: Charism and Power* became a best-seller in Europe and sold 50,000 copies in Brazil; he even became something of a celebrity among poor Brazilians. According to Brazilian Bishop Adriano Hipólito: "These [poor] are humble people. . . . Before, they did not know who Leonardo Boff was and they didn't know or care much about liberation theology. Now, everyone knows" (quoted in Lernoux, 1989, p. 110). Seeing the mess made by the affair, John Paul moved to mend fences with the Brazilian Church in a way that affirmed the validity of liberation theology.

John Paul also has been willing to cooperate with secular powers on matters of common concern, as with the mutual U.S.-Vatican distaste for clerics in the Sandinista government. Even here, however, John Paul's pragmatism emerged when it appeared that White House efforts to dislodge the Sandinistas might not work and that the priests would stay despite Church disciplinary measures. Toward the end of the Sandinistas' tenure, the Vatican brought pressure to bear on pro-contra Cardinal Miguel Obando y Bravo of Managua to improve relations with the Nicaraguan government (Lernoux, 1989, p. 387).

Without a doubt, the method most feared by liberation theology supporters has been the replacement of progressive bishops (at retirement, death, or by administrative maneuver) with conservatives. Progressive Catholic publications regularly run alarmed headlines on yet another papal appointment sure to bring down the curtain on liberation theology and similar innovations (for example, Martins, 1989a).

The importance of this power to appoint bishops—which the papacy acquired only in recent times—is considerable. If applied single-mindedly, and over a long enough period, one pope can indeed dramatically affect later events. Were John Paul to appoint enough bishops opposed to the anticapitalist trend in the Latin American Church, eventually this might undermine my argument (and become a nonstructural but entrenched factor rather than a contingent one). But for a variety of reasons, this appears most unlikely; the impact of episcopal appointments on changing the anticapitalist movement in the Church seems to be vastly overrated, serving more to rally progressives than anything else. This is the case for three reasons.

For one, the primary criteria that seem to operate in John Paul's choices for bishops are not directly related to liberation theology, capitalism, or economic justice. Rather, they are concerns with women, sex, and authority. There are many examples of bishops who publicly support traditional teachings on sex, offer deference to Rome, and do not endorse ordination of women, but who nonetheless are opposed to capitalism and support liberation theology. John Paul is indeed appointing a disproportionate number of conservatives, but that in itself predicts nothing relevant to the thesis at issue. There is a poor fit between the apparent selection criteria and economic/social views, which would seem to dilute the impact of episcopal appointments as a means of blunting the anticapitalist trend.

Second, bishops are affected by their surroundings in ways that make predictions based on their preappointment views open to question. The "conversion of bishops" is an ongoing process, one that may affect even John Paul's appointees to Third World dioceses. While such changes in direction cannot be predicted in individual cases, neither can they be discounted. Many episcopal "radicals" (for example, Helder Camara, Romero) were appointed with impeccable conservative credentials, only to be changed by their pastoral experiences (Adriance, 1986).

Finally, papal mortality must be considered. It assumes too much to predict that bishops will behave similarly under the next pope as under the present one. Should the next conclave choose someone whose temperament and vision are more like John XXIII's or Paul VI's, bishops appointed as conservatives by John Paul II may well behave in surprising ways—much as those appointed by Pius XI and Pius XII produced Vatican II and Medellin.

SUMMARY: POLITICAL ECONOMY, ECCLESIOLOGY, AND THE ANTICAPITALIST TREND

One is struck by the structural nature of political and economic problems of Latin America in particular, and Third World regions more generally. Also strikingly apparent is the limited number of options available to the Church in pursuing its many objectives. Overall, these processes, limits, and objectives suggest a more anticapitalist direction for the Latin American Church in the years to come.

This position can be affirmed, as demonstrated, with full recognition of countertrends and contrary evidence. Stated simply, the factors supporting an anticapitalist direction are more fundamental, more deeply rooted, than are those undermining it; the latter depend more fully on multiple contingencies and confluences and thus are less reliable as future indicators. A summary is offered in table 5.

Chapter 2 suggested that political economy and ecclesiology might provide useful axes of analysis in this study. The present chapter provides evidence that political economy and ecclesiology, considered separately and in tandem, do indeed advance understanding of the Church and social ethics.

The Church in Latin America clearly stands on a political-economic base of poor and uninfluential people (level one PE). Unlike those in the U.S. Church, the faithful are not primarily middle-class or among the

Table 5   Will the Latin American Church Become More Anticapitalist?

	Yes		No	
Level	Political/ Economic Factors	Religious Factors	Political/ Economic Factors	Religious Factors
Structural	Endurance of core-periphery relations Secular trends in the world-system Antisystemic movements	Religious competition Clergy shortage Diversity of ecclesial actors Class composition of Latin American Church	Capitalist opposition	Curial bureaucracy
Non-structural but Entrenched	Periodic crises (e.g., debt)	Papal/official documents Pastoral innovations/ experiences Religious orders/con-gregations Grass-roots resistance Support from other churches Quality of theologians	Neo-conservative movement	Opposition within Third World churches Opposition from First World churches
Contingent				Pope John Paul II

powerholding sectors; the Latin American Church is relatively poor, not affluent.

The political-economic critique of society offered by the Latin American Church at nearly all levels is a radical one (level two PE), one likely to become more radically anticapitalist in years ahead. While that critique is not unchallenged (for example, CELAM's retreat), it is sufficiently well-entrenched to have shifted the terms of discussion sharply away from procapitalist orientations.

Examining these two levels of political economy, one sees no fundamental contradiction between the composition of the Church's base and the nature of its political-economic critique of the status quo. That critique, although radical in substance, accords with the lived reality of the bulk of Church members. It further enhances the Church's credibility with the poor.

In addition, the structural nature of the region's political and economic problems is likely to increase social pressures and hardships on the poor. This ongoing squeeze, from crises rooted in the region's peripheral location in the world economy, will make the Church's radical political-economic critique even more compelling. A retreat from this critique in the face of increased impoverishment and exploitation would be suicidal for the Latin American Church—a point not lost on Pope John Paul II.

This alignment of political-economic base and critique is neither automatic nor inevitable; indeed, the Latin American Church operated for decades without such a convergence. What made it possible was a set of intervening variables best understood as a shift in ecclesiology. Without such a shift, the convergence would have been improbable at best, and one unlikely to endure.

This ecclesiological shift is best manifested, not surprisingly, in the CEBs. By providing a space for nurturing and protecting a more demanding idea of faith, the CEBs embody a "tight ecclesiology" operating within the Latin American Church. In terms of the two levels of political economy considered here, the CEBs act as vehicles for poor, marginalized Catholics, places where they can reflect on their situation and praxis without the smothering presence of upper-class believers. The CEBs act as two-way conductors for the radical political-economic critique; they make such a critique both possible and necessary.

Significantly, however, the CEBs as a tight ecclesiological manifestation are not isolated from the larger Church. The critical importance of para-ecclesial actors is apparent, for such agents link together the two ecclesiological tendencies—often with stress and negotiation, to be sure. These agents make possible the preservation of a congregational element within Catholicism, a development that would have surprised (or refuted) Weber.

This tight ecclesiology is a development with a future in the Latin American Church. Although not a majority phenomenon, the CEBS are setting much of the agenda for the rest of the Church; the tight ecclesiology sector is more dynamic, creative, and capable of solving problems than the loose ecclesiology sector, especially with regard to the problems and faith of the poor and marginal. The CEBS and similar manifestations of tight ecclesiology would not be easily replaced in Latin America, so critical have they become in many areas.

So, political economy and ecclesiology do seem to help advance our understanding of the prospects of the Latin American Church. Those prospects are likely to involve a greater faith-based opposition to capitalism and its attendant social order.

4

U.S. CATHOLIC NATIONALISM

What I do mean by Americanization is the filling up of the heart with love for America and her institutions. It is the harmonizing of ourselves with our surroundings, so that we will be as to the manner born, and not as strangers in a strange land, caring but slightly for it, and entitled to receive from it but meagre favors. It is the knowing of the language of the land and failing in nothing to prove our attachment to our laws, and our willingness to adopt, as dutiful citizens, all that is good and laudable in its social life and civilization.—Archbishop John Ireland

U.S. Catholic Nationalism is used here to describe the ideological position that posits a harmony between living out one's Catholic religious convictions and the obligations of American citizenship and civic responsibility. More than positing a lack of conflict between religious and political loyalties, U.S. Catholic Nationalism at its strongest maintains a special affinity between the two: the United States as the hope of the world, and the Church as the hope of the United States. This vision is of Church and Republic joined "in thorough harmony," in a common destiny, bringing out the best in one another (Dolan, 1985, pp. 308–9).

The legacy of U.S. Catholic Nationalism is firmly rooted in the history of the U.S. Church. While it did not arise without opposition, by the early twentieth century it had been established as the dominant position across the U.S. Catholic spectrum. And while some dissenting voices in

The quotation from Archbishop John Ireland is given in Gleason (1973, pp. 291–92, and Dolan (1985, p. 302).

the Church have risen against it in this century, it remains the dominant, barely examined ideology of most American Catholics.

EARLY U.S. CATHOLIC NATIONALISM

Two major U.S. Catholic writers of the mid-nineteenth century, Orestes Brownson and Isaac Hecker, gave voice to the emergent religious nationalism of the era. Brownson, writing in 1858, insisted that "our Catholic population shall feel and behave that a man may be a true American and a good Catholic." He said that Catholic immigrants should shed their national identities and embrace Anglo-American culture in order to become true Americans (Dolan, 1985, p. 296).

Brownson and Hecker, both influenced by Enlightenment ideals and enthusiasm, adopted the Puritan idea of American mission and destiny, but with the twist that Catholics, not Protestants, best represented that hope (Dolan, 1985, pp. 307–8). As Brownson wrote:

> The salvation of the country and its future glory depend on Catholics, and therefore they must prove themselves superior in intelligence, independence, public spirit, all the civic virtues, to non-Catholics, or else they will do nothing to save and develop American civilization. (quoted in Deane, 1978, p. 265)

Hecker, the founder of the Paulist Fathers, had a progressive view of history in which the Holy Spirit becomes more manifest over time. As Dolan notes, Hecker believed

> that a new age was dawning and that the United States had a special destiny to usher in this new age for both church and world. The key to it was Roman Catholicism. According to Hecker, the destinies of the United States and American Catholicism were so bound together that Catholics alone would be able to guide the nation toward "its highest destinies." (1985, p. 308)

The drive to "prove" one's loyalty to the United States was a commonplace throughout the immigration decades. This desire to harmonize patriotism and creed received ongoing reinforcement from the anti-Catholic opposition that began in the mid-nineteenth century (Dolan, 1985, p. 295). As Dolan observes:

> Strengthening the tenacity of the [Catholic] Americanists was the fear of public opinion. Catholics generally saw themselves as outsiders in the United States, a minority group that was forced to suffer

persecution because of their religion. But the hierarchy desperately wanted to become insiders and be accepted as part of mainstream America. To gain such acceptance, Catholics had to shed any taint of foreign loyalties, customs, and languages. Time and again this argument was used in Rome in defense of an Americanization policy. If the [ethnic] nationalists were to win the day, then Catholics would continue to remain outsiders and possibly even suffer because of such foreign separatism. Viewed in this manner, more than just the desires of one group were at stake: the very future of Catholics in the United States appeared to hang in the balance. (pp. 301–2)

Opposition to the largely Irish-born and descendant Americanizers came from several European ethnic groups, most notably the Germans and Poles. With leaders like Bishop Thomas Foley of Chicago setting the pattern, the establishment of national (ethnic language) parishes became the norm in helping and controlling new non-English-speaking groups (Coughlin and Riplinger, 1981, pp. 102–3). The national parish scheme allowed for a more gradual assimilation process, a protection of national heritage and culture, and a structural network with interests often at odds with the hierarchy's aims.

The anti-Americanists carried ambiguous and ultimately contradictory ambitions. As much as the Americanizers, they wanted to demonstrate their loyalty to the United States; on the other hand, they "wanted to remain loyal to their own national heritage and strongly resisted any attempt to force them to abandon it" (Dolan, 1985, p. 302). Particularly for the German-Americans, the balancing act fell apart with the arrival of World War I. Given the manic patriotism of the era, their and other groups' arm's-length treatment of effusive Catholic-and-American rhetoric proved untenable (Dolan, 1985, p. 299).

World War I and its aftermath had a decisive impact on the further development of U.S. Catholic Nationalism.

The outbreak of World War I gave the Catholic hierarchy an opportunity to demonstrate its patriotic Americanism, and the bishops did so with vigor. . . .

World War I intensified the spirit of 100 percent Americanism to the point that all foreigners were suspect. Within the Catholic community, herculean efforts were made to demonstrate Catholic loyalty to the American republic. War-bond drives, fund-raising rallies, loyalty banquets, promotion of recruiting for the military, and episcopal statements of patriotism were the order of the day. (Dolan, 1985, pp. 344, 299)

The war smothered whatever doubts lingered about equating the Catholic heritage with the advancement of the United States. The National Catholic War Council, formed by the bishops in 1917 (and renamed the National Catholic Welfare Conference after the war) to coordinate Catholic patriotic activities, continued the patriotic thrust during the postwar years. During the 1920s, as the Church's commitment to the national parish concept waned, the NCWC orchestrated a massive "Campaign for Civic Instruction" to encourage citizenship and assimilation (Dolan, 1985, pp. 363–64). George Cardinal Mundelein, installed in Chicago in 1916 and an avowed Americanizer, boasted to Theodore Roosevelt that "there is hardly any institution here in the country that does so much to bring about a sure, safe and sane Americanization of immigrant peoples as do our parochial schools" (Kantowicz, 1983, p. 25).

The postwar era, in another shift toward further Americanization, saw most Catholic leaders, lay and clerical, abandon their opposition to immigration restrictions (Linkh, 1975, p. 177). The wartime halt on immigration gave Church leaders a glimpse of what might be possible, both in protecting the newcomers' faith and developing their patriotism, if large-scale immigration were ended (Linkh, 1975, pp. 180–81).

U.S. CATHOLIC NATIONALISM THROUGH MIDCENTURY: THE NEW DEAL AND ANTICOMMUNISM

Catholic involvement in social reform efforts is of relatively recent origin. The Church's ideas of charitable care, which were institutionalized during the immigrant period, "reiterated the tradition of the old country and never sought to challenge the economic system" (Dolan, 1985, p. 126). Fundamentally, the conservative, defensive cast of the Church's outlook during the nineteenth century—suspicious of Protestants, wary of government reform efforts, and outside the reaches of progressive thinking (Dolan, 1985, p. 311)—made it largely a political spectator until the early twentieth century. The Church's support for the labor movement, while reaching back to the 1870s, did not represent a dramatic exception.

In February 1919 the NCWC released the "Bishops' Program of Social Reconstruction," a manifesto of social reforms that the Church would advocate throughout the coming two decades. Written by Father John A. Ryan (later nicknamed "the Right-Reverend New Dealer" by one critic), the document advocated a minimum wage, a minimum working age, public housing, laws enforcing the right of workers to organize, old age insurance, sickness and unemployment insurance, regulation of public utilities, control of monopolies, and labor-management partnerships in the form of co-ops and worker stock ownership. The unprecedented document reflected the growing institutional confidence of the Church hierarchy and the strong role that Ryan would continue to play in Catholic activist circles for decades to come. As Dolan (1985, pp. 343–44) observes:

> The genius of Ryan was his ability to merge Catholic social thought with the American current of reform. The basis for this merger was the natural-law tradition. . . . Prior to him, Catholic reformers had operated more from the principle of expediency, what the times demanded, than from principles articulated in a coherent social ethics. Ryan changed that by formulating a system of social ethics that was both very Catholic and very American. Thenceforth, the natural-law tradition would become the keystone of American Catholic social thought.

Another factor pushing Church leaders into the eventual New Deal coalition was their extreme antiradical, anti-Bolshevik orientation. In the United States the primary use of *Rerum Novarum* (1891), Leo XIII's landmark encyclical legitimating labor organizing for Catholics, was as an antisocialist cudgel aimed at the Catholic working class (Dolan, 1985, pp. 336–37). In the wake of the Bolshevik Revolution and later the Spanish Civil War, the U.S. Catholic leadership was ahead of the rest of the country in opposing communism. These leaders, including liberal organs such as *Commonweal*, criticized FDR's decision to recognize the USSR in 1933. In 1938 the U.S. bishops warned the faithful on the "spread of subversive teachings" and called for a Crusade for Christian Democracy to instill civic and social virtues (Crosby, 1978, p. 6). It was not long before the benefits of an anticommunist stance became apparent to U.S. Catholic leaders. As David O'Brien observed: "In fighting the red peril the Catholic could dedicate himself to action which was both Catholic and American. Few would disagree that he was proving his worth as an American and demonstrating the compatibility of faith and patriotism" (O'Brien, 1968, p. 96).

Anticommunism was to be the final cement in U.S. Catholic Nationalism. Nearly all sectors of the Church could join in this common religious-patriotic exercise. Church liberals in the labor movement were especially active in the purge of communists in the post-World War II era and in establishing rivals such as the Association of Catholic Trade Unionists (Crosby, 1978, pp. 21–22).

Catholic anticommunism was reinforced by the anticommunism of the American political culture. Anticommunism had become a common denominator, the bulwark of both true Americanism and authentic Catholicism. The Catholic leadership, in combining these explosive elements, had mixed a heady brew that fired the blood of American Catholics for at least two decades. (Crosby, 1978, p. 11)

Communism, to the Catholic leadership of the 1950s, represented both the oppression visited on Catholics behind the Iron Curtain and a threat to the prosperity and freedom the Church had come to enjoy in the United States. It threatened the "brick-and-mortar" Catholicism of the 1920–60 era, when "it was a matter of pride to have a magnificent church and a large complex of parish buildings housing school, faculty, and clergy" (Dolan, 1985, pp. 350–51). The Church's institutional capabilities also had grown during the period, with systematization of finances and management proceeding apace and priests often made bishops because of their fund-raising acumen (Dolan, 1985, pp. 354–55).

McCarthyism marked the apex of Catholic anticommunism. Correct or not, the anticommunist zeal of the 1950s has become identified in a special way with Catholic anticommunism. While many Catholic liberals—those at *Commonweal*, Bishop Bernard Sheil of Chicago, and others—attacked McCarthy throughout his crusade, they did so as part of a disagreement over means, not ends. Liberals were often embarrassed by McCarthy's crude style and more concerned with advocating anti-poverty reforms to eviscerate Marxism's appeal (Crosby, 1978, pp. 19–20, 55–56).

For all their differences, however, both Catholic liberals and conservatives shared a core of common values and beliefs. Both were passionately, even obsessively, opposed to communism, profoundly convinced that it represented the greatest of all possible dangers to both church and Republic. Both shared a brand of patriotism that one can only describe as strident, though the conservatives outdid the liberals in this department. Both liberals and conservatives found inspiration in the teachings of the church, though they selected different traditions. . . . Neither, finally, doubted the gravity of the church's confrontation with communism, though the liberals were quicker to perceive the reduction of tensions that came in the early 1950s.

Most important of all, [Catholic anticommunism] demonstrated that the religious and political convictions of American Catholics had become inextricably entwined. Religious practice had become politicized, and political beliefs had been elevated to the status of religious creed. Religious and political values were thus tending to merge and to reinforce each other. (pp. 22–23, 171–72)

The convergence of anticommunism and Catholic acceptability reached one peak, to be sure, with the presidential election of John F. Kennedy in 1960. While many scholars point to the event as proof of the fully Americanized status of Catholics, it may be true that Kennedy would have remained unelectable without the previous decade's anticommunist crusade; the 1950s was also an era of insurgent anti-Catholicism, led by Paul Blanshard. Kennedy's willingness, even eagerness, to reassure Protestant clergy in Houston that his Catholicism would affect his policies not at all was also important (Cuddihy, 1978, p. 71).

CIVIL RELIGION AND U.S. CATHOLICS

A series of setbacks, progressions, and paradoxes for religious communities in the United States occurred during the 1960s. For Catholics, it was the era of Vatican II, a time of renewed openness to "the world" and its problems, a reorienting in liturgy, spirituality, and self-definition (ecclesiology), and a time of dashed hopes, undermined truths, and a plummet in clergy vocations. For the Protestant mainstream in the United States it was a time of falling numbers and even faster-falling confidence as movements of blacks, women, and minorities undermined the false universalism of the mainstream's cultural discourse (Coleman, 1988, p. 244). For all believers and unbelievers it was the era of civil rights and black power, Vietnam and the counterculture, and the end of U.S. worldwide hegemony—in all, an era of profound structural changes in the world economy, national politics, and political culture.

While debate on the utility of civil religion as an analytic framework continues, I am persuaded that many powerful groups and institutions seek to fashion ideologies and discourses best described as types of civil religion. Robert Bellah is perhaps the most important sociologist studying U.S. civil religion. He defines civil religion as "that religious dimension found, I think, in the life of every people, through which it interprets its historical experience in the light of transcendent reality" (1975, p. 3). Such a definition seems too abstract in its processes, as if the "people" (rather than identifiable blocs, groups, and individuals) together construct and promote such interpretations. More to my liking, Coleman describes civil religion as those stories, symbols, metaphors, and myths which a nation's elite seeks to

> make some sense of [the nation's] continuity and meaning in world history and its collective identity and vocation vis-à-vis other nations and its own citizens. What does it mean—in terms of ultimate vocation and moral identity—to be an Israeli, an American, or a Frenchman? (Coleman, 1982, p. 109)

Civil religion, in this perspective, must be "carried" by organizational "vehicles" (Hammond, 1980, p. 44). Until recent years the mainline Protestant denominations carried this cultural self-understanding with support from the secular state. In its fundamentals all civil religion acts as an integrative force affirming the status quo in the sense meant by Rousseau, for whom

> Civil religion was not to be just another religion; its purpose was precisely to harmonize religion and politics. . . . Civil religion is religious because it is necessary that citizens be disposed to "love their duties." It is civil because its sentiments are those of "sociability, without which it is impossible to be either a good citizen or a faithful subject." (Hammond, 1980, pp. 42–43)

U.S. civil religion, as Bellah has maintained in works as diverse as *Beyond Belief* and *Habits of the Heart*, has been characterized by overlapping and often conflicting strains of biblical virtue and ethics and a utilitarian, maximizing individualism. The former, focusing on norms such as liberty, justice, and charity, "understood in a context of theological and moral discourse which led to a concept of personal virtue as the essential basis of a good society," has suffered greatly at the hands of a utilitarianism that has eroded personal virtue in the direction of a generalized "decline of belief in all forms of obligation" (Bellah, 1975, pp. ix–x).

Detailed analyses of the religious and secular contents of American civil religion have been produced in recent years (Bellah 1975; Bellah and Hammond, 1980; Wuthnow, 1980; Tipton, 1982; Lee and Cowan, 1986). The fate of the carriers of that civil religion until recent times, the so-called mainline churches, deserves further attention.

Roof and McKinney (1987, pp. 73–75) offer five qualities that typify a mainline denomination: group size, power, vitality, support for the "American Way," and a lack of religious/secular tension. The mainline civil religion was traditionally carried by churches associated with the National Council of Churches, including the Episcopal and Presbyterian churches, the United Church of Christ, the United Methodist Church, and two of the major Lutheran denominations. As has been documented, all suffered serious declines in numbers and influence beginning in the 1960s and continuing into recent years (Roof and McKinney, 1987, p. 150; Hoge and Roozen, 1979; Roozen, 1984; McKinney and Hoge, 1983; Hoge, 1979; Kelley, 1972). During the 1970s mainline denominations saw numbers decline as follows: United Presbyterian (19 percent); Disciples of Christ (17 percent); Episcopalian (15 percent); United Church of Christ (11 percent); United Methodist (9 percent) (Chalfant et al., 1981, pp. 455–60). Roof and McKinney, in situating the significance of this mainline decline, observe:

> The mainline churches over the years have served as bridging institutions, as "trustees" of the society's values. Stressing nurture as well as conversion, and public as well as private faith, they have played an important role as a culture-shaping force; by linking the fate of individuals and congregations with the country, they helped create a sense of moral community and national unity. In actual practice they have engaged in what Benjamin Franklin described as a "publick religion": the interpretation of American life in relation to a transcendent order. This has meant reflecting critically upon national and group experience from the vantage point of the Judeo-Christian heritage an inclusive vision of public order and societal well-being. (1987, p. 26)

Mainline Protestantism no longer effectively serves in such a capacity. Martin Marty notes that the mainline churches benefited from their close ties with the dominant order up through the 1950s and suffered significantly when that order's world power and credibility began declining in the 1960s (1976, p. 71). According to Roof and McKinney, "So wedded were the liberal, mainline churches to the dominant culture that their beliefs, values, and behavior were virtually indistinguishable from the culture" (1987, p. 22). Hammond points beyond numerical shifts to other evidence of decline in mainline civil religion, including the increased appearance of cults and the rise of Evangelicalism, which, along with the abrupt turnabout in the "200-year pattern of mainline growth," all "reflect a weakening of people's national identity, a reduction in their national faith" (1983, pp. 156–57).

Having grown close to the mainstream by the late 1950s, the U.S.

Catholic Church experienced its own share of traumas during the 1960s. According to Roof and McKinney (1987, p. 21):

> Though liberal Protestantism was the hardest hit, Catholicism hardly escaped the strains and tensions. Catholic membership grew during this period but at a slowing rate. More noticeable were the declines in religious participation, from 74 percent attending Mass weekly in 1958 to 51 percent in 1982. Declines in Mass attendance were most pronounced for young, upwardly mobile Catholics. Rising socioeconomic levels and rapid assimilation into American life after World War II led many Catholics to disregard much of their immigrant heritage, and Vatican II brought about a new climate of lay participation and freedom, inspiring greater religious individualism and choice. . . . Catholics joined the ranks of the mainline and in so doing took on both the burdens and the glory of identifying with the dominant culture.

A decisive challenge to U.S. Catholic Nationalism, and to the prospect of a culture-shaping role for Catholicism in the United States, was the Vietnam War. The leadership of the U.S. Catholic community, its bishops and many theologians and laity, had never met a war it didn't like before Vietnam. They continued to like—or at least support—the U.S. presence in Vietnam much longer than much of society, being among the last to abandon the war effort.

During the Vietnam era protests, as Dolan writes (1985, p. 451):

> the bishops were notably absent. As a group they remained publicly silent until the early 1970s, when opposition to the war had already become quite widespread throughout the nation. Their one major contribution was a 1968 pastoral letter which supported the right of Catholics to conscientious objection.

The bishops in a 1971 pastoral finally concluded that "at this point in history it seems clear to us that whatever good we hope to achieve through continued involvement in this war is now outweighed by the destruction of human life and moral values which it inflicts" (Benestad and Butler, 1981, p. 78). Throughout the era the bishops continued to grant "a presumption of justice" to U.S. government policies toward Vietnam. Their pivotal statement on the war, although it was the first time as a body that the bishops had publicly opposed the government on a major foreign policy issue, generated little attention by 1971, so far were they in the rear of antiwar sentiment within the country (Au, 1987, p. 180).

While the bishops took some severe criticism for their long support of the war, Catholicism as a whole managed to avoid losing its legitimacy as an independent social force as the war's unpopularity grew. This may have resulted from the emergence and visibility of the Catholic peace movement during the era, a "Catholic left" of laity and lower clergy that were among the more visible elements of the antiwar movement. At the episcopal level the National Conference of Catholic Bishops learned the advantages of a more critical brand of patriotism; by appropriating some of the moral force and themes of the Catholic left, but avoiding their fundamental critique of American imperialism and its irreformability, the Church's institutional leaders steered a path from blind patriotism to the role of friendly critic necessary for establishment legitimacy in the post-Vietnam era. A similar course was steered by other establishment institutions, most notably the news media (Herman and Chomsky, 1988). U.S. Catholic Nationalism, shorn of its naive excesses but with its fundamentals intact, survived Vietnam.

A COMING "CATHOLIC MOMENT"?

The U.S. Catholic Church moved through the 1980s with several serious internal problems—an aging and diminished number of clergy, conflicts over the role of women and minority groups, resistance to official teachings on sexual ethics, and more—but, from another angle, presenting evidence of considerable strength and potential as a cultural and political force.

Catholics in the United States have been the largest "denomination" since the Civil War, now three times more numerous than the largest Protestant group (Southern Baptists) (Coleman, 1988, p. 236). Approximately 28 percent of the U.S. population can be described as Catholic, between 53 and 67 million (the wide variation reflects differences in official Catholic Directory statistics and Gallup self-identification data; see Gallup and Castelli, 1987, pp. 1–9). Catholics now rank even or ahead of most Protestants, including mainline denominations, in most measures of educational achievement, income, and social status; they are overrepresented in political leadership roles relative to population (for example, the U.S. House of Representatives and state governorships); and they are well represented among the CEOs of top U.S. corporations (Coleman, 1988, p. 236). The United States is home to more Catholic colleges and universities (235) than any other nation in the world; and although down from a high of 5.6 million students in 1964, the Catholic parochial school system still educates 2.7 million students (Coleman,

1988, p. 242). So thoroughly and decisively have Catholics entered the middle class that one sociologist, David Leege, has remarked that "the GI bill may have had more of an impact on the Catholic Church than the Second Vatican Council" (J. Berger, 1987, p. 64).

Having survived the 1960s more intact, confident, and energetic than the Protestant mainstream, the Catholic Church is seen by many observers as well positioned to assume the culture-forming responsibilities once borne by the mainstream denominations. Among the most visible advocates of such a role is Richard John Neuhaus, a Catholic convert who as a longtime Lutheran theologian was associated with the neoconservative Institute for Religion and Democracy. Neuhaus lays out his view (in which he is joined by such liberals as William Lee Miller) in *The Catholic Moment: The Paradox of the Church in the Postmodern Era* (1987). As he summarized it in another work, Neuhaus argues:

> I mean that this is the historical moment at which Roman Catholicism has a singular opportunity and obligation to take the lead in reconstructing a moral philosophy for the American experiment in republican democracy. . . . One critical piece of the proposition is the manifest decline, if not collapse, of the Anglo-Saxon Protestant cultural hegemony in American life. The hegemony of "mainline" or "old-line" Protestantism has been on the skids for at least four decades, and its slide gives every appearance of being irreversible. (1986, p. 46)

Neuhaus, Marty, and others are suggesting the time is ripe for something like a "Catholic moment," in which the Catholic community takes the lead in helping forge a religiously inspired but publicly accessible language of political discourse and norms. One Catholic commentator has noted that the Catholic community does occupy the geographic and social-class "center" of American life and that it possesses a distinctive social agenda and moral language (Coleman, 1988, p. 245). Another wonders whether the Catholic moment must come on neoconservative terms (Higgins, 1988), without apparently doubting that such a moment is indeed possible or desirable.

Many Catholic leaders are aware of the prospects for a "Catholic moment" and are moving forward to meet it. Archbishop J. Francis Stafford of Denver spoke for many when, in an address on Catholics in the Bicentennial of the U.S. Constitution, he asserted that "the American Catholic community is in a distinctive position to offer leadership in the building of a community of virtue capable of sustaining and developing the American democratic experiment today" (1987, p. 57). Stafford offers three reasons supporting his claim: one, that Catholics have proved their loyalty to the American system; two, that "the classic Catholic natural law approach to moral reason may well become increasingly important as America works to create a contemporary community of virtue," providing "moral concepts and language that can speak across the many pluralities of American culture"; and third, that the numerical and social strength of U.S. Catholicism suggests that "our community should assume a considerable burden of leadership in helping to define the terms of argument over civic virtue in the American third century." Stafford notes that the "task of renewing the American experiment" is not solely for Catholics, but instead must be "a genuinely ecumenical and interreligious enterprise." Still, he argues, "the possibilities of leadership in that common effort are now open to Catholics in a historically distinctive way" (1987, pp. 57–58).

No formal invitation has been issued to the U.S. Catholic Church to play such a role in American culture. Nevertheless, at the highest levels, the Catholic Church has moved to assume the role, to fill the void created by the declining mainline hegemony. Whether by intuition or conscious design, the episcopacy in the United States has moved to position itself as a central voice in political/ethical discussions on the fundamentals of the American system. The most evident examples of this are the pastoral letters authored by the NCCB on nuclear weapons and the U.S. economy.

THE PASTORAL LETTERS

Rather than being the products of establishment, flag-waving insiders, large parts the two major pastoral letters issued by the hierarchy in the 1980s appear to some like an attack on the United States. To conservative critics like Michael Novak, *The Challenge of Peace: God's Promise and Our Response* (1983) ignored the perils of communism and the special promise of the American experiment. Similarly, numerous businesses and government leaders chided the bishops for economic naïveté and ingratitude in the pastoral *Economic Justice for All: Catholic Social Teaching and the U.S. Economy* (National Conference of Catholic Bishops, 1986). The letters, which are major policy and teaching instruments of the highest levels in the U.S. Church, do indeed criticize many important policies and practices of the U.S. government and American society. By leveling a religious, and specifically Catholic, critique against the workings of national economic and military policy, the demise of U.S. Catholic Nationalism would seem to have arrived; the Church is now willing to be a "sign of contradiction," standing against much of the dominant American mainstream, according to former NCCB Chairman James Malone (1986, p. 396).

Such a conclusion, derived from a reading of the final texts of the two pastoral letters, might draw some support. More correct, however, is to read the entire pastoral process—the consultations, draftings, revisions, and implementation—through the perspective of U.S. Catholic Nationalism. Rather than being rejected or even called into serious question, that ideological commitment framed, limited, and guided the "prophetic" movements of the Catholic hierarchy.

The bishops have issued position papers on social topics throughout the twentieth century and on a regular basis since the formation of the USCC and NCCB in 1966. Most of these statements have been written by staff members, often presented in testimony before government agencies, and usually ignored. "Typically, bishops' statements are published in pamphlet form and receive passing coverage in the press," note Benestad and Butler (1981, p. v.). The process and attention given to the two 1980s pastoral letters were altogether different. For both, the drafting committees (five bishops and various staff members and advisers) met with hundreds of experts in law, theology, economics, strategic studies, sociology, and related fields, with more than a dozen public hearings also involving testimony from the laity across the country (Gannon, 1988, p. 5). Each letter went through three drafts, with comment periods producing important revisions after each in a process lasting more than two years. In its breadth of consultation, openness of participation, and amount of attention it drew from people outside Church activist circles, the pastorals' process was a genuine innovation.

The internal structure of each letter reflected important value choices made by the bishops' conference in matters of epistemology, audience, and competence. Both letters, in their first sections, develop distinctively Christian themes relevant to their subject matter; a strong emphasis on biblical revelation is evident, supplemented by sections on Catholic social teaching and Church history. In *The Challenge of Peace* (1983), a sustained theological examination of peacemaking, the life of Jesus and the biblical norms of reconciliation and conversion of life-style are developed in a systematic and nuanced fashion. Similarly, *Economic Justice for All* initially outlines "The Christian Vision of Economic Life," a scriptural and theological evaluation of God's lordship over created goods and the earth, the demands of discipleship, and the norms of the kingdom of God that are relevant to the community Jesus calls.

After outlining the general principles and values they believe relevant to the issue areas, the bishops move into the realm of application and public policy. Whereas the first sections were heavily dependent on Scripture and Christian theological insights, each letter employs a natural law methodology when considering policy choices and options. This shift in epistemology, in turn, is related to the various audiences the bishops hope to address. Realizing that their theological arguments and language will apply primarily (and probably only) to committed Christians, they adopt a natural law framework to make themselves understood by state leaders, non-Christians, and other "people of good will." This appeal to two audiences—to Catholics and to "men of good will"—was first used in John XXIII's *Pacem in Terris* encyclical in 1963; before then, modern papal encyclicals were largely in-house matters for the Church.

Finally, the bishops recognize that the pastorals' sections on principles and applications carry different moral weight. Catholics are expected to give greater heed and respect to the principles the bishops derive from Scripture and tradition, and the bishops hope their policy choices, which they consider "prudential judgments," will receive serious consideration, even while they acknowledge that different conclusions can be drawn by Catholics and other "people of good will" (*Economic Justice* (*EJ*), chap. 3, sec. 135).

While the pastorals' thematic first sections on war and peace, the just war and pacifism, and on the fundamental norms of economic justice are more radical in their implications than are their policy judgments, the latter still are critical of many policies and priorities. *The Challenge of Peace* rejects any use of nuclear weapons against civilian population centers, advocates a no-first-use policy, calls for an international political authority that is truly effective, and links peacemaking to cooperative world development. It grants nuclear deterrence policy a "strictly conditional tolerance," so long as efforts toward disarmament are making true progress. *Economic Justice for All* calls for experiments in workplace democracy and other labor-capital arrangements, rejects unregulated free-market approaches to social problems, calls for full employment, jobs programs, increased support for domestic and international antipoverty and pro-development efforts, greater efforts on behalf of women and minorities, more generous and effective welfare programs, and support for family farms, among other things. By implication as much as by direct statement, it criticizes many of the postwar economic policies of the United States.

Conservative critics of the two pastorals have assailed the bishops for being unpatriotic, ill-informed, captive to anticapitalist ideologies, and more. In contrast, the conclusion I advance is just the opposite. The pastorals gave the bishops yet another opportunity to demonstrate their patriotism, their political acumen, and their belief in a capitalist world economy. U.S. Catholic Nationalism, rather than being undermined, stands affirmed and as definitive of the U.S. Catholic mainstream.

Support for this admittedly controversial position can be found by carefully examining *Economic Justice for All*, the most recent and more far-reaching of the major pastorals. Four points are particularly relevant and should be discussed at length.

(1) The bishops assume from the outset that the United States is a force for good in the international order, and they do not seriously consider that such a view might not accord with the lived experience of their coreligionists in other countries. The bishops' judgment is that "U.S. policy toward the developing world should reflect our traditional regard for human rights and our concern for social progress" (*EJ*, sec. 264). Questions of imperialism, political or economic, do not merit even passing consideration. Nowhere do they confront—even to dismiss—assertions like those of the Brazilian Frei Betto, who claims that "the supposedly freest nation—the United States—is undoubtedly the one that most oppresses the Third World" (1988, p. 56).

In their uncritical belief in the fundamental goodness of the United States—in which "mistakes" or "errors" have been made, to be sure, but none that change the nation's fundamental benevolence—the bishops demonstrate one of the fundamental ideological pillars of U.S. elite opinion. Herman and Chomsky have noted the phenomenon as it relates to U.S. intervention in Vietnam—a result of "good intentions," a "noble purpose" pursued naïvely, an example of America's "selfless policies" in the world—in which no amount of evidence could shatter the assumption of U.S. virtue and goodness (Herman and Chomsky, 1988). The bishops' pastorals point out where "regrettably, we have fallen short" in our attempts to do good in the world (*EJ*, sec. 264). That the United States might be experienced as anything but a virtuous presence scarcely seems to have occurred to them.

(2) For all their "prophetic" and courageous rhetoric, at no point do the bishops seek a structural analysis of U.S. power and prosperity. In short, as the brothers Boff correctly note, "what is missing . . . is an analysis and a critical understanding of what capitalism really represents" (Boff and Boff, 1987, p. 23). Rather than examine capitalism, the bishops seek to hide behind an economic agnosticism that is "pragmatic" in nature. They are content to note that "we live in a "mixed" economic system which is the product of a long history of reform and adjustment. It is in

the spirit of this American pragmatic tradition of reform that we seek to continue the search for a more just economy" (*EJ*, sec. 131). The bishops claim that Catholic social thought has rejected the "ideological extremes" of laissez-faire and communism, along with the view that "the capitalist system is inherently inequitable and, therefore, contradictory to the demands of Christian morality . . ." (*EJ*, secs. 128–29). The statement, as a summary of twentieth-century papal encyclicals (through the 1960s), is minimally correct as it stands; that the bishops use it to signal their unwillingness to discuss the legitimacy of capitalism is unfortunate. It is a selective appeal to authority of a rather dubious nature, and it can only undermine the bishops' desire to be taken seriously as a group knowledgeable about how their society functions. This refusal to examine the fundamental workings of capitalism is all the more curious since it comes less than fifteen years after they approved a more systematic, structural examination of world capitalism and the United States. That document was entitled "Development-Dependency: The Role of Multinational Corporations," and was issued by the U.S. Catholic Conference's Department of Social Development and World Peace in August 1974.

The Canadian Catholic bishops, in a major pastoral on their country's economy, dared to provide a structural analysis of their situation. By focusing on the distortions and injustices intrinsic to capitalism (and recent changes in the composition of capital worldwide), the Canadian bishops brought down on themselves a storm of criticism from Canadian business and government elites within and outside the Church. The different analytic methodologies of the U.S. and Canadian hierarchies is instructive and illustrates the degree to which the U.S. Church is unwilling to scrutinize the system in which it has prospered.

(3) Many considerations and factors converge to form a nonconflictive, functionalist picture of U.S. society and world politics that pervades the bishops' social vision in the pastoral. The bishops continue a traditional Catholic reliance on the "common good" as a prime criterion for evaluating public policy (see, for example, *EJ*, intro., sec. 23; sec. 296). Difficult questions of what the common good might be in a seriously class-divided country and world are avoided insofar as the bishops have decided against any serious analysis of capitalism. Allied with ethics of the common good is a sense that a renewed spirit of cooperation among powerful groups can help reconcile differences; the possibility of fundamentally contradictory interests, either domestically or internationally, is nowhere entertained. The bishops title their last section, encompassing their boldest policy recommendations, "A New American Experiment: Partnership for the Common Good." In it, they assert:

The United States prides itself on both its competitive sense of initiative and its spirit of teamwork. Today a greater spirit of partnership and teamwork is needed. . . . Only a renewed commitment by all to the common good can deal creatively with the realities of international dependence and economic dislocations in the domestic economy. (*EJ*, sec. 296)

The pastoral's call for "experiments in economic democracy" and cooperation—in the workplace, at local and regional levels among business, labor, and government, and at the national and international levels —seems to repackage the organicist, corporatist view of society typical of medieval Catholic moral theology and expressed in the twentieth century in *Quadragesimo Anno* (1931). The pastoral's recommendations throughout have a distinct corporatist flavor to them, albeit of a more modern, tripartite variety. The bishops call on elites to renew their "civic commitment" to the common good, warning that "in the absence of a vital sense of citizenship among the businesses, corporations, labor unions and other groups that shape economic life, society as a whole is endangered" (*EJ*, intro., sec. 66).

Having avoided any consideration of potential class conflict, the bishops seek to portray social reality in as nonconflictual a light as possible in the face of glaring evidence to the contrary. Like the political elites whom Alan Wolfe (1981) claims have chosen high levels of economic growth as a way to avoid divisive questions of distributive justice, the bishops seek high-growth, nonconflictive, positive-sum solutions to economic problems. These fit the pastoral's functionalist assumptions and "pragmatic" unwillingness to challenge the legitimacy of existing institutions and processes.

Building on their notions of a generalizable common good and politics as a cooperative enterprise, the bishops hope to speak a moral word to powerholders. Indeed, one of the most significant qualities of both pastoral letters is the extent to which they are addressed to persons of power rather than to the dispossessed or oppressed on whose behalf the bishops claim to speak. This "Constantinian bias" of seeking influence through the consciences of powerholders dates back at least to the fourth century; its accommodationist perspective fits well with the nonconflictual posture the bishops adopt.

So, despite their intention "to stand with the poor everywhere" (*EJ*, sec. 260), the bishops do so in ways that do not at all confront the limits of existing arrangements. Powerholders in U.S. capitalism are urged to act more charitably and morally, with the bishops never questioning whether even the saints would find it possible to humanize a capitalist system. Seeking the common good primarily by means of appeals to the powerful allows the bishops to appropriate the prophetic and moral legitimacy of the "option for the poor" in ways that do not call into question their fidelity to U.S. capitalism and the system that has been so good to the U.S. Catholic middle class.

(4) A methodological strategy of considerable importance undergirds the bishops' main pastorals in a way that strengthens the dominance of U.S. Catholic Nationalism. Both pastorals are divided into biblical/theological and public policy sections. The former use the language of faith, see themselves as addressed to committed Christians, and seek to describe distinctively Christian or Catholic perspectives on the matters at hand. The policy sections employ the language of natural law (ethical reasoning open to all, without theological or religious orientations); address themselves to all people "of good will," especially to powerholders (Christian and non-Christian); and seek to define policy directions acceptable to a wide range of people, including those far removed from a Christian or Catholic moral perspective.

The pastorals claim greater authority for their biblical/theological reflections than for their policy recommendations, on which they acknowledge people of good will may disagree. And while the biblical/theological material could have been interpreted in a more radical or demanding way, the nature of the texts and theological traditions used by the bishops push their reflections in a more radical direction (at the level of principle at least) than the bishops might otherwise be inclined to travel. The pastoral on economics talks of the demands of discipleship (chap. 1, pt. 4), the purpose of created goods (chap. 1, sec. 34), Old and New Testament reflections on wealth (chap. 1, secs. 30–39, 41–52), and more—all themes that, on their own terms, challenge the legitimacy of existing relations under capitalism.

But if the biblical/theological reflections promise potential conflict with secular power, the policy sections quickly minimize that potential. As Stanley Hauerwas observes, the two sections are poorly, if at all, integrated; the moral demands of the first section are quickly watered down or forgotten in the policy sections (1985, pp. 15–16, 179). So little impact do the biblical/theological reflections have on policy (in accordance with natural law methodology) that the former begin to look like religious gloss on an essentially nonreligious document. In terms of size and public attention, the natural law policy sections dwarf the biblical/theological ones; the two stand more like unrelated treatises than as parts of a whole. The biblical/theological perspectives do not stand in judgment of the policy recommendations, for as products of natural law reasoning the latter must be evaluated with concepts open to all people and not with "confessional" criteria.

Without taking a position for or against the legitimacy of natural law theology, one can still observe that while a natural law perspective undermines the pastoral's worth as a Christian document (in terms of helping Christians explore the implications of their specifically religious commitments), it does serve to reinforce the citizenship credentials of the U.S. Catholic community. By using a natural law approach, the bishops can plead innocent to trying to impose their religious vision on secular society; rather, they seek merely "to add our voice" to the public discussion in tasks that "seek the cooperation and support of those who do not share our faith tradition" (EJ, chap. 1, sec. 27). This return to an ethic centered in natural law, after a move toward more biblically based ethics since Vatican II (Curran, 1982), is part of the larger movement to fill the void in public culture mentioned earlier. A biblical and theological orientation speaks primarily to the Christian community—its obligations and traditions, its values and discipleship—and little, if at all, to secular power. Natural law, in contrast, seeks common ground with secular norms—invariably, it seems, by watering down Christian norms to a "least common denominator" sufficiently nonthreatening to secular power—and says little of substance regarding the implications of the distinctively Christian vocation.

The choice is clear: natural law approaches are more serviceable in cooperating with secular power (at least on economic and military matters) than are some biblical/theological approaches. The former are perfectly compatible with acting as good and loyal citizens who, far from challenging the system's legitimacy, add to it by providing a revitalized language of public discourse and civil religion. Biblical/theological modes of discourse, which had received renewed appreciation since Vatican II, are again consigned to "sectarians" whose "privatized morality" cannot be expected to help build the moral and spiritual fiber of the United States.

In weighing the tasks—dialogue with the faithful or dialogue with secular power—the bishops have chosen the latter as more important. Dialogue with the faithful on matters of economic justice, were it done seriously and without regard to secular opinion, would open the Church to renewed charges of "separateness" or "un-American-ness." Dialogue with secular power, particularly on terms amenable to that power, enhances the respectability and American-ness of U.S. Catholic spokesmen—another step ahead in the history of U.S. Catholic Nationalism.

U.S. CATHOLICISM AND HISPANICS

At least a few commentators have expressed the belief (or hope) that the middle-class bias of the U.S. church might be mitigated by the influx of new immigrant (primarily Hispanic) Catholics into the United States (Coleman, 1988). As the largest minority group within the Church, so the scenario goes, poor and newly arrived Hispanics might constitute a powerful counterpoise to the world of U.S. Catholic Nationalism by forcing the Catholic mainstream to take account of the Church's reality as a Third World institution (as well as its own roots as a multinational community of poor and working-class migrants).

This thesis has a surface plausibility. According to some estimates (Greeley, 1988), Hispanics will make up about one-fourth of the U.S. Catholic Church by the year 2000. The new Hispanic immigrants are in fact poorer, less educated, and younger than the rest of U.S. society and the U.S. Church (Gonzales and LaVelle, 1985, chap. 1). In terms of sheer size (currently around 12 million U.S. Catholics are of Hispanic origin, according to Greeley, 1988, p. 61) and demographic/cultural qualities, the new immigrants cannot help but change the nature of the U.S. Catholic Church away from nationalism and middle-class values, at least according to people subscribing to this position.

A more nuanced evaluation suggests, on the contrary, that the new Catholics are unlikely to weaken the hold of U.S. Catholic Nationalism as the mainstream ideology of American Catholics. Several factors indicate that the Hispanic (or Asian) Wave will not alter the Church in ways remotely comparable to the surge in Catholic immigration between 1820 and 1920.

The first, and most important, barrier to such transformation is class. Nineteenth-century immigrants were greeted on arrival by a multiclass, relatively small Church community. Current immigrants are confronted by a Church of "comfortable middle-class status," large and powerful, that is not "immersed in the lives of the newcomers as it was with the European immigrants" (Fitzpatrick, 1988, p. 11). The newcomers are neither numerous nor powerful enough to remake the U.S. Church; they will be fitted to it, or they will leave (as have nearly 1 million Hispanic Catholics since 1973) (Greeley 1988, p. 61).

Second, this merger will take place on terms that put forward mainstream Catholicism as normative, to the detriment of immigrants' native culture. Despite assurances from the U.S. hierarchy that "integration, not assimilation" is their goal (National Conference of Catholic Bishops, National Pastoral Plan, 1987, p. 451), what is emerging is much more assimilative than not. The Hispanics, like the Italians before them, arrive without the presence of indigenous clergy; where the Italians received their Catholicism from clergy with a distinctive Irish brogue, the Hispanics are ministered to by middle-class Anglo clergy primarily in geographic (as opposed to ethnic or national) parishes. Without indigenous clergy to defend immigrant religious sensibilities and culture against native secular and religious norms, or to negotiate a more tolerant modus vivendi, the new immigrants are left with a choice: Catholicism à la middle-class Anglos (Spanish-speaking or not), or leaving the Church (usually for a Pentecostal group) (Deck, 1988, p. 485).

Some have called for a return to national parishes to better integrate Hispanics into the U.S. Church (Fitzpatrick, 1988, p. 12). Others point not to its national quality, but to the parish system itself, as the root of the problem. As Deck observes:

> The problem is that the parish, at least in California, is too big. Efforts to make the parish into a "community of communities," to break it down into smaller faith-sharing units, have been less successful than we might have expected. As Robert Bellah and other researchers have begun to demonstrate, Anglo-American Catholics may talk about community and family, but they have a hard time subjecting themselves to these very demanding realities. There has been, therefore, a lot of talk about small community, basic ecclesial community, or whatever you want to call it, but the results have been exceedingly more modest than the rhetoric. . . . The fundamental problem is the inflexibility of the parish. (1988, p. 486)

Whatever else may be said about the episcopal leaders of the U.S. Church, they remain committed to the parish structure as foundational (Murnion, 1982, p. 46). Some efforts have attempted to graft a base community model onto the parish structure, in part as a tactical concession to Hispanic Catholics. These moves have remained marginal and usually uninspiring. The parish (on average ten times larger in numbers than Protestant congregations) (Hoge, 1981, p. 10) is fundamental to the U.S. Catholic bishops, despite its many deficiencies as an organizational model. Further, the move away from national parishes to "American" ones seems irrevocable; as Deck notes, the idea of the parish as an Americanizing vehicle remains popular among many Church leaders (1988, p. 487).

For these and other reasons, it seems unlikely that Hispanic Catholics will alter or undermine the significance of U.S. Catholic Nationalism in the U.S. Church. That ideology is shaping the Catholicism experienced by the new immigrants more than the reverse; its strength is evidenced by surveys that show increasingly "Anglo" styles and patterns of worship as Hispanic Catholics rise economically (for example, marriage; Gonzales and LaVelle, 1985, p. 16) and in the pastoral plans designed to combat incursions by Pentecostal evangelization.

SUMMARY: ECCLESIOLOGY, POLITICAL ECONOMY, AND U.S. CATHOLIC NATIONALISM

Chapter 2 described the U.S. Catholic Church as one with a loose ecclesiology, a middle-class base, and a weak PE critique of its society. This chapter's study of U.S. Catholic Nationalism suggests how these three qualities reinforce one another and why substantive strengthening of the Church's PE critique is likely to require (or prompt) change in ecclesiology and perhaps in the Church's social base. It further suggests why, in the absence of such changes, the U.S. Church is unlikely to break free of U.S. Catholic Nationalism and will be at odds with its Third World coreligionists on a range of theological and political commitments. That this is so can be seen in summarizing the present chapter, with more explicit correlation with the ecclesiology/PE axes outlined in chapter 2.

ECCLESIOLOGY IN THE U.S. CATHOLIC CHURCH

The first important trait of the U.S. Catholic Church in ecclesiological terms is its minimalist demands for membership. "Cultural Catholics," people of religious indifference or noninvolvement, all have the same rights and privileges as those for whom their faith is a more demanding reality affecting their fundamental life commitments—work, worship, personal and political witness, and more. Church leaders explicitly reject the notion that being a Christian ought to make great demands on adherents (National Conference of Catholic Bishops, 1980, p. 4); Church membership and participation belong to all, sinners and saints alike, for those who try to live lives of Christian discipleship and those whose religious sensibilities demand of them nothing beyond prevailing cultural norms. Despite occasional rhetoric to the contrary, being "of the Church" makes few if any demands in important areas of personal and social life.

Critical to this minimalist conception of "church" is the centrality of the parish as the structural core of U.S. Catholicism as a social reality. As a sacramental and social dispensary, the parish provides few opportunities for forming genuine "communities" or for learning a distinctive way of life and virtues not derivable from secular culture (Hauerwas, 1985, pp. 42–43). The U.S. Catholic bishops are committed to the centrality and primacy of the parish form, often in tones giving it a normative historical authority far beyond its barely 300-year dominance in Church life (Dolan, 1974). One recent document calls the parish "for most Catholics the single most important part of the church" (Murnion, 1982, p. 46), while another claims that "parishes are places where people take root and where their religious sensibilities begin to take concrete forms" (Greeley et al., 1981, p. 10).

Despite awareness of the inadequacies of parish life (one bishop observes that "the parish structure is so outmoded that it becomes a painful work place for priests, sisters and lay people . . ." (Ottenweller, 1978, p. 15), and despite many attempts to revitalize parish life, the parish remains unchanged in its essentials—too large to provide a sense of belonging, too narrowly sacramental in emphasis to engage in ongoing "formation of character," and too often mirroring the secular opinions and prejudices of its surroundings to make faith come alive "as a strenuous and fateful adventure, catching up men's [sic] lives in a surge of significance and purpose. . ." (Kelley, 1972, p. 56).

Unlike the Latin American Church, no alternative or supplement to the parish exists for the vast majority of U.S. Catholics. Attempts to copy the base community model have been feeble, appealing to a few disgruntled Catholics (usually homogeneously comfortable in economic terms; see, for example, National Conference of Catholic Bishops, 1980, p. 4; Pravera, 1981, pp. 253–54). The USCC Secretariat for Hispanic Affairs in 1979 claimed the existence of 12,000 BCCs in the United States, a figure that in retrospect seems inflated and in any event not likely to have come to terms with criticisms of assumptions of a "natural affinity" between Hispanics and BCCs (Deck, 1988).

The fact remains that the parish is a poor structure for forming much beyond "cultural Christians," those whose religious convictions blend harmoniously with the fundamentals of the dominant secular culture. For those Catholics who desire a more intense experience of community, who seek forms of worship and practice more demanding than the "dilute residue of former vitality" (Kelley, 1972, p. 56), options are few. There is no experience of a strong ecclesiology coexisting alongside (or within) a loose one, as with the BCCs in the Latin American Church, and there are no significant moves to develop or nurture such structures or practices.

This should not seem surprising since U.S. Catholic Nationalism so thoroughly harmonizes Christian and secular values that the need for developing character-forming structures of a more intensive nature scarcely appears. Indeed, the centrality of a loose, minimalist, parish-based ecclesiology makes sense principally in relation to the affinity between religious and secular roles propounded in U.S. Catholic Nationalism. Given the "strong continuity between Christian and non-Christian morality, especially in a liberal society" (Hauerwas, 1985, p. 2), why would a tighter ecclesiology be either necessary or desirable? If being a good Catholic and a good American are mutually supporting, why would there ever be a need for a tighter ecclesiology capable of "sustain[ing] a people who are not at home in the liberal presuppositions of our civilization and society," or for a sense of ecclesial mission at odds with the welfare of the U.S. national state (Hauerwas, 1985, pp. 11–12)? The affinities between Church and state that undergird U.S. Catholic Nationalism help maintain the loose ecclesiology of the U.S. Church; they figure largely in its leaders' weak critique of American political-economic arrangements; and they also play a part in the bishops' inability or reluctance to challenge the loyalties of the Catholic middle class.

POLITICAL ECONOMY AND THE U.S. CATHOLIC CHURCH

Chapter 2 divided our consideration of political economy into (1) a sociological level, Level One PE, of the membership of the Catholic Church and (2) an ideological level, Level Two PE, reflecting the strength or weakness of the Church's critique of political-economic arrangements. This chapter has shown that Catholics in the United States have become overwhelmingly middle class, thoroughly integrated into all levels of power and privilege in society, and well positioned to assume a role of cultural leadership following the decline of Protestant civil religion and the subsequent search for a "language of public discourse." Catholics in the United States are eager participants in the exercise of economic and political power, both in their professional roles and through the leadership of the U.S. bishops. The middle-class character of the Church is unlikely to be diminished by the rising Hispanic population within it.

The nature of the PE critique of the U.S. Catholic leadership remains weak, as is evident in the bishops' much-celebrated pastoral letters on American society. The bishops assume the fundamental goodness and legitimacy of the United States, its institutions, and its role in the world. Whatever criticisms they offer are in a spirit of "fraternal correction" rather than outright opposition; in any event, they remain committed to preventing any possible rift between the religious and political identities of U.S. Catholics (Au, 1987, p. 251).

The bishops' PE critique is one that avoids an analysis of capitalism, avoids any serious engagement with dependency or world systems theory, and avoids the disturbing possibility of seeing the United States as the source of serious human suffering in the world. Their critique, mild as it is, is directed primarily to people and institutions of secular power, most of them presumably non-Catholics; it follows a long line of (primarily Protestant) social ethics concerned primarily with "how to sustain the moral resources of American society" (Hauerwas, 1985, pp. 35–36). The bishops' critique is that of a sharer of secular responsibilities and power, not of a religious community "formed by a language that the world does not share" (Hauerwas, 1985, pp. 11–12).

One can see, then, how ecclesiology and both aspects of political economy link together in the mainstream of U.S. Catholicism. A loose ecclesiology with minimal demands fits well with a middle-class, increasingly powerful community at peace with its religious and political self-understanding. In turn, a weak PE critique helps to avoid the troublesome prospects of a conflict between self-interest and the welfare of others (especially the poorest) and legitimates a position of loyal critic rather than one of prophetic denunciation. Further, a weak PE critique (weakened at many points to pacify political, corporate, and conservative religious elites—see, for example, Au, 1987, pp. 229–33) provides nothing to offend or alienate the Church's middle-class membership, thus acting to sustain the Church's presently constituted social base.

Changing one element in this relationship without changing others would be extremely difficult. A more demanding form of ecclesiological mission by itself would not affect the PE base or critique of the Church; but attempts to strengthen the Church's PE critique would likely fail without some elements of a tighter ecclesiological arrangement (such as the BCCs, for example). This latter prospect reflects the ease with which conservative or affluent actors can and do undermine more critical efforts and actions within a purely loose ecclesiological framework. Were a more radical PE critique joined to a normative and structural tightening in ecclesiology, the Church's social base would almost certainly change— many people of weak religious commitment or socially privileged means would likely depart, leaving only those of strong religious commitment and those not threatened by radical social analysis. Overall, the relations suggested in the political-economy/ecclesiology matrices in chapter 2 seem to be supported by the past and present experiences of the U.S. Catholic Church.

5

RESOURCES FOR CHANGE?
U.S. CATHOLIC SOCIAL ETHICS

Chapters 1 through 4 have illustrated the growing split between core and peripheral Catholicism by providing evidence of the widening rift between rich and poor Catholics in the Americas. Particularly noteworthy is the apparent inability, based on historical and contemporary experiences and ideas, of the U.S. Catholic Church to respond sympathetically to the challenges in political economy and ecclesiology offered by Latin American Catholics. But if past and present are not encouraging in this regard, what of suggestions for the future? What resources are offered by U.S. Catholic social ethicists, those theologians writing about Christianity and social issues?

This chapter examines a number of recent works in U.S. Catholic social ethics. While not intended to be a representative sampling—these authors are all males within the Church's broad mainstream and are most likely to be given a sympathetic hearing by most Church leaders—they do cover a range of political convictions (generally, from social democratic to neoconservative). If the U.S. Catholic Church is to find common ground with its Latin American coreligionists on political economy and ecclesiology, social ethicists may well play an important role, suggesting forms of religious presence and action in the world more conducive to religious solidarity and cooperation.

But while theology has a role in such a movement toward solidarity—should one arise—it is far from the only factor (or the most important one) influencing change in the Church. As we have seen, a variety of nontheological forces affect the rate and direction of religious change. To promote close scrutiny of social ethics as one important factor is not to argue for it as the only one deserving such treatment; it does suggest, however, that social ethics is particularly important when considering the interrelations of political-economic and religious ideas.

Theology in general, and social ethics in particular, can influence change through a variety of vectors. Three of the most important ones will be outlined here:

(1) *Service to Hierarchy*: Some theologians act as Church intellectuals for hierarchical members and leaders. This magisterial service might be based in the chancery, in pastoral programs under direct episcopal control, in service organizations controlled by the hierarchy (for example, U.S. Catholic Conference), or perhaps even in Church schools.

(2) *Nonhierarchical Organizations*: Some theologians exercise influence through independent religious institutes (for example, the Center of Concern in Washington, D.C.), through pastoral programs outside direct episcopal control (various Bible study programs, for example), through religious media (for example, *The National Catholic Reporter*, *The Wanderer*, Orbis Books), and through seminaries, colleges, and universities outside direct episcopal control.

(3) *Via Secular Vehicles*: An increasing number of theologians operate independently of religious institutions altogether, taking advantage of secular organizations to disseminate religious ideas. In the United States most Catholics receive the bulk of their religious information from the secular media; worldwide, Hanson has documented the role of mass communications in disseminating and transmuting religious messages (Hanson, 1987, pp. 5–9). Particularly on matters of controversy, secular media have been willing participants in religious discussions. Secular institutions like universities have served as refuges for theologians purged from Church-affiliated institutions, providing such dissidents a base to continue their theological activities (although as the travails of Charles Curran at Auburn University indicate, secular universities in the Bible Belt South also can be inhospitable places).

Of course, in practice, all three means of influence overlap and interact. A theologian might advise a bishops' conference, for instance, on the contents of a pastoral letter, which is then communicated to the faithful principally by means of television and secular print media.

RESOURCES FOR CHANGE IN U.S. CATHOLIC SOCIAL ETHICS?

Do U.S. Catholic social ethicists provide intellectual resources and suggestions for the future that are useful in closing the gap between U.S.

and Latin American churches? As a sampling of mainstream theological opinion, the writers examined here display diverse political and theological opinions. None of them are unknowns, and all are among the more respected U.S. Catholic theologians. The most glaring omission might be J. Bryan Hehir, arguably the most influential Catholic social ethicist in the United States. The source of Hehir's influence is his role in drafting the U.S. bishops' pastoral letters on nuclear weapons and the national economy. Since the bishops have adopted his substantive and methodological positions in their entirety (and since the documents reflecting them have been discussed in previous chapters), it seemed appropriate to seek out other writers for discussion here.

In evaluating these social ethicists, each will be introduced with brief biographical information and background on the major work that is the center of discussion. The particulars of their respective studies are not of primary interest in all cases; rather, three specific concerns will be examined: each authors' political presuppositions, evaluations of the United States and capitalism, and ecclesiological and methodological positions.

INTERLUDE: HAUNTED BY THE GHOST OF MURRAY

No figure has dominated Catholic theology in the United States more than John Courtney Murray. The Jesuit scholar and author, longtime editor of the prestigious *Theological Studies* and product of an elite New York family, continues to dominate the practice of Catholic social ethics in the United States even two decades after his death.

At least part of Murray's ongoing importance flows from his stature as a world-class theologian, perhaps the only U.S. Catholic theologian worthy of such a designation. As a peritus (expert) working through his sponsor, Francis Cardinal Spellman of New York, Murray had a decisive role at Vatican II through its *Declaration of Religious Freedom*. The declaration adopted Murray's primary themes—affirming the validity of religious freedom and pluralistic societies, moving beyond the confessional state ethics of the medieval era, and recognizing constitutional democracy as a political system Catholics could support. Equally as important to modern theologians was Murray's effectiveness in defining the terms of discussion (and seeing his views prevail) both in the United States and in the worldwide Church.

Murray's status in U.S. theological circles remains high; indeed, all the theologians discussed here bow before him as the U.S. Catholic theologian par excellence. Numerous works seek to continue the "Murray project," or extend "Murray's method," or hope to assume the "Murray mantle." In addition to his attractiveness as a role model for theologians (perhaps a tribal loyalty toward the brightest star in an otherwise undistinguished universe), Murray's disciples argue for the continued validity of his style of social ethics.

Murray's primary concerns, his theological methodology and presuppositions, and his assessment of political life can all be found in *We Hold These Truths*, a loosely unified series of essays (written in the 1950s) published in 1960. Murray sought to defend Catholicism in the United States from nativist attacks on its compatibility with American democracy; he pushed the Church to come to terms with religious pluralism on principled, not merely expedient, grounds. Throughout the book, he speaks to secular and religious elites on the proper relations of religion and society, on Catholicism and civic responsibility, and on the need for a common moral language appropriate to political community.

Many of Murray's concerns emerged from his contention that the Founding Fathers believed that

> the life of man in society under government is founded on truths, on a certain body of objective truth, universal in its import, accessible to the reason of man, definable, defensible. If this assertion is denied, the American Proposition is, I think, eviscerated at one stroke. (1960, p. ix)

It is this "objective truth," accessible to reason, that provides the basis for civic consensus, an absolute necessity for authentic political civilization. Political association, to Murray, is fundamentally rational and deliberative, with its "permanent cohesiveness" dependent on argument among men (1960, pp. 6, 10).

> The whole premise of the public argument, if it is to civilized and civilizing, is that the consensus is real, that among the people everything is not in doubt, but that there is a core agreement, accord, acquiescence. We hold certain truths; therefore we can argue about them. (1960, p. 10)

Threatening the entire "American Proposition," to Murray, has been the erosion of consensus or a language appropriate to it, as well as a declining sense that such consensus is either possible or necessary.

Within the tradition of politics as rational discourse discovering universal truths stands, of course, the Catholic natural law tradition. It has been the Catholics, to Murray, who have preserved the natural law tradition in the United States, even as it was abandoned in the universities. Murray argues that the natural law tradition, far from being a peculiarly Catholic concept, has been operative in the United States since the nation's founding and has been critical in maintaining the American consensus. It has been the natural law tradition that has allowed Catholics to participate freely and enthusiastically in American public life.

> Catholic participation in the American consensus has been full and free, unreserved and unembarrassed, because the contents of this consensus—the ethical and political principles drawn from the tradition of natural law—approve themselves to the Catholic intelligence and conscience. Where this kind of language is talked, the Catholic joins in the conversation with complete ease. It is his language. The ideas expressed are native to his own universe of discourse. Even the accent, being American, suits his tongue. (1960, p. 41)

Murray argues against assuming that the decline of consensus concerning the fundamentals of American society must be temporary. However, he also argues that the consensus on a universal moral law, fundamental rights, and a nation under God *will* be preserved within the Catholic community, if nowhere else. If the trends he observed in the 1950s continue,

> the results would introduce one more paradox into history. The Catholic community would still be speaking in the ethical and political idiom familiar to them as it was familiar to their fathers, both the Fathers of the Church and the Fathers of the American Republic. The guardianship of the original American consensus, based on the Western heritage, would have passed to the Catholic community, within which the heritage was elaborated long before America was. (1960, pp. 42–43)

Murray anticipates by thirty years arguments for the "Catholic Moment" in revitalizing political discourse and pursuit of the common good. It has been this thrust of Murray's thought—the validity of natural law methodology, the compatibility of the Church and the American system, and the responsibilities of Catholics in that system—that has been most attractive to later theologians. Still, Murray's other concern— to replace the normativeness of the unitary state (and its provisional, grudging tolerance of pluralism when state sponsorship of Catholicism was not possible) with an ethically grounded idea of religious freedom— was important since, by the 1950s, Catholics' actual assimilation "had outrun its legitimations" (Cuddihy, 1978, p. 60). Abandoning the unitary state norm (which was the effect of the *Declaration on Religious Free-*

dom) would rob nativists of their most serious anti-Catholic charge and would allow Catholics to assimilate and assume power more completely and unreservedly as loyal Americans.

In the course of his argument, Murray makes important assumptions concerning the operation of American politics, the state, the international system, and more. While such are historically limited, they are important in grounding his philosophical concordance between Catholicism and the American Proposition. This will be reviewed later in this chapter in analyzing U.S. Catholic social ethics.

CONTEMPORARY U.S. CATHOLIC SOCIAL ETHICS

CHARLES E. CURRAN

Past president of the Catholic Theological Society of America (and recipient of its John Courtney Murray Award), Curran is a Catholic priest of some notoriety. His dismissal as professor of moral theology at the pontifically chartered Catholic University of America generated a storm of protest, extended litigation, and much media attention. Curran has turned increasingly to social ethics in recent years, although his reputation (and controversial impact) was made as a moral theologian writing on sexuality, reproduction, and Church doctrine.

An important book is Curran's *American Catholic Social Ethics: Twentieth-Century Approaches* (1982). While most of it is a survey history of important U.S. Catholic social theologians, its concluding chapter situates Curran's own beliefs and views. As he notes:

> Can one be both a good Catholic and a good American at one and the same time? No other single question has been of such practical significance for the life of the Catholic Church in the United States. No other problematic has been as influential in shaping American Catholic social ethics. (1982, pp. 4–5)

After chapters summarizing the answer to that question formulated by Catholic actors like John A. Ryan, the Central-Verein, the Catholic Worker movement, Murray, and the Catholic peace movement, Curran offers his own position. Despite his reputation (undeserved) as a radical in moral theology, Curran's own social ethics are decidedly middle-of-the-road. On being Catholic and American, he writes, "In general my approach avoids the extremes of either complete identification or of total opposition" (1982, p. 283).

Curran rejects the Catholic Worker/Catholic peace movement position that nonviolence and pacifism should be normative for all Christians. He holds a positive view of the state, claiming that it "exists to secure and promote the common good which redounds to the good of individual persons" (1982, p. 288).

Ecclesiologically, Curran accepts the church/sect typology of Troeltsch and uses it to argue for a dualistic ethic of radical demand—acceptable for the select few with "a special vocation," but in no way binding on all Catholics (1982, pp. 290-91).

Methodologically, while noting that the trend in Catholic ethics since Vatican II has been toward greater reliance on evangelical norms, Curran hopes to blend in the Catholic natural law approach. He sees no fundamental conflict between the two approaches and presumably favors the structure of the bishops' recent pastorals as an attempt to "speak to Christians and to non-Christians alike" (1982, pp. 286–87).

Curran does not address the role of the United States in the world, nor the Church's proper response to capitalism. While he does warn of "the danger of losing the critical element which must always be associated with the gospel and the church" (Curran, 1987, pp. 59–60), his overall tenor is one of reform and loyal correction.

RICHARD P. MCBRIEN

McBrien is a renowned ecclesiologist, chairman of the theology department at the University of Notre Dame (until 1991), and author of the two-volume catechism *Catholicism* (1981). His major work in social ethics is *Caesar's Coin: Religion and Politics in America* (1987).

The first half of *Caesar's Coin* examines ecclesiology, theological method, and theoretical concerns; the second half explores current controversies, including abortion, state aid to private schools, and nuclear weapons. While the extended attention to ecclesiological concerns is notable, the substance of his explorations is unremarkable. Throughout the book, McBrien employs Troeltsch's church/sect typology, accepting Troeltsch's contention that the central ideals and values of Christianity "cannot be realized within the world apart from compromise." While noting the intermingling of both types within U.S. Catholicism, McBrien maintains the normativity of the church model, which "is for all the masses" (1987, pp. 18–19).

Like Curran, McBrien quotes approvingly from Murray throughout and derives his definition of politics from the Jesuit. To McBrien, "politics has to do with the public forum and with the process of decision making that occurs there. A political community is one in which its members are 'locked together in argument' [quoting Murray]." (1987, p. 20). Similarly, McBrien agrees with Joseph Cardinal Bernadin, who said in a major Georgetown address:

> I stand with Murray in attributing a public role to religion and morality in our national life. But I also stand with him in the conviction that religiously rooted positions must somehow be translated into language, arguments and categories which a religiously pluralistic society can agree on as the moral foundation of key policy positions. (Bernadin, 1984, p. 343)

This need to "translate" religiously derived positions into terms acceptable to secular society undergirds McBrien's approach to specific questions of religion and politics. For example, he approves of the ways in which the U.S. bishops attempted to address the nuclear weapons issue:

> Unlike sectarians, the bishops accepted responsibility for addressing not only their own fellow Catholics but also the wider civil community. As a consequence, they were required to develop arguments that they hoped would be compelling even for those who did not share Catholic, Christian, or any other religious faith.

> Unlike fundamentalists, whenever the bishops appealed to the authority common to all Christians, that is, the Bible, they did so in a manner that reflected some of the complexities of modern biblical scholarship and of historical consciousness. They recognized, in other words, that the Bible does not yield ready-made answers to current political, economic, social, military, or even moral problems. Instead, it provides a vision, a set of values, a sense of moral direction. (1987, p. 201)

At no point in *Caesar's Coin* does McBrien examine matters of political economy, the role of the United States in the world, or similar questions. Neither does he suggest that U.S. Catholic ecclesiology is anything but adequate.

DENNIS MCCANN

Trained at the University of Chicago Divinity School, Dennis McCann is a professor of religious studies at DePaul University. He may well be the politically most progressive of the ethicists examined here, at least on the basis of his *New Experiment in Democracy: The Challenge of American Catholicism* (1987a).

McCann applauds the economic democracy recommendations of the

U.S. bishops' pastoral, which, if fully implemented, would lead toward a thoroughgoing social-democratic system. His interest goes beyond that, however, insofar as McCann seeks "new experiments in democracy" within the Church. He argues for a notion of justice as participation, employs it in examining internal Church decision-making, and considers the possibilities that would emerge from such a program.

McCann claims to have appropriated the philosophical notion of justice-as-participation from the American experiment in constitutional democracy. He self-consciously adopts the mantle of the Americanist movement and calls on the Church to embrace the Americanist intent to synthesize the best of Catholicism and the United States. The American legacy of self-governing associations, he suggests, may someday become the U.S. Church's contribution to the universal Church.

The Church in the United States can best serve religiously and socially, to McCann, by functioning as a forum for public moral discourse, allowing for pluralism, mutual engagement, and the formation of new communal norms. To this end, he endorses a Murray-like role for natural law tradition; McCann, however, situates this within a wider notion of communicative competence that generates procedures for ethical reflection (derived from Habermas; McCann, 1987a, pp. 100, 108–9). McCann and a coauthor have devoted an entire book to a Habermasian approach to theology and social ethics (McCann and Strain, 1985).

Given his interest in the Church as a forum for generating specifically public, nonreligious social norms, McCann's ecclesiology is appropriately loose. He dismisses the criticism of Methodist theologian Larry Rasmussen (who suggests that ecclesiological error has plagued the Church since Constantine):

> Rasmussen to the contrary notwithstanding, the admittedly diverse biblical legacies cannot be played off against each other when it comes to discerning the will of the Holy Spirit for these communities today. Nor can they, either singly or collectively, be used to dismiss the greater part of the Catholic community's own experience as a "long Constantinian hangover." However inadequate the theology and institutions characteristic of the Constantinian period may be for our purposes, they, too, continue to make a contribution, despite their corruption, to the work of the Holy Spirit in history. (1987a, p. 129)

Overall, ecclesiology concerns McCann only as it affects his primary value of participation. He is cautious about making an "option for the poor," because such might stifle the dialogic participation of social and religious influence wielders (1987a, p. 128).

Like many contemporary Catholic ethicists, McCann sees internal Church reforms as helpful in creating a new public ethic similar to Neuhaus' "Catholic Moment":

> The democratization of the church is not just desirable from the perspective of Catholic ecclesiology, but may also hold the key to various efforts in American Christianity today to renew itself as a "public church" and thus continue the work of building "the kingdom on earth". . . . If the Church expects this nation's economic institutions to democratize themselves so that all may share in "basic justice," the church must lead the way by democratizing its own institutions. (1987a, p. 186)

McCann further argues that, to participate in public discussion, religious communities must rely on "middle axioms" to act as a bridge between theological principles and social applications. Middle axioms, to him, reflect a community's "generalizable interests," which must be:

> (1) an authentic reflection of the [religious] community's own particular tradition of moral discernment, and once recognized as such by members of the community it serves as the focal point for their contribution to public dialogue.

> (2) at the same time, the policy guideline must be regarded as appropriate to society as a whole, in the sense that it could and should become the basis for consensus, not just within the religious community but also within the civil community as a whole. (1987a, pp. 113–15)

McCann insists his approach is no mere ratification of the social status quo. He says the substance of the new Americanist agenda is not easily specified, but "it cannot be answered simply by taking the current pulse of the nation and the Catholic community within it. For the Americanist agenda is not, and never was, merely a baptism of the *Zeitgeist*" (1987a, p. 157).

Overall, McCann says little on international issues or problems, and political economy is a given as presently constituted.

GEORGE WEIGEL

Few U.S. Catholic theologians combine scholarship with polemic as effectively or provocatively as does George Weigel. His *Tranquillitas Ordinis: The Present Failure and Future Promise of American Catholic Social Thought on War and Peace* (1987) swings from carefully reasoned philosophy and theology to political ad hominem. People whose views differ from his receive a most uncharitable handling. More than any of the current works in social ethics examined here, Weigel's book may have the most staying power and thus deserves more extended treatment.

Weigel's generally conservative worldview is mixed with world-order internationalism and concerns for international law and organization, reflecting his time as scholar in residence at the World Without War Council in Seattle. Presently, he is director of the Ethics and Public Policy Institute in Washington, D.C.

In postwar conservative fashion, *Tranquillitas Ordinis* identifies the twin dangers of the modern world as war and totalitarianism (1987, p. 5). Weigel's notion of the latter is similarly conservative: "totalitarianism began with a moral imperative; it arose from a passion to close the painful gap between things as they are and things as they ought to be" (1987, pp. 11–12).

Given this starting point, Weigel offers three theses:

> The first is that American Catholicism's elites—its bishops, priests, religious, intellectuals, and publicists—were the bearers of a heritage well equipped to define, with wisdom, a moral imagination capable of facing the threats of modern war and totalitarianism. The second thesis is that this heritage was largely abandoned by the most influential sectors of the American Catholic elite in a short decade after Vatican II, and that, under the influence of this shift, the official organs of the Church in the United States became, not the shapers of a new and wiser moral argument, but antagonists in old ones. (1987, p. 21)

Weigel's third thesis is that the resources of that abandoned heritage can be reclaimed with sufficient diligence in the present era. The content of that heritage Weigel describes as tranquillitas ordinis, literally the "tranquillity of order" (1987, p. 28). Throughout, he uses the term to mean "the peace of public order in dynamic political community" (1987, p. 31). He claims to root the heritage in Augustine, whose fundamental concern Weigel sees as trying "to establish the realistic conditions for the possibility of a politics of virtue, even in a fallen world" (1987, p. 27). Weigel dismisses the New Testament as a source of ethics on war and peace because of the "interim ethic" of its era (among those rejecting the interim ethic thesis, see Myers, 1988). The "realist" tradition of Augustine Weigel properly situates as an outgrowth of the changed circumstances of the Church: "Given its post-Constantinian position within the empire, Christianity had to face questions of social ethics and political theory that would have been inconceivable before the Edict of Milan" (1987, p. 26).

Weigel claims that Augustine's just war thinking did not reflect a relativizing or accommodating process within Christianity, but was instead "a necessary development in Christian self-understanding, once the decision had been made to leave the religious ghetto and undertake a transforming mission in the world" (1987, p. 30). After tracing the tradition from Augustine through Aquinas and the Middle Ages, Weigel summarizes it as "the Catholic tradition of moderate realism," built on three core convictions:

Politics is an arena of rationality and moral responsibility . . . political community is a good in its own right, an institutional expression of the sociability that is part of the God-given texture of human life.

Power should be understood in classical terms: as the ability to achieve a corporate purpose, for the common good.

Peace should be understood as tranquillitas ordinis, a dynamic, not static, concept. Peace provides the stability that allows social life to grow and develop. . . . The dimensions of justice that are most relevant to the creation of a morally worthy peace of tranquillitas ordinis are those that derive from Augustine's constitutionalism; concepts of the limited authority of the state, and of the importance of consent for the proper exercise of authority. (1987, pp. 43–44)

This moderate realism, to Weigel, fits well with ecclesiological developments through Vatican II:

The Council's ecclesiology of the laity was thoroughly transformationalist (or "conversionist," in H. Richard Niebuhr's typology): the Church was not a sect set over against the world, but a leaven within it. This mission of leavening the affairs of the world with the values of the Gospel was specifically and properly the mission of the laity, according to the Council. (1987, p. 104)

Both the tranquillitas ordinis tradition and the transformationalist ecclesiology Weigel ascribes to Vatican II, in his view, have been abandoned by U.S. Catholic elites of the post-Murray generation. He finds both the tradition and the ecclesiology intact and reflected in Murray (Weigel devotes his entire fourth chapter to "The John Courtney Murray Project"), but points to a number of well-known Catholics—Dorothy Day, Gordon Zahn, Thomas Merton, James Douglass, and Daniel and Philip Berrigan—as having led the rush to abandon the previous consensus. Weigel frequently uses the Berrigan brothers as examples:

> If there has indeed been an abandonment of the heritage of tranquillitas ordinis as it has been received and developed in American Catholicism through the Second Vatican Council, then no two men share a larger portion of the responsibility than Daniel and Philip Berrigan. To them, of course, whatever "abandonment" there has been has been all to the good. (1987, p. 164)

> The Berrigans taught an ecclesiology of repristination. Only the early Church, the Church of martyrs and nonviolence, was authentic. For those who wished to take up the task of institutional reform, that was the goal to be sought: the Church of the catacombs, a classically sectarian view. But even here, New Left politics obtruded. The classic, sectarian Peace Church was a Church that had eschewed the task of culture-formation in society; that was not the Berrigan view. The sectarian Church was to bring society to judgment, by its own witness and by building cadres for revolutionary social change. (1987, p. 169)

Unlike many more liberal or moderate social ethicists, Weigel shows no reluctance to identify the importance of evaluations of the United States in ecclesiological and other decisions. The impact of the New Left on U.S. Catholicism, to Weigel, was to shift the "center of gravity" in debate toward "a profound moral and political skepticism about the American capacity to act for peace, security, freedom or justice in the world" (1987, p. 214). Weigel claims that more eschatological understandings of peace deemphasized the value of tranquillitas ordinis, with the former "a neo-isolationist view of American foreign policy; that minimized the possibility of the legitimate use of force; that urged anti-anticommunism on the Church; and that questioned the moral worthiness of the American experiment" (1987, p. 237).

The loose, transformationalist ecclesiology also was challenged. To Weigel, "Sectarian currents of thought, emphasizing the corruption of the Church through its interaction with civil authority, came to the fore" (1987, p. 238). The relationship between views of the United States and ecclesiology also receive extended attention from Weigel:

> Various theological vectors of influence contributed to American Catholic sectarianism. Liberation theology was not classically sectarian in its ecclesiology (because it envisioned an important public role for the church as an agent of revolutionary change); but its radical critique of the organization of power in the West caused the question of whether the Church had become an unwilling accomplice to oppression by taking a transforming approach to its mission in the world. Ecumenical theological dialogue contributed to this evolution of thought. Mennonite theologian John Howard Yoder, for example, brought the classically sectarian ecclesiology of his traditional "peace church" into active conversation with Catholic theologians, publicists and activists.

> New Left political themes were influential in driving the ecclesiology of the Berrigan brothers in a sectarian direction. If America was really Babylon, a principal bearer of the world's evil, then the Church had no business making common cause—even in a critical vein—with the principalities and powers of that oppressor state. Rather, the Church's essential business was judgment. Its mission was to shout a judgment from the rooftops: to call down fire from heaven (in the form of revolutionary action) on the present order of corrupt power.

> Confusions abounded here. Whereas classic, sectarian, "witness" ecclesiology stood radically over against "the world," eschewing political prescription, the Berrigans and many others who shared their view of the Church did not hesitate to make numerous policy prescriptions. Ecclesiological sectarianism was married to political activism in a new hybrid. However one sorts out the various influences at work in the creation of that hybrid, it clearly represented a break with the transformationalist perspective of the Catholic heritage on the relationships between Church and world. (1987, pp. 238–39)

Weigel forthrightly offers his own understanding of the United States and its political and economic institutions. He criticizes the U.S. bishops in their discussion of active nonviolence for not having identified "democratic governance" as "the world's most successful and widespread form of nonviolent conflict resolution" (1987, p. 283). He further argues that "the dignity and end of the human person" are "the moral substance of the American proposition and experiment" (1987, p. 340). After quoting Peter Berger on economic growth being essential for development and democracy, Weigel argues that

> economic growth leading to the alleviation of poverty is a sine qua non of the evolution of tranquillitas ordinis. The peace of rightly ordered community cannot be built in a zero-growth world" (1987, pp. 369–70).

On this basis, Weigel argues that a market economy and capitalism are essential for the development and extension of democracy (1987, p. 370). He lauds U.S. accomplishments in wealth creation and points to "success stories" in Southeast Asia as further legitimation for capitalism (1987, pp. 368–69).

All things considered, Weigel argues, "There is no contradiction between the truth claims of Catholicism and commitment to the American democratic experiment" (1987, p. 385). One way for the Church to play a creative role in the world would be "to provide critical support for the efforts of quasi-public agencies like the National Endowment for Democracy, which works through private sector instruments to help build the infrastructure of democracy abroad" (1987, p. 385).

ANALYSIS AND SUMMARY

As is evident, all of the theologians discussed here pay homage to Murray; all see themselves as continuing his work, applying his methodology, and extending the discussion of Catholicism and the American Proposition. A critical look at Murray will therefore reflect on this more recent generation of social ethicists. If, as this book has suggested, the U.S. Church needs a more critical appraisal of capitalism and changes in its ecclesiology to maintain religious solidarity with the Latin American Church, then social ethicists should have something constructive to say on one or both counts. At a minimum, their methodologies and assumptions should offer some hope for such development in the future.

MURRAY

Political Assumptions. Murray's conceptual apparatus can be faulted on several fundamental points. His insistence on politics as a thoroughgoing rational undertaking seems profoundly at odds with the everyday realities of political life. Murray's theory of the state, such as it is, can only be described as naive, almost a direct transferral from civics texts to political description (1960, p. 159). This naive view of the state is best illustrated by the "consent of the governed" and consensus he finds throughout American political life. No testing of reality seems to have affected his assessment of American political institutions:

> Through the American techniques of the constitutional convention and of popular ratification, the American Constitution is explicitly the act of the people. It embodies their consensus as to the purposes of government, its structure, the extent of its powers and limits on them, etc. (1960, p. 32)

> Not only do the people adopt the Constitution; through the techniques of representation, free elections, and frequent rotation of administration they also have a share in the enactment of all statutory legislation. . . . The people are governed because they consent to be governed, and they consent to be governed because in a true sense they govern themselves. (p. 33)

> Policy is made by society, especially in a democratic context; and society bears the moral responsibility for the policy made. As a problem in justice, the problem of war is put to the People, in whom, according to good medieval theory, the sense of justice resides, and from whom the moral judgment, direction, and correction of the policy must finally come. . . . Here, if anywhere, "The People shall judge." (p. 257)

Such an effusive faith in the People, and in the People as architects of social policy and public consensus, is contradicted throughout Murray's work by his unyielding elitism and low opinion of the average person's intellect (O'Brien, 1986, p. 14); this active, populist picture of American politics clashes with his view that elaborating the "public consensus"

> is not the work of the public at large. It is not the job for sheer common sense. The public consensus is not formally public opinion. Its elaboration is the task of the wise and the honest. . . . These tasks lie beyond the competence of the generality. It is for the wise, who develop the consensus, to give "instruction" to the generality, in the meaning of its principles as "matters of necessary observance," and also in the manner of their application. (1960, pp. 118–19)

Murray also claims the public consensus, once formulated, works through disinterested academics, honorable politicians, responsible journalists, and other professionals (1960, p. 104).

Throughout his essays, Murray's political vision is limited by his relentless adherence to consensus views of history, derived from Boorstin and Rossiter (O'Brien, 1986, p. 11). This consensual framework similarly affects his evaluation of the United States and capitalism.

The United States and Capitalism. As of the 1950s, Murray accepts the notion that poverty in the United States had been eliminated except for a few depressed areas and underprivileged groups (1960, p. 179). He notes that capitalism concentrates power in the hands of a few, but argues that the "public consensus" helps keep corporate power in check (1960, pp. 94–101, 104).

His conclusion on limits to capitalist power draws directly on A. A. Berle's *Power Without Property* (1959). Murray summarizes Berle's conclusion as being that

> the present concentration has in recent years been (on the whole) relatively free from the excesses which often make concentrated power odious. . . . Checks (not "balances") appeared in the form of periodic political interventions demanded by American public opinion. (1960, p. 101)

Further summarizing Berle, Murray argues that the

> public consensus furnishes the "reality of the corporate conscience" as it recognizes limits on corporate power and submits uses of economic power to public judgment. Finally, because concentrated economic power is checked by, and responsible to, the public consensus, the American economy qualifies as "democratic." (1960, p. 104)

As if to remove any lingering suspicion, Murray goes on to affirm that the American consensus "is not in any sense an ideology. Its close relation to concrete experience rescues it from that fate. The thought it embodies is not visionary or doctrinaire. Nor does it reveal any trace of class consciousness or partisan group interest" (1960, p. 106).

This ironic view of economic power accords well with Murray's belief in the United States as a force for good in the world (1960, p. 88). This view is foundational to his cold war ideology, which lays the blame for East-West conflict solely on the intrinsic nature of the USSR (Murray's relevant chapter title is "Doctrine and Policy in Communist Imperialism"). His international analysis sees the Soviet Union as driven relentlessly by ideology, incapable of change, and restrained only by the willingness of the United States to use force against it, and he offers many strategies for the United States to go on the cold war offensive (1960, pp. 231, 233–35).

Ecclesiology and Methodology. No suggestion of ecclesiological shift appears in *We Hold These Truths*. Murray's ecclesiology is loose in all respects, which is necessary given the primacy he accords natural law in conducting social ethics.

Murray discounts any role for biblical or evangelical criteria in conducting social ethics (1960, p. 275); indeed, one searches *We Hold These Truths* for much more than throwaway Scripture citations, so dominant are philosophical categories and arguments. One of the few places where he does reference the New Testament in *We Hold These Truths* is when, following Reinhold Niebuhr, he cites Luke 16:9, comparing the USSR with the Children of Darkness and the United States with the Children of Light (1960, p. 244). In all instances Murray's use of natural law reasoning is incapable of challenging anything significant about U.S. power (including its imperialism, which he admits exists, only to argue against feeling guilty about it) (1960, p. 281). He substantiates Cuddihy's contention (in reference to Reinhold Niebuhr, but analogically to Murray) that: "Presumably, one cannot hold and interest for long an audience composed of agnostic and atheist academicians . . . [and other of] Christianity's "cultural despisers," without something happening to Christianity" (Cuddihy, 1978, pp. 42–43).

A loose ecclesiology makes an exclusively natural law focus possible (and perhaps necessary); natural law theology, at least as used by Murray, accommodates secular power at almost every turn and nowhere seems to stand against it in significant ways.

CURRAN

Political Assumptions. Curran's view of the modern state is similar to Murray's: "The state exists to secure and promote the common good which redounds to the good of individual persons" (1982, p. 288). Throughout *American Catholic Social Ethics*, Curran offers little political analysis of any kind; one gets from him no opinion of the origin of social problems, mechanisms of social change or cohesion, or relations among institutional sources of power. In practice, this absence of political analysis puts Curran's middle of the road position much closer to the accommodationism of the Americanists than to the resistance of the Catholic Worker and similar forces. With no framework offered for analyzing social relations, Curran instead considers social problems as discrete and amenable to reformist measures.

The United States and Capitalism. Curran's lack of political analysis puts him in the position of rejecting radical groups like the Catholic Worker, but without answering their critiques of capitalism or the United States. One is left to conclude that "extremist views" must be rejected if only because of a predisposition favoring a "golden mean" in intellectual matters.

Curran provides no insights into the nature or significance of capitalism, or the role of the United States in the world economy. Both exist, in his framework, as given, legitimate loyalties for Catholics. With no investigation—or even defense—of these questions, Curran cannot claim a middle position except on a most unusual range of attitudes.

Ecclesiology and Methodology. Curran's heavy reliance on Troeltsch's typology leads him (as it does others) to ascribe normativity to the "church" type. His description of a more demanding ecclesiology (1982; e.g., pp. 290–91) seems more like a caricature than a position seriously encountered.

Curran's attempt to combine the energies of a more radical ecclesiology with the dominant loose ecclesiology is unpersuasive. Instead, he merely revives a dualistic ethic—one standard for the minority, a lesser one for the masses—as when he states (without much discussion): "In my judgment the total church cannot be absolutely pacifist or committed to total poverty, but individuals and prophetic groups within the church bearing witness to these virtues are very important and significant for the life of the whole church" (1982, p. 292).

This traditional limitation of a more demanding sense of church to those with a "special vocation" (1982, p. 292) is no more persuasive in Curran's hands than in others. It is particularly unpersuasive here, insofar as Curran makes no attempt whatsoever to link ecclesiological choices to evaluations of the social situation confronted by the Church. The latter requires political analysis, which is outside Curran's area of interest; instead, one is left with an ecclesiological choice (loose) divorced from historical challenges. Presumably, Curran would then opt for the same ecclesiology in situations of dictatorship, colonization, slavery, etc. Such a position may be defensible, but Curran nowhere ventures such a defense.

MCBRIEN

Political Assumptions. Political naïveté again surfaces, this time in McBrien's foundations. He defines the state as "that part of society concerned with public order and the enforcement of social justice" (1987, p. 204). It appears that several decades of theorizing on the modern state (for example, by Milliband, Offe, O'Connor) have made no inroads into the cloisters of most theology departments.

McBrien's rosy view of the state is complemented by his view of politics. Quoting Murray, he writes: "Politics has to do with the public forum and with the process of decision making that occurs there. A political community is one in which its members are 'locked together in argument'" (1987, p. 20). Such an understanding of politics is extraordinarily narrow; it ignores, for example, the activities of corporations and other nonpublic powers. It also is incapable of investigating the exercise of power in preventing matters from entering the public forum (for an example, see Gaventa, 1980).

The United States and Capitalism. Such a narrow scope becomes understandable when reviewing McBrien's case studies on issues of contemporary religion and politics. His limited definition of politics leads him to focus solely on nation-level, state-centered controversies; he is free to ignore larger questions on capitalism or the role of the United States in the world. The status quo escapes scrutiny in McBrien's analysis, except to be affirmed by his ecclesiological position.

Ecclesiology and Methodology. McBrien's reliance on Troeltsch's typology is by far the strongest among the writers examined here. His collapsing of categories into normative judgments is even more pronounced than Curran's. His adherence to Murray's natural law methodology causes him to overlook the problems inherent in translating theologically derived positions into philosophical, nonreligious categories and concepts. In practice, much of what happens is not translation, but rather allowing the desire to be relevant or understandable to nonreligious elites to circumscribe the religious discussion from the outset, rendering some conclusions (however theologically defensible) simply out of bounds. One will wait in vain with this translation approach for attempts to relate "love your enemies" or "turn the other cheek" in terms understandable to secular powerholders.

McBrien's problems do not end here. His view of Scripture as providing "a vision, a set of values, a sense of moral direction," rather than specific ethical guidelines (the practice of "fundamentalists"), is no less arbitrary than the position he ridicules (1987, p. 201). Which biblical values will

McBrien privilege? Based on what? On whose authority? His natural law approach to Scripture is no less selective than the approach he rejects, so that in practice it elevates to normativity those biblical themes judged a priori compatible with natural law translations for unbelievers.

His ecclesiological discussion, further, is diminished by his dismissal of theologians such as Yoder and Hauerwas as "sectarians," without engaging them in any way. Such an omission is all the more curious given the pair's presence in the theology department chaired by McBrien (Hauerwas has since moved to Duke), and given the influence they have had in recent Catholic theology (e.g., Clapp, 1988, p. 979; Weigel, 1987, pp. 238–39).

MCCANN

Political Assumptions. While McCann seems more politically sophisticated than McBrien or Curran, there are several weaknesses in his political reasoning. Foremost among these is the extent to which he assumes correspondence between U.S. political values/rhetoric (for example, democracy, participation) and their real-world manifestation. Nowhere does he question the realities or limitations of participation in U.S. politics (Ferguson, 1989; Dolbeare and Edelman, 1985); he assumes as empirical realities fundamentals that, given his overall argument, deserve substantiation.

Further, McCann's work suggests (largely in *Christian Realism and Liberation Theology*, 1977) that any political praxis beyond his manner of reform is "utopian" (e.g., *Christian Realism*, p. 18). McCann is not alone in such a practice (see the conservatives Mary Douglas and Aaron Wildavsky, *Risk and Culture*, 1983, for a notorious example), but it does not reflect well on his intellectual range.

The United States and Capitalism. McCann's case for Americanism (that is, compatibility between Catholicism and American values) suffers from his equation of values and performance. At the level of values or rhetoric, Catholicism might have fit even better with the USSR, a position, given the gap between theory and practice in that country, not held seriously by anyone. While McCann may feel no such gap exists in the United States, he owes his readers a defense of such a position; contrary evidence (from critics including Chomsky, Zinn, and the Berrigans) is certainly not lacking.

McCann's attempt to stress the Americanists' independence from dominant culture seems lame for similar reasons ("the Americanist agenda is not, and never was, merely a baptism of the *Zeitgeist*"; 1987a,

p. 157). Nothing McCann says suggests any place where he stands against the zeitgeist of the United States. He says little about the role of the United States in the world and offers no observable distance from the presuppositions of the dominant ideology.

As a nationalist, he is understandably hostile to liberation theology, although his argument against it is undermined by his tendency to caricature those to his left (e.g., 1987a, p. 89). Correspondingly, he is optimistic about the extent to which Americanist Catholicism can revitalize public theology in the United States, situating him with Murray, Neuhaus, and others anticipating with eagerness the coming "Catholic Moment."

Ecclesiology and Methodology. McCann is a Murray enthusiast, and he sees his own work as following similar lines (1987a, pp. 108–9). His loose ecclesiology encounters problems when the "middle axioms" principle he adopts for social ethics is looked at more closely. In particular, questions can be raised about the criteria used in deriving such axioms:

(1) How broad a community faith tradition should one consider? The national community? That unit may be too small and insular for a universal communion like the Catholic Church. If the world Church and its traditions are the norm, McCann may be faced with increasingly anticapitalist views if he takes the "moral discernment" of Third World churches seriously. Such would not fit well with his Americanist, nationalist loyalties.

(2) If policy must be "appropriate" to the Church's larger secular society, it must fit with the existing "consensus" of powerholders. The Church thus maintains no basis to challenge society in any of its fundamentals. This norm gives the status quo a veto in advance and is a prescription in every respect for a culture-affirming theology. All of which may be consistent with McCann's hostility to "utopianism," but it bears a disquieting similarity to a "baptism of the *Zeitgeist.*"

McCann's ecclesiology is troubled in another respect. Given his emphasis on participation, it is odd that he leaves unclear whether ecclesiological changes might be necessary as preconditions (or predictable as effects) of increased lay participation in Church decision-making. Does he envision voting for bishops, referenda on chancery revenues, or other forms of indirect participation? If his commitment to a loose ecclesiology is as thoroughgoing as it appears, he may have foreclosed in advance participation that changes the Church's self-definition—a difficult position to defend on his own terms, if in fact he holds it.

Finally, his dismissal of Rasmussen's critique (by appealing to the Holy Spirit's protective influence) smacks of irenicism worthy of Eusebius.

McCann's argument here looks like a form of "theological Parsonianism"—if a Church practice survives, it must have been theologically legitimate. Using the Holy Spirit as a theological trump card allows McCann to avoid the possibility of serious error in Church practice or history, or the need ever to rethink fundamentals. This type of avoidance can make the "Catholic Moment" possible, but it also can make necessary the shock of the Reformation.

WEIGEL

Political Assumptions. Unpacking Weigel's political assumptions is particularly important, given the radical nature of the charges he makes. His initial definition of totalitarianism and war as the paramount political challenges in the world (1987, p. 5) frames the discussion on terms he finds favorable. Beyond that utility, Weigel's definition provides no reason to exclude other possible issues from the same status (for example, starvation, ecology).

Having framed the world problematic in these terms, Weigel proceeds to tie totalitarianism to radicalism (1987, p. 12), thereby setting up anyone who is not an incrementalist of his sort as a potential moral tyrant. Weigel thus constructs a polemical tool he does not hesitate to use later in his book.

Weigel's political analysis is weakened by his refusal to define "dynamic political community," part of his definition of tranquillitas ordinis. Depending on one's perspective, absent further guidance, the modern USSR seems more like a "dynamic political community," with the Gorbachev revolution and autonomy movements under way, than does the comparatively static U.S. system.

Historian Jay Dolan takes issue with Weigel's entire thesis of tranquillitas ordinis as developed since Augustine (doubtful, in Dolan's view) and supported and developed as a critical commentary on American power by the U.S. bishops up to the 1960s ("simply not true," says Dolan). Dolan, considered by many scholars as among the best and most respected current historians of U.S. Catholicism, thus undermines Weigel's attempt to legitimate tranquillitas ordinis as a concept with some distance from the political status quo (1987, p. 30).

Other questions arise from examining Weigel's notion of "moderate Catholic realism." Its excessive rationalism is manifest, as is an unreflective view of political power, which, like McCann's, equates normative and descriptive usages. Weigel's emphasis on consent as the foundation for peace is underdeveloped; one wonders how serious Weigel is here—

for example, whether consent is relevant in the anticommunist dictatorships he supports. Similarly, his undefined uses of "order" and "anarchy" make for much question-begging. Finally, like McCann, Weigel assumes much about U.S. performance that he bases on U.S. rhetoric (e.g., 1987, p. 141), a practice he would reject when done by ideological opponents.

The United States and Capitalism. Weigel's assumptions about the American system are undisguised, for example, that the "dignity and end of the human person" are "the moral substance of the American proposition and experiment" (1987, p. 340). His avowal of U.S./Catholic affinity is no less forthright (1987, p. 385). And his defense of the superiority of capitalism leads him to reject the entire Latin American economic critique; like Novak, he blames Latin American destitution on Catholicism and other cultural factors (1987, p. 300).

Curiously, however, in his defense of capitalism as necessary for liberal democracy, Weigel unintentionally draws attention to a major contradiction. If it is true, as he argues, that unending economic growth is necessary for tranquillitas ordinis, then surely his is the most utopian position available, for few things seem more ecologically impossible than endless, Western-style economic growth (Gurr, 1988; Daly, 1980; Ophuls, 1977; Georgescu-Roegen, 1973).

Weigel's analysis carries other contradictions as well. He wants a greater role for international law in the future, but he makes no mention of U.S. violations of international law in the present (for example, the World Court's judgment on CIA mining of Nicaraguan harbors, violations of the UN refugee treaties) (1987, pp. 363–69). Such a conflict between Weigel's internationalism and nationalism may well be fundamental.

Similarly, he stresses the importance of human rights (1987, pp. 366–67), but he backs away from Pope John Paul II's expansive sense of economic and political rights. His support for the Nicaraguan contras, or the "democratic opposition" as he calls them, is difficult to reconcile with a serious commitment to human rights. His advice that the Church should support the National Endowment for Democracy, part of the Iran/Contra mechanism funneling CIA funds to groups that were seeking the overthrow of the Nicaraguan government, provides a humorous interlude, if nothing else.

Perhaps the capstone on Weigel's political, partisan selectivity can be discerned from his concern with "state terrorism":

State-sponsored terrorism is incompatible with the international stability that is the prerequisite for the pursuit of peace, security, and freedom among nations. General principles, under the burden of necessity, may have to be subordinated to choosing necessary evils, but there seems little point in maintaining more than minimal diplomatic intercourse with states that have consistently set themselves outside the framework of orderly international public life. Developing the means to sequester outlaw nations that harbor, sponsor, or give material assistance to international terrorists, and achieving the agreement necessary to make such means effective, would be a step toward, not away from, peace. (1987, p. 382)

One wonders whether Weigel would stick to this view if confronted with evidence of U.S.-supported terrorism in world affairs (in Nicaragua, Angola, or elsewhere). Many of the New Left types that Weigel savages have examined the international role played by the United States and have done what Weigel recommends regarding state terrorists. It may well be that Weigel's advice may be followed more consistently by the Berrigans, the Pledge of Resistance, and similar groups opposed to U.S.-sponsored terror than by Weigel or his friends among U.S. foreign policy makers. State terror as applying only to ideological enemies (the USSR, Libya) and never to the United States is a conclusion consistent with Weigel's practice of assuming (rather than demonstrating) equivalence between virtuous rhetoric and political practice.

Ecclesiology and Methodology. Weigel consistently uses ecclesiology to bludgeon those critical of the United States, for example, describing the Berrigans as "sectarians" in a most pejorative sense. To his credit, however, Weigel at least recognizes the relationship between ecclesiology and evaluations of the Church's secular political environment (1987, pp. 238–39). A tight ecclesiology would seem to be less necessary if one found the secular environment in accord with religious principles.

Weigel consistently offers false choices in matters of ecclesiology, as when he presents an all-or-nothing decision between "witnessing over against the world" or "transforming and healing in a broken and divided human community" (1987, p. 238). He refuses to recognize the possibility of different forms and terms of religion-and-politics engagement, that the either/or choice he sets up does not necessarily exhaust all possibilities.

In fact, it may well be that his favorite whipping boys, the Berrigans, recognize "witnessing vs. transforming" as a false choice. Their praxis was and is both oppositional and activist, evidencing a tight ecclesiology and an active participation in political struggles; Weigel dismisses that manner of praxis as an ecclesiological aberration, rather than considering it a refutation of the "sectarian=withdrawal" equation.

Weigel's own ecclesiology is one he describes as transformationalist, which he says derives from H. Richard Niebuhr's typology. But apart from his condemnation of anti-Americanism and softness on communism, it is not clear what in the United States Weigel wants to transform.

CONCLUSIONS

This sampling of social ethicists reveals a high degree of political naïveté and unreflective political reasoning. Such lapses include an unrelenting equation of professed political values with what is actually practiced, an overly rationalistic view of politics, an unreflective notion of "common good" ideology, and a civics text understanding of the modern state.

Ecclesiologically, except for Weigel, none of these ethicists seriously consider the relationship between ecclesiology and one's view of the surrounding secular culture (in this instance, capitalism and the world role of the United States). The dominant assumption is that a loose ecclesiology is normative for the Church, and that the possibility of a historical wrong turn in ecclesiology is inadmissible. More radical or tighter ecclesiologies are consistently caricatured. Throughout all of their work, Troeltsch's church/sect typology can be described as hegemonic.

Despite their diverse political stances, all of these theologians hold fundamentally similar views on the United States. Weigel is the most up-front with his nationalism; the others claim to have a critical capacity but cannot seem to find much to criticize. Weigel simply says there is nothing in the fundamentals to criticize, but much to champion. Concerning capitalism, these theologians again appear similar; either capitalism is not a factor in their social ethics, or it is a positive good. Again, Weigel is the most intellectually forthright of the lot.

In summary, this group of U.S. Catholic theologians does not appear to offer much help in moving the U.S. Catholic Church closer to the Latin American and other Third World churches. To the extent that other social ethicists are similar to those examined (those here span the mainstream of U.S. Catholic social ethics), so too can the U.S. Church expect little guidance or exhortation relevant to future religious solidarity.

6

CONCLUDING THOUGHTS

COLLAPSING COMMUNISM

AND THE FUTURE OF

RELIGIOUS ANTICAPITALISM

As argued throughout this book, I believe that worldwide the Catholic Church, led by its Third World majority, will continue to develop in an anticapitalist direction. Changes within the Church, as well as the processes of the capitalist world system, combine to provide the interactive dynamics that will drive the institution further from the procapitalist sympathies of its North American and Western European churches.

The dramatic events in Eastern Europe and the USSR since 1988 would seem, to some critics, to cast doubt on *any* sustained opposition to capitalism in the future. With the collapse of state socialism and a rush toward fully market-oriented economies, many commentators have hastened to proclaim "victory" for capitalism over all serious opposition. Nobel laureate James Buchanan (1990) asserts that recent developments prove that "socialism is dead." "Socialism promised quite specific results," he argues. Quite simply, "it did not deliver."

Does the collapse of state socialism signal the collapse of my argument as well? Will the rising tide of anticapitalism in Third World Catholicism recede in tandem with the centrally planned economies of the USSR and its former satellite states? Dealing with such questions, even provisionally, seems appropriate in this final chapter. For a variety of reasons, I suggest that the collapse of state socialism does not undermine my argument. Two of these reasons can be stated briefly, while two others deserve more extended examination.

(1) First, except in unusual circumstances, the anticapitalist ethos within the Catholic Church in recent decades has not relied on the Soviet model for inspiration or as an alternative. Virtually no base community

leaders, theologians, or clergy will likely feel betrayed or demoralized by the collapse of the Soviet bloc command economy. The Soviet Union as "The God That Failed" was a trauma for radicals of the 1930s and '40s, not those of the 1990s and beyond. To the extent that the collapse also heralds the death of the cold war and the bogeyman of the world communist conspiracy, many Third World Christians celebrate the removal of at least one of the primary rationales offered by repressive forces persecuting the Church in Latin America and elsewhere. With the fig leaf of world communism torn away, perhaps the real reasons for widespread repression will become more visible to the world community.

(2) Second, given the interlocked nature of the world economy, it is possible that the changes in Eastern Europe and the USSR may *worsen* conditions in many poor countries—hardly likely to generate increased enthusiasm for the capitalist order. Already many Latin American countries—most notably the U.S. client states of Nicaragua and Panama— are finding promised bilateral aid being postponed, reduced, or forgotten as the debt-laden U.S. government scrambles to find aid for the Eastern European embrace of capitalism.

Consistent with the commercial interests of their core state directors, increased amounts of capital from multilateral agencies like the IMF and World Bank are flowing to Eastern Europe. There are now many more nations competing for the limited supply of multilateral capital, and the new competitors appear, for many reasons, more attractive than much of Latin America, Africa, or Asia. Already there is evidence of increased competition among East European countries for international assistance and investment, Poland being bypassed in favor of Hungary and Czechoslovakia, for example (Weschler, 1990, p. 21).

It also is possible that some multinational corporations may seek greater proximity to the West European market by moving production from Mexico or Thailand to Poland or to the former German Democratic Republic (East Germany), eliminating whatever meager contributions these activities provided to the former two countries.

Further, the collapse of the Soviet Union as a world power, however tightfisted it had been toward Third World actors, removes even a hypothetical counterweight to U.S. aspirations throughout the peripheral regions of the world economy. However meager or illusory the Soviet involvement in past Third World distributional struggles, at least it sometimes encouraged a degree of caution in core state aspirations. With the USSR seemingly (as of mid 1991) on the edge of internal breakup or military repression, Third World elites and their Western sponsors can pursue their economic and political objectives with greater latitude—to the detriment of the rights and living conditions of popular movements, trade unions, and poor people.

While these first two reasons—the irrelevance of the USSR as a political or economic model for most Third World Christians, and the increased hardships capitalism is likely to bring to many people in poor countries in the wake of East European developments—are straightforward enough, two other considerations merit a more complete explanation. These involve the likely role of the former command economies in the capitalist world system, and the place of the East European churches in their societies and in world Catholicism.

(3) Considerable controversy within world-systems literature has focused on how to understand state socialism and the capitalist world economy. Whether one views the former Soviet system as an area external to the capitalist system, as an independent system of its own, or as a component of the capitalist system, the recent changes will dramatically deepen the penetration of capitalism in the region.

However one views them, it seems unlikely that the former Comecom countries will achieve identical places in the post-cold war international division of labor. It does seem likely that the former East Germany will, in the reunited German state, eventually reap benefits as part of a major core actor. No other East European country's future seems as promising, nor does that of the USSR; as one observer notes, while the other countries of Eastern Europe believe their future will look like life in Sweden, more probably it will resemble life in Mexico (Weschler, 1990, p. 212). Another observer suggests that "at best, some parts of the East may become another Southern Europe, albeit at the cost to both of competing with each other" (Frank, 1990, p. 43).

While the specifics of market development and privatization of the economy are at various stages of being implemented (see Jefferson and Petri, 1990, p. 6), in no country does it appear that productive assets will be widely distributed on an enduring basis—Poland's tepid "people's capitalism" move being no exception (see Wellisz, 1990, p. 11; also Rule, 1990, p. 426). There are many barriers to the widespread distribution of productive assets, including a lack of purchasing power among the majority of East European citizens. In the case of Hungary, for example, "the maximum private liquid assets in the hands of individuals available for the purchase of the state's industrial assets is so small that it would take more than a hundred years for individuals to buy up all state-owned and enterprise-owned firms in the country" (Marer, 1990, p. 8).

More widespread will be the creation of what one wag sees not as market socialism, but the "socialist market" in which former government and party apparatchiks sell off productive assets among themselves (or to outside investor partners) and thus reconstitute their influence as the new national capitalist class.

If the beneficiaries of the transition are likely to be few, the wrenching dislocations involved—massive unemployment, decreasing purchasing power, homelessness, and more—are likely to fall most heavily on working-class majorities in most countries (Frank, 1990, p. 48–49). While the costs of transition seem to be most pronounced thus far in Poland, other states may be seeing their future in that present. Hungary may be cushioned somewhat by its ties with Austria, but prosperity for most of the rest is hardly around the corner (Frank, 1990, p. 48).

In fact, the East European countries may well experience the burdens of marketization—unemployment, inflation, and decline in living standards—without any protection from the few positive accomplishments of the command economy system: namely, the public goods of housing, basic foodstuffs, public health, and the like. However inadequate or stifling the bureaucracies that provided such measures, they constituted a social safety net, the abolition of which members of the working class are only now coming to see as the price demanded by foreign investors and the IMF (Frank, 1990, p. 48).

If this scenario holds, the world may yet see how thin is the enthusiasm for capitalism among the peoples of Eastern Europe and the USSR. They may come to discover too late that life under capitalism holds burdens not explored on "Dallas" or Voice of America. As one scholar observes:

> Admiration for capitalism in real life is limited to a small section of the populace. For example, most East Europeans I speak to love the market abstractly. The market they love means a guaranteed job for them and their children and relatives and of course their friends, cheap housing, public health, free education, and a pension. Provided they have all these things they would love to have a market in which they could get jeans that fit. But that's not what the market is about. Most of the free-market supporters in Eastern Europe would be utterly shocked at the poverty and social injustice imbedded in American society. Poor as many of the Eastern European cities are, you will not find people sleeping in the street. Nor in most of Western Europe. (Denitch, 1990, p. 179)

Another recent visitor observes that in one East European country

> three factors have been at work: [the people] have learned to reject
> everything they read or hear in the communist-controlled media;
> they are inclined to believe everything they hear on the BBC or Voice
> of America; they are, and always have been (since I was a boy there)
> [,] inclined to believe that most people in America live the American
> Dream every day. (reported by Haskell, 1990, p. 157)

The newly established business class—built on undervalued state
properties sold to political cronies and on ties to transnational investors—may well find the struggles worth the prize. For the majority of
the population, who have gained the ballot but lost their ability to earn a
livelihood, the triumph of capitalism may soon ring hollow. The honey-
moon for capitalism in Eastern Europe and the USSR may prove to be
short. As a force obstructing the anticapitalist trend that I see growing in
world Catholicism, the collapse of state socialism may be less important
than some people assume.

(4) But what of the Christian churches in general, and the Catholic
Church in particular, in the formerly state socialist countries? How are
they likely to affect the growing anticapitalist ethos in world Catholicism?

As noted by many observers, the Catholic Church throughout Eastern
Europe is institutionally weak after years of state oppression and hostility ("Religious Liberty and Eastern Europe," 1990; "Theses of Czechoslovak Catholics," 1988). The notable exception of course is Poland, in
which, according to Hanson, the Eastern bloc's strongest church squared
off against its weakest communist party (Hanson, 1987, p. 310). A clergy
shortage, while uneven in distribution, affects many national churches;
ecclesially, the Church's structures are underdeveloped and strained.
While no state pursued an exterminative policy toward organized religion as ambitious as that of Albania (Janz, 1990), communist party domination has left most Catholic churches in need of pastoral adaptation and
innovation. The need for more facilities, educational resources, training
centers, and increased interaction with coreligionists worldwide are only
a few of the deficits that require redress in the post-cold war era.

In many of these countries, especially Poland and Czechoslovakia, the
bulk of Catholic membership is among non-elite sectors. The former
elite in those countries—members of the communist party—had few
personal ties to the Church, although most hammered out working
relationships with the hierarchy after 1956 (Mojes, 1990). In particular,
governments sought to influence papal appointments to the episcopate,

as when the Czech government agreed to the appointment of Frantisek Tomasek as archbishop of Prague because he was perceived as a weak and unthreatening leader (Hanson, 1987, pp. 220–21).

In Hungary the Church's close ties with political elites before and after World War II have weakened its credibility as a social actor (Hood, 1990). And in countries like East Germany, the Protestant churches have been in the forefront of efforts at radical change; many in these churches retain profound skepticism about the capitalist system that now surrounds them (see Downey, 1990).

The ecclesiology of East European Catholic churches can be described as loose, although some have had experiences more akin to the tighter ecclesiologies that undergird phenomena like the BCCs. Specifically, where an underground church has developed in reaction to state pressures to join conformist institutions (like Pacem in Teris in Czechoslovakia, Hanson, 1987, pp. 221–22), some members have experienced the sense of distance from secular norms, high demands on adherents, and intensity of faith more common in tight ecclesiological formations. In some places, notably Hungary, actual base communities remained vital and forthright despite hostility from state and ecclesial authorities through the 1970s and 1980s (Hood, 1990). The phenomenon is not limited to Catholic congregations; alternative groups thrived for many years within larger structures in East German Protestant churches (Burgess, 1990).

How the East European Catholic churches respond to the resurgence of capitalism will depend, to a large degree, on whether pastoral innovations provide vehicles for a tighter ecclesiology within the more latitudinarian ecclesiology of the Church as a whole. If they do, the lived experiences and protests of the working classes upended by capital's inroads may find expression and support within the Church. If no tighter ecclesiology develops, the ravages of economic transition may cost the Church—once again—the support of the European working class.

Even if the scenario of grave dissatisfaction with the new capitalist order proves unfounded, it is not clear that the East European or Soviet churches can or will reverse the anticapitalist direction of world Catholicism. For one, the East European and Soviet Catholic churches have been largely cut off from ecclesial and theological developments in the Church at large; they have a fair amount of updating to do before their voices will likely be important on questions of international economics. Second, the churches of East Europe and the USSR will likely be preoccupied with internal problems, not international Church issues, for the next several years. Many will be seeking to preserve what they see as the good features of state socialism threatened by the advance of capitalism (see "Religious Liberty and Eastern Europe," 1990).

Third, it is well to remember that the East Europeans, even when counted with their coreligionists of Western Europe, will constitute a minority voice within Roman Catholicism. They will be outnumbered by Third World Catholics even if they retain whatever vitality and strength they had before the cold war's end. If they encounter mass defections and declines similar to their Western cousins, their numerical weight in the world Church will decline more rapidly.

SUMMARY

While a more detailed examination of changes in Eastern Europe and the USSR is beyond the scope of this book, a review of the preceding pages suggests that attention to world-systems and ecclesiological concerns might frame our expectations on how developments in the former state socialist countries may affect the anticapitalist trend within Roman Catholicism.

Of the four factors that tend to minimize the impact of state socialism's collapse on economic ethics within the Church, three of them touch directly on world-systems or ecclesiological concerns. Future research specifically concerned with the international division of labor and Church groups in the region might produce additional insights. Whether other scholars choose such a path depends in part, perhaps, on whether the framework used in this book seems worthwhile.

I believe world-systems theory helps provide a coherent picture of the political, economic, and social environment that confronts the Catholic Church in core and peripheral regions. That environment shapes many of the challenges, opportunities, and limitations that the Church encounters; changes in that environment cannot help but change the situation of local and national churches and, ultimately, the Church as a worldwide phenomenon.

But while the Church is profoundly affected by its immersion in the capitalist world economy, its actions and objectives are not determined by it. Not only does capitalism affect the Church (and, by extension, other social/cultural institutions), but the Church, by its activities, affects the future development of the political/economic system. The ease or difficulty (or impossibility) of capitalist reproduction is increasingly affected by actors outside the productive or state sectors—by cultural agents such as religious groups, for example. As illustrated in chapters 3 and 4, matters of ecclesiology are important in framing how churches are likely to respond to conditions and changes in the world economy. Continued attention to both sets of factors is necessary to avoid constructing either an agentless determinism or an unfettered social actor.

Looking at ecclesiology and political economy, I suggest that world Catholicism, led by the Latin American churches, will continue to develop an anticapitalist animus. That anticapitalism, I suggest, draws on diverse sources and does not rise or fall with the fortunes of liberation theology or the secular left. With Roman Catholicism well under way in its transformation from a core-based to a periphery-based religious phenomenon, many earlier understandings of Church and society will need to be revised.

How will the core churches respond to this transformation? As islands of affluence in a sea of impoverished coreligionists, will the churches of Western Europe and North America be able to support their brothers and sisters in their critique of capitalism? With the U.S. Catholic Church as my example, I again examine matters of political economy and ecclesiology to search for likely directions of development. The most likely scenario is one of serious class conflict within world Catholicism: a majority increasingly antagonistic to capitalism and its effects, and a minority who defend the capitalist order from which they have benefited substantially. An important consideration is the acceptance of what I call U.S. Catholic Nationalism by leaders and many mainstream theologians of this important core Church. This is a form of religious nationalism that legitimates capitalism and the state structures that reinforce it; its widespread adoption suggests that U.S. Church leaders will be unwilling to introduce ecclesiological changes that might later enable them to support their Third World coreligionists in their religiously informed condemnation of capitalism as a world order and system. Those who want a more socially radical Catholic church in the United States and other core countries would do well to direct their efforts toward challenging the dominant ecclesiology while constructing more demanding alternatives within it.

Finally, I expect these cleavages to grow despite the collapse of state socialism. Here, too, the workings of the international division of labor and ecclesiological considerations provide plausible reasons for such expectations. It appears that a question once thought settled—the relation between Christianity and capitalism—will need to be reconsidered in the Church and in the world.

BIBLIOGRAPHY

Abalos, David T. (1986). Latinos and the Sacred. *Cross Currents* 36.

Adams, John (1979). *International Economics*. New York: St. Martin's Press.

Adriance, Madeleine (1986). *Opting for the Poor: Brazilian Catholicism in Transition*. Kansas City: Sheed and Ward.

——— (1988). Brazil and Chile: Seeds of Change in the Latin American Church. In Thomas Gannon (ed.), *World Catholicism in Transition*. New York: Macmillan.

African Cities and the Church (1981). *Pro Mundi Vita* 17.

Africa's Opaque Reality: Marxism and Christianity (1982). *Pro Mundi Vita*, Dossier 23.

Aguilar-Monsalve, Luis (1984). The Separation of Church and State: The Ecuadorian Case. *Thought* 59(233).

Aguirre, Luis Perez (1989). The Theological Arm of the Armed Forces. *LADOC* New Keyhole Series 4.

Albano, Peter J. (1987). The Contributions of Johannes B. Metz to a Political Theology. *Thought* 62(244).

Alford, Robert and Roger Friedland (1986). *Powers of Theory: Capitalism, the State and Democracy*. Cambridge: Cambridge University Press.

Allen, Charles W. (1987). Review of *Polity and Praxis*. *Journal of Religion* 67.

Alter, Robert (1981). *The Art of Biblical Narrative*. New York: Basic Books.

Aman, Kenneth (1984–85). Marxism(s) in Liberation Theology. *Cross Currents* 34.

——— (1987). Being Church in Chile. *Christianity and Crisis*, June 8.

Amin, Galal (1976). Dependent Development. *Alternatives* 2.

Amir, Samir (1977). *Imperialism and Unequal Development*. Sussex: Harvester Press.

Anderson, Gerald, and Thomas Stransky (eds.) (1976). *Mission Trends No. 3: Third World Theologies*. New York: Paulist Press.

Anderson, Gerald, and Thomas Stransky (eds.) (1979). *Mission Trends No. 4: Liberation Theologies*. New York: Paulist Press.

Angus, Ian, and Sut Jhally (eds.) (1989). *Cultural Politics in Contemporary America*. New York: Routledge.

Antonio, Robert, and Tim Knapp (1988). Democracy and Abundance. *Telos* 76.

Arrighi, Giovanni, Terence K. Hopkins, and Immanuel Wallerstein (1987). Dilemmas of Antisystemic Movements. *Social Research* 53(1).

Arrighi, Giovanni, and John Saul (1973). *Essays on the Political Economy of Africa.* New York: Monthly Review Press.

Artellano, José Pablo (1989). The 10 Years Since Medellin. *Origins* 18(44).

Ashe, Kay (1983). *Today's Woman, Tomorrow's Church.* Chicago: Thomas More Press.

Assman, Hugo (1986). Democracy and the Debt Crisis. *This World* 14.

Associated Press (1988). Vatican Reports It Had 2d Worst Deficit in 1987. *Chicago Tribune*, October 16, p. 3.

Au, William A. (1987). *The Cross, the Flag, and the Bomb.* New York: Praeger.

——— (1988). Review of *Tranquillitas Ordinis. Catholic Historical Review* 74(1).

Augustine (1958). *City of God.* Garden City, N.Y.: Doubleday.

——— (1986). *Confessions.* New York: Penguin Books.

Avery, William, and David Rapkin (eds.) (1982). *America in a Changing World Political Economy.* New York: Longman.

Avila, Charles (1983). *Ownership: Early Christian Teaching.* Maryknoll, N.Y.: Orbis Books.

Azvedo, Marcello (1987). *Basic Ecclesial Communities in Brazil.* Washington, D.C.: Georgetown University Press.

Baccheta, Vittorio (1989). LP Interview with Bishop Pedro Casaldaliga. *Latinamerica Press*, February 16, p. 5.

Bahro, Rudolf (1981). *The Alternative in Eastern Europe.* London: Verso.

——— (1984). *From Red to Green: Interviews with* New Left Review. London: Verso.

——— (1986). *Building the Green Movement.* Philadelphia: New Society Publishers.

Bakunin, Mikhail (1985). *From Out of the Dustbin: Bakunin's Basic Writings, 1869–1871.* Ann Arbor, Mich.: Ardis Publishers.

Balasuriya, Tissa (1988). Emerging Theologies of Asian Liberation. *Concilium* 199.

Bamat, Tomas (1988). Ecuador: Bishops Lament Recent Elections' Demagogic Use of Religious Language. *Latinamerica Press*, June 30, p. 5.

Barreiro, Alvaro (1977). *Basic Ecclesial Communities: The Evangelization of the Poor.* Maryknoll, N.Y.: Orbis Books.

Barrett, David B. (1987). Annual Statistical Table on Global Mission. *International Bulletin of Missionary Research* 11(1).

Barry, Tom (1987). *Roots of Rebellion: Land and Hunger in Central America.* Boston: South End Press.

Barth, Maurice (1983). Basic Communities Facing Martyrdom: Testimonies from the Churches of Central America. *Concilium* 163.

Basic Christian Communities in Argentina (1985). *LADOC* 16(8).

Basic Ecclesial Communities: The People of God in Search of the Promised Land (1986). *LADOC* 17(9).

Baum, Gregory (1985). Call for Social Justice: A Comparison. *Christianity and Crisis*, January 21.

——— (1986a). A Response to David Tracy. *CTSA Proceedings* 41.

——— (1986b). The Catholic Church's Contradictory Stances. In William K. Tabb (ed.), *Churches in Struggle.* New York: Monthly Review Press.

——— (1986c). The Social Context of American Catholic Theology. *CTSA Proceedings* 41.

——— (1986–87). Catholicism and Secularization in Quebec. *Cross Currents* 36.

——— (1987a). The Impact of Marxism on the Thought of John Paul II. *Thought* 62(244).

——— (1987b). An Option for the Powerless. *The Ecumenist* 26(1).

——— (1988). Victims in the Affluent Society. *Concilium* 198.

Bazdresch, Juan, and Ernest Sweeney (1988). The Church in Communist Cuba. *Thought* 63(250).

Bell, Daniel (1976). *The Cultural Contradictions of Capitalism*. New York: Basic Books.

Bellah, Robert N. (1970). *Beyond Belief*. New York: Harper and Row.

—— (1975). *The Broken Covenant: American Civil Religion in Time of Trial*. New York: Seabury.

—— (1978). Religion and Legitimation in the American Republic. *Society* 15.

—— (1982). Religion and Power in America Today. *Commonweal*, December 3.

—— (1985). *Tokugawa Religion: The Cultural Roots of Modern Japan*. New York: Free Press.

Bellah, Robert N., and Philip E. Hammond (1980). *Varieties of Civil Religion*. New York: Harper and Row.

Bellah, Robert N., Richard Madsen, William M. Sullivan, Ann Swidler, and Steven M. Tipton (1985). *Habits of the Heart*. Berkeley: University of California Press.

Benestad, J. B., and Francis Butler (eds.) (1981). *Quest for Justice: A Compendium of Statements of the United States Catholic Bishops on the Political and Social Order, 1966–1980*. Washington, D.C.: United States Catholic Conference.

Berger, Joseph (1987). Being Catholic in America. *New York Times*, August 23, p. 64.

Berger, Peter (1980). *The Heretical Imperative*. Garden City, N.Y.: Anchor Press.

—— (1986). *The Capitalist Revolution*. New York: Basic Books.

—— (1987). Different Gospels: The Social Sources of Apostasy. *This World*, Spring.

Berger, Suzanne (ed.) (1981). *Organizing Interests in Western Europe*. Cambridge: Cambridge University Press.

—— (1987). Religious Transformation and the Future of Politics. In Charles S. Maier (ed.), *Changing Boundaries of the Political*. Cambridge: Cambridge University Press.

Bergeson, Albert (1982). The Emerging Science of the World-System. *International Social Science Journal* 34(1).

—— (1984). The Critique of World-System Theory: Class Relations or Division of Labor? *Sociological Theory*.

Bernadin, Joseph (1984). Address at Georgetown University. *Origins* 14.

Bernadin, Joseph, et al. (1986). *Shepherds Speak: American Bishops Confront the Social and Moral Issues That Challenge Christians Today*. New York: Crossroad.

Bernal Sahagun, Victor M. (1989). The Foreign Debt and Beyond: Alternatives to the Latin American Economic Crisis. *Latin American Perspectives* 16(1).

Bernstein, Richard J. (1971). *Praxis and Action*. Philadelphia: University of Pennsylvania Press.

—— (1978). *The Restructuring of Social and Political Theory*. Philadelphia: University of Pennsylvania Press.

—— (1985). *Beyond Objectivism and Relativism*. Philadelphia: University of Pennsylvania Press.

Berrigan, Daniel (1971). *No Bars to Manhood*. New York: Bantam Books.

—— (1972). *The Dark Night of Resistance*. New York: Doubleday.

—— (1981). *Ten Commandments for the Long Haul*. Nashville: Abingdon.

—— (1983). *The Nightmare of God*. Portland, Ore.: Sunburst Press.

—— (1985). *Steadfastness of the Saints*. Maryknoll, N.Y.: Orbis Books.

—— (1987). *To Dwell in Peace: An Autobiography*. San Francisco: Harper and Row.

Berrigan, Daniel, and Robert Coles (1972). *The Geography of Faith*. Boston: Beacon Press.

Berrigan, Philip. (1971). *Prison Journals of a Priest Revolutionary*. New York: Ballantine Books.

—— (1973). *Widen the Prison Gates*. New York: Simon and Schuster.

Berrigan, Philip, and Elizabeth McAlister (1989). *The Time's Discipline*. Baltimore: Fortkamp.

Berryman, Phillip (1984a). "Basismo and the Horizon of Change." *Journal of Inter-american Studies and World Affairs* 26(1).

———— (1984b). *The Religious Roots of Rebellion*. Maryknoll, N.Y.: Orbis Books.

———— (1987). A Theology for North America. *Kosmos*, January/February.

———— (1989). *Our Unfinished Business: The U.S. Catholic Bishops' Letters on Peace and the Economy*. New York: Pantheon.

Betto, Frei (1987). *Fidel and Religion*. New York: Simon and Schuster.

———— (1988). The Prophetic Diakonia: The Church's Contribution to Forming Humanity's Future. *Concilium* 198.

Bill, James A., and John Alden Williams (1988). Shi'i Islam and Roman Catholicism: A Comparative Analysis. *New Catholic World*, November/December.

Billings, Dwight (1990). Religion as Opposition: A Gramscian Analysis. *American Journal of Sociology* 96.

Bishops and the Bomb: Nine Responses to the Pastoral on Peace and War, (1982) [special issue]. *Commonweal*, August 1.

Bleicher, Josef (1982). *The Hermeneutic Imagination*. London: Routledge and Kegan Paul.

Boesak, Allan A. (1977). *Farewell to Innocence*. Maryknoll, N.Y.: Orbis Books.

———— (1978). Coming Out in the Wilderness. In Sergio Torres and Virginia Fabella (eds.), *The Emergent Gospel: Theology from the Developing World*. Maryknoll, N.Y.: Orbis Books.

———— (1987). *Comfort and Protest: The Apocalypse from a South African Perspective*. Philadelphia: Westminster Press.

Boff, Clodovis (1987). *Feet-on-the-Ground Theology: A Brazilian Journey*. Maryknoll, N.Y.: Orbis Books.

Boff, Leonardo (1978). *Jesus Christ Liberator*. Maryknoll, N.Y.: Orbis Books.

———— (1981). Ecclesiogenesis: Ecclesial Base Communities Re-Invent the Church. *Mid-Stream* 20(4).

———— (1982). *Way of the Cross, Way of Justice*. Maryknoll, N.Y.: Orbis Books.

———— (1985). *Church, Charism and Power: Liberation Theology and the Institutional Church*. New York: Crossroad.

Boff, Leonardo, and Clodovis Boff (1987). Good News of Bishops' Economics Pastoral, and Bad News Left Unmentioned. *National Catholic Reporter*, August 28.

Boff, Leonardo, and Virgil Elizondo (eds.) (1988). Theologies of the Third World: Convergences and Differences. *Concilium* 199.

Bolivian Bishops' Conference (1987). A Call to Hope. *LADOC* 17.

Bonhoeffer, Dietrich (1963). *The Cost of Discipleship*. New York: Macmillan.

———— (1966). *Letters and Papers from Prison*. New York: Macmillan.

Bonpane, Blase (1984). The Church in the Central American Revolution. *Thought* 59(233).

———— (1987). *Guerrillas of Peace: Liberation Theology and the Central American Revolution*. Boston: South End Press.

Borrat, Hector (1982), The Future of Religion in Latin America: Divergences in Brazil. *PMV Bulletin* 90.

Brandt Commission (1983). *North/South: Cooperation for World Recovery*. London: Pan Books.

Brantlinger, Patrick (1983). *Bread and Circuses: Theories of Mass Culture as Social Decay*. Ithaca, N.Y.: Cornell University Press.

Bray, Marjorie Woodford (1989). Latin America's Debt and the World Economic Crisis. *Latin American Perspectives* 16(1).

Brazilian Bishops' Conference (1989). Press Statement from the Bishops' Conference. *LADOC* 19.

Brenner, Robert (1977). The Origins of Capitalist Development: A Critique of Neo-Smithian Marxism. *New Left Review* 104.

Brett, Donna, and Edward Brett (1988). *Murdered in Central America: The Stories of Eleven U.S. Missionaries.* Maryknoll, N.Y.: Orbis Books.

Bright, Charles, and Susan Harding (eds.) (1984). *Statemaking and Social Movements.* Ann Arbor: University of Michigan Press.

Brooke, James (1991). Rural Leader Is Slain in Brazil. *New York Times*, February 5, p. A-7.

Brown, Dale W. (1986). *Biblical Pacifism: A Peace Church Perspective.* Elgin, Ill.: Brethren Press.

Brown, Delwin (1985). Struggle 'til Daybreak: On the Nature of Authority in Theology. *Journal of Religion* 65.

Brown, Raymond E. (1981). *The Critical Meaning of the Bible.* New York: Paulist Press.

—— (1984). Liberals, Ultraconservatives, and the Misinterpretation of Catholic Biblical Exegesis. *Cross Currents* 34.

Brown, Robert McAfee (1986). *Saying Yes and Saying No: On Rendering to God and Caesar.* Philadelphia: Westminster Press.

Brownson, Orestes (1858). *Brownson Quarterly Review* 3 April.

Bruneau, Thomas (1979). Basic Christian Communities in Latin America: Their Nature and Significance (Especially in Brazil). In Daniel H. Levine (ed.), *Churches and Politics in Latin America.* Beverly Hills: Sage Publications.

—— (1982). *The Church in Brazil: The Politics of Religion.* Austin: University of Texas Press.

—— (1986). Brazil: The Catholic Church and Basic Christian Communities. In Daniel H. Levine (ed.), *Religion and Political Conflict in Latin America.* Chapel Hill: University of North Carolina Press.

—— (1988). Cooperation or Conflict? The Church in the Brazilian Transition. *Thought* 63(250).

Buchanan, James (1990). Socialism Is Dead; Leviathan Lives. *Wall Street Journal*, July 18.

Budde, Michael L. (1983). Basic Christian Communities: Changing Church and State? Unpublished seminar paper, Department of Politics, Catholic University of America.

—— (1984a). *My Neighbor, My Ally: Perspectives on Immigration.* Chicago: Catholic Charities of Chicago.

—— (1984b) Participation, Self-Reliance and the Poor: In Search of an Alternative Theory of Development. Unpublished seminar paper, Department of Politics, Catholic University of America.

—— (1985). Reaching Back and Looking Ahead: Catholic Theories of Property. Unpublished seminar paper, Department of Political Science, Northwestern University.

—— (1986a). *Mission and Community.* Chicago: Catholic Charities of Chicago.

—— (1986b). Religion, World-Systems Theory and the Case of Liberation Theology. Unpublished seminar paper, Department of Political Science, Northwestern University.

—— (1986c). Thomas Aquinas and Property Theory. Unpublished seminar paper, Department of Political Science, Northwestern University.

—— (1987). Christian Theology in Africa: A Role for Class Analysis? Unpublished seminar paper, Department of Political Science, Northwestern University.

—— (1991). Pope John Paul II's (Non)Theory of Capitalism in *Centesimus Annus.* Unpublished manuscript.

Buhlmann, Walbert (1986). *The Church of the Future.* Maryknoll, N.Y.: Orbis Books.

Building Christian Basic Communities (1978). *Pro Mundi Vita* 29.

Burgess, John (1990). Church-State Relations in East Germany: The Church as a "Religious" and "Political" Force. *Journal of Church and State* 32.

Butalid, Ted (1982). People's Movements: A Response to Man-Made Oppressive Structures. *Pro Mundi Vita*, Dossier 21.

Cadorette, Curt (1988). Basic Christian Communities: Their Social Role and Missiological Promise. *Missiology* 15(2).

Calderon, Gaspar (1987). Reconciliation or Option for the Poor? *Christianity and Crisis*, February 16.

California Hispanic Bishops (1988). Responding to Proselytism. *Origins* 8(6).

Canadian Catholic Conference, Social Affairs Commission (1983). Alternatives to Present Economic Structures. *Origins* 12(33).

Caporaso, James, and Behrouz Zare (1981). Interpretation and Evaluation of Dependency Theory. In Heraldo Munoz (ed.), *From Dependency to Development*. Boulder, Colo.: Westview Press.

Cardenal, Ernesto (1977). *The Gospel in Solentiname*. Maryknoll, N.Y.: Orbis Books.

Cardman, Francine (1984). The Church Would Look Foolish Without Them: Women and Laity Since Vatican II. In Gerald Fagin (ed.), *Vatican II: Open Questions and New Horizons*. Wilmington, Del.: Michael Glazier.

Cardoso, Fernando Henrique, and Enzo Faletto (1979). *Dependency and Development in Latin America*. Berkeley: University of California Press.

Carey, Patrick W. (ed.) (1987). *American Catholic Religious Thought*. New York: Paulist Press.

Carnoy, Martin (1984). *The State and Political Theory*. Princeton, N.J.: Princeton University Press.

Carter, Samuel (1988). The Priority of Labour. *LADOC* 19.

Casaroli, Agostino Cardinal (1986). The Dialogue Between Church and Economy. *Communio* 13.

Casey, William Van Etten, and Philip Nobile (eds.) (1971). *The Berrigans*. New York: Avon Books.

Castillo, José Maria (1981). Basic Christian Communities. *Pro Mundi Vita* 30.

Castles, Stephen, and Godulka Kosack (1973). *Immigrant Workers and Class Structure in Western Europe*. London: Oxford University Press.

CELAM (1988). Message to the People of Latin America. *LADOC* 18.

Central American Kairos, The (1988). *LADOC* 19.

Chalfant, Paul, Robert Beck, and Eddie Palmer (1981). *Religion in Contemporary Society*. Palo Alto, Calif.: Mayfield.

Chandler, William M., and Alan Siaroff (1986). Post-Industrial Politics in Germany and the Origins of the Greens. *Comparative Politics* 18.

Chayanov, A. V. (1986). *The Theory of Peasant Economy*. Madison: University of Wisconsin Press.

Chicago Tribune (1986). *The American Millstone: An Examination of the Nation's Permanent Underclass*. Chicago: Contemporary Books.

Chomsky, Noam (1985). *Turning the Tide: U.S. Intervention in Central America and the Struggle for Peace*. Boston: South End Press.

——— (1987). *The Chomsky Reader*. New York: Pantheon Books.

Chung, Hyung-Kung (1988). Opium or the Seed for Revolution? Shamanism: Women-Centered Popular Religiosity in Korea. *Concilium* 199.

Church and State (1990). Religious Liberty and Eastern Europe. 43(8).

Church in Zimbabwe: The Trauma of Cutting Apron Strings, The (1982). *Pro Mundi Vita*, Dossier 21.

Clapp, Rodney (1988). Catholics, Anabaptists and the Bomb. *Christian Century*, November 2.

Clark, Thomas E. (1983). A New Way: Reflecting on Experience. In James E. Hug (ed.), *Tracing the Spirit: Communities, Social Action, and Theological Reflection.* New York: Paulist Press.

Clarke, Tony (1982). Witness to Justice: A Catholic Reflection on Small Communities. *International Review of Mission* 71(283).

Clevenot, Michel (1985). *Materialist Approaches to the Bible.* Maryknoll, N.Y.: Orbis Books.

Cohen, Dennis, and John Daniel (eds.) (1981). *Political Economy of Africa.* Essex: Longman.

Cohen, Youssef (1989). *The Manipulation of Consent: The State and Working-Class Consciousness in Brazil.* Pittsburgh: University of Pittsburgh Press.

Cohn, Norman (1970). *The Pursuit of the Millennium.* Oxford: Oxford University Press.

Coleman, John A. (1981). The Future of Ministry. *America,* March 28.

———— (1982). *An American Strategic Theology.* New York: Paulist Press.

———— (1988). American Catholicism. In Thomas Gannon (ed.), *World Catholicism in Transition.* New York: Macmillan.

Coles, Robert (1987). *Dorothy Day: A Radical Devotion.* Reading, Mass.: Addison-Wesley.

Coll, Regina (ed.) (1982). *Women and Religion: A Reader for the Clergy.* New York: Paulist Press.

Collett, Merrill (1987). The Cross and the Flag: Right-Wing Evangelicals Invade Latin America. *Progressive,* December.

Collier, David (ed.) (1979). *The New Authoritarianism in Latin America.* Princeton, N.J.: Princeton University Press.

Collum, Danny Duncan (1989). Doing the Lord's Work: Churches Energize the Left. *Progressive,* February.

Colombia: Basic Ecclesial Communities Meet (1987). *LADOC* 17(2).

Comblin, José (1979). *The Church and the National Security State.* Maryknoll, N.Y.: Orbis Books.

Cone, James H. (1986). *Speaking the Truth: Ecumenism, Liberation and Black Theology.* Grand Rapids, Mich.: Eerdmans.

———— (1988). Theologies of Liberation Among U.S. Racial-Ethnic Minorities. *Concilium* 199.

Cone, James, and Gayraud Wilmore (eds.) (1980). *Black Theology: A Documentary History, 1966–1979.* Maryknoll, N.Y.: Orbis Books.

Cook, Guillermo (1985). *The Expectation of the Poor: Latin American Basic Ecclesial Communities in Protestant Perspective.* Maryknoll, N.Y.: Orbis Books.

———— (1987). Grassroots Churches and Reformation in Central America. *Latin American Pastoral Issues* 14(1).

———— (1990). The Evangelical Groundswell in Latin America [review article]. *Christian Century,* December 12.

Cooke, Bernard (1976). *Ministry in Word and Sacraments.* Philadelphia: Westminster Press.

Corner, Mark (1988). Liberation Theology for Britain. *New Blackfriars* 69(813).

Costello, Gerald M. (1979). *Mission to Latin America.* Maryknoll, N.Y.: Orbis Books.

Coughlin, Roger, and Cathryn Riplinger (1981). *Charitable Care.* Chicago: Catholic Charities of Chicago.

Cox, Harvey (1984). *Religion in the Secular City.* New York: Simon and Schuster.

———— (1988). *The Silencing of Leonardo Boff: The Vatican and the Future of World Christianity.* Wilmington, Del.: Michael Glazier.

Cox, Robert W. (1979). Ideologies and the New International Economic Order: Reflections on Some Recent Literature. *International Organization* 33(2).

Crews, Clyde F. (1984). American Catholic Authoritarianism: The Episcopacy of William George McCloskey, 1868–1909. *Catholic Historical Review* 70.

Crosby, Donald F. (1978). *God, Church, and Flag: Senator Joseph R. McCarthy and the Catholic Church, 1950–1957.* Chapel Hill: University of North Carolina Press.

Crozier, Michel, Samuel Huntington, and Joji Wataniski (1975). *The Crisis of Democracy.* New York: New York University Press.

Cuddihy, John Murray (1978). *No Offense: Civil Religion and Protestant Taste.* New York: Seabury.

Cunningham, Agnes (ed.) (1982). *Early Church and the State.* Philadelphia: Fortress Press.

Curran, Charles E. (1977). *Themes in Fundamental Moral Theology.* Notre Dame, Ind.: University of Notre Dame Press.

────── (1982). *American Catholic Social Ethics: Twentieth-Century Approaches.* Notre Dame, Ind.: University of Notre Dame Press.

────── (1987). Being Catholic and Being American. *Horizons* 14(1).

Curran, Charles, and Richard McCormick (eds.) (1986). *Readings in Moral Theology No. 5: Official Catholic Social Teaching.* Mahwah, N.J.: Paulist Press.

Cussianovich, Alejandro (1975). *Religious Life and the Poor.* Maryknoll, N.Y.: Orbis Books.

Cypher, James M. (1989). The Debt Crisis as "Opportunity": Strategies to Revive U.S. Hegemony. *Latin American Perspectives* 16(1).

Dalton, George (ed.) (1968). *Primitive, Archaic and Modern Economies: Essays of Karl Polanyi.* New York: Anchor Books.

Daly, Herman (ed.) (1980). *Ecology, Economics, Ethics: Essays Toward a Steady-State Society.* San Francisco: W. H. Freeman.

Dassin, Joan (1986). *Torture in Brazil.* New York: Vintage Books.

Day, Dorothy (1963). *Loaves and Fishes.* New York: Harper and Row.

Day, Mark (1988). *LP* Interview with Former CELAM Head. *Latinamerica Press*, June 30, p. 4.

Deane, Dennis (1978). The Theological Importance of Orestes Brownson and Isaac Hecker on John Ireland's Ecclesiology. Unpublished Diss., Catholic University of America.

DeBernardo, Francis (1988). Engaging Words: The Bishops Get Their Message Across. *Commonweal*, June 3.

DeBroucker, José (1979). *Dom Helder Cámara: The Conversion of a Bishop.* London: Collins.

Deck, Allan Figueroa (1988). Proselytism and Hispanic Catholics: How Long Can We Cry Wolf? *America*, December 10, p. 405.

Declaration on Religious Freedom. (1966). In Walter M. Abbott (ed.), *The Documents of Vatican II.* New York: Herder and Herder.

Degen, Johannes (1988). Diakonia as an Agency in the Welfare State. *Concilium* 198.

DeJanvry, Alain (1981). *The Agrarian Question and Reformism in Latin America.* Baltimore: Johns Hopkins University Press.

Delgado, Gary (1983). Organizing Undocumented Workers. *Social Policy* 3.

Denemark, Robert A., and Kenneth P. Thomas (1988). The Brenner-Wallerstein Debate. *International Studies Quarterly* 42.

Denitch, Bogdan (1990). The Triumph of Capitalism? *Dissent* Spring.

DeSanta Ana, Julio (ed.) (1980). *Separation Without Hope? The Church and the Poor During the Industrial Revolution and Colonial Expansion.* Maryknoll, N.Y.: Orbis Books.

────── (1988). The Situation of Latin American Theology (1982–1987). *Concilium* 199.

de Soto, Hernando (1989). *The Other Path.* London: Tauris.

Devoy, Juliana (1988). Whither the Catholic Church in China? *America*, August 27.

Dewey, John (1934). *A Common Faith*. New Haven, Conn.: Yale University Press.

Diefenbacher, Hans (1988). Armaments and Poverty in the Industrial Nations. *Concilium* 195.

Dieter, Richard, and Barbara Cullom (eds.) (1986). *Set My People Free: Liberation Theology in Practice*. Hyattsville, Md.: Quixote Center.

Dietz, James L. (1989). The Debt Cycle and Restructuring in Latin America. *Latin American Perspectives* 16(1).

Digan, Parig (1984). *Churches in Contestation: Asian Christian Social Protest*. Maryknoll, N.Y.: Orbis Books.

Dinges, William (1988). Lefebvre Abandons Ship. *Commonweal*, August 12.

Dinham, Barbara, and Colin Hines (1984). *Agribusiness in Africa*. Trenton, N.J.: Africa World Press.

Diskin, Martin (ed.) (1983). *Trouble in Our Backyard: Central America and the United States in the Eighties*. New York: Pantheon.

Dodson, Michael (1986). Nicaragua: Struggle for the Church. In Daniel H. Levine (ed.), *Religion and Political Conflict in Latin America*. Chapel Hill: University of North Carolina Press.

——— (1988). The Church and Political Struggle: Faith and Action in Central America [review article]. *Latin American Research Review* 23(1).

Dodson, Michael, and T. S. Montgomery (1982). The Churches in the Nicaraguan Revolution. In Thomas Walker (ed.), *Nicaragua in Revolution*. New York: Praeger.

Dolan, Jay P. (1974). The Parish—Past and Present. *National Catholic Reporter*, May 31.

——— (1977). *The Immigrant Church: New York's Irish and German Catholics, 1815–1865*. Baltimore: Johns Hopkins University Press.

——— (1985). *The American Catholic Experience*. Garden City, N.Y.: Doubleday.

——— (1987). Review of *Tranquillitas Ordinis*. *New York Times Book Review*, April 26, p. 30.

Dominican Community of Bogotá (1987). The Church of the Poor. *LADOC* 17.

Donders, Joseph G. (1985). *Non-Bourgeois Theology: An African Experience of Jesus*. Maryknoll, N.Y.: Orbis Books.

Dorman, William, and Mansour Farhang (1987). *The U.S. Press and Iran: Foreign Policy and the Journalism of Deference*. Berkeley: University of California Press.

Dorr, Donal (1983). *Option for the Poor: A Hundred Years of Catholic Social Teaching*. Maryknoll, N.Y.: Orbis Books.

Douglas, Mary (ed.) (1982). *Essays in the Sociology of Perception*. London: Routledge and Kegan Paul.

Douglas, Mary, and Aaron Wildavsky (1983). *Risk and Culture: An Essay on the Selection of Technological and Environmental Dangers*. Berkeley: University of California Press.

Downey, William (1990). For German Pastors, A Bitter Taste. *Christian Century*.

Dubofsky, Melvin (1969). *We Shall Be All: The History of the IWW*. New York: Quadrangle/New York Times Books.

Dulles, Avery (1973). *The Survival of Dogma*. Garden City, N.Y.: Doubleday.

——— (1978). *Models of the Church*. Garden City, N.Y.: Doubleday.

——— (1982). *A Church to Believe In: Discipleship and the Dynamics of Freedom*. New York: Crossroad.

——— (1985). *Models of Revelation*. Garden City, N.Y.: Doubleday.

Durkheim, Émile (1968). *The Elementary Forms of Religious Life*. New York: Free Press.

Durkn, Gloria (1982). Is Partnership Possible? Ordained Men and Unordained Women in Ministry. In Regina Coll (ed.), *Women and Religion: A Reader for Clergy*. New York: Paulist Press.

Dussel, Enrique (1976). *History and the Theology of Liberation*. Maryknoll, N.Y.: Orbis Books.

Eagleson, John, and Philip Scharper (eds.) (1979). *Puebla and Beyond*. Maryknoll, N.Y.: Orbis Books.

Eckstein, Susan, and Frances Hagopian (1983). The Limits of Industrialization in the Less Developed World: Bolivia. *Economic Development and Cultural Change* 32(1).

Edelman, Murray (1988). *Constructing the Political Spectacle*. Chicago: University of Chicago Press.

Edwards, Chris (1985). *The Fragmented World: Competing Perspectives on Trade, Money and Crisis*. London: Methuen.

Eliade, Mircea, and Joseph M. Kitagawa (eds.) 1959. *The History of Religions*. Chicago: University of Chicago Press.

Elizondo, Virgil, and Norbert Greinacher (eds.) (1981). Tensions Between the Churches of the First World and the Third World. *Concilium* 144.

Ellacuria, Ignacio (1988). Violence and Non-violence in the Struggle for Peace and Liberation. *Concilium* 195.

Eller, Vernard (1987). *Christian Anarchy*. Grand Rapids, Mich.: Eerdmans.

Ellis, John Tracy (1987). Reflections on the Legacy of Religious Freedom. *Origins* 17(13).

Ellis, Kail C. (1988). Vatican II and Contemporary Islam. *New Catholic World*, November/December.

Ellsberg, Robert (ed.) (1983). *By Little and By Little: The Selected Writings of Dorothy Day*. New York: Alfred A. Knopf.

Ellul, Jacques (1980). Anarchism and Christianity. *Katallagete*, Fall.

——— (1984). *Money and Power*. Downers Grove, Ill.: Inter-Varsity Press.

Escobar, Samuel (1987a). Base Church Communities: A Historical Perspective. *Latin American Pastoral Issues* 14(1).

——— (1987b). Mission and Renewal in Latin-American Catholicism. *Missiology* 15(2).

Evans, Peter (1979). *Dependent Development: The Alliance of Multinational, State and Local Capital in Brazil*. Princeton, N.J.: Princeton University Press.

Everett, William Johnson (1988). God's Federal Republic. *New Catholic World*, July/August.

External Debt, The (1988, January/February). *LADOC* 18.

Fabella, Virginia, and Sergio Torres (eds.) (1985). *Doing Theology in a Divided World*. Maryknoll, N.Y.: Orbis Books.

Fagin, Gerald (ed.) (1984). *Vatican II: Open Questions and New Horizons*. Wilmington, Del.: Michael Glazier.

Falk, Richard (1984). Militarisation and Human Rights in the Third World. In Charles K. Wilber (ed.), *The Political Economy of Development and Underdevelopment*, 3rd ed. New York: Random House.

Ferguson, Tom (1989). The Hidden Election. Z Magazine, January.

Feyerabend, Paul (1984). *Against Method*. London: Verso.

Fichter, Joseph H. (1989). The Church: Looking to the Future. *America*, March 4.

Final Document of the Third General Conference of the Latin American Episcopate (Puebla, Mexico) (1979). Reprinted in John Eagleson and Philip Scharper (eds.), *Puebla and Beyond*. Maryknoll, N.Y.: Orbis Books.

First Andean Congress of Basic Ecclesial Communities (1987). *LADOC* 17(36).

Fitzpatrick, Joseph P. (1984). The Latin American Church in the United States. *Thought* 59(233).

——— (1988). The Hispanic Poor in a Middle-Class Church. *America*, July 2.

Five Hundred Years in Latin America (1988). *LADOC New Keyhole Series* 3.

Fogarty, Gerald P. (1985). *The Vatican and the American Hierarchy from 1870 to 1965*. Wilmington, Del.: Michael Glazier.

Folliard, Dorothy (1988). Theological Literature of the USA Minorities. *Concilium* 199.

Foucault, Michel (1980). *Power/Knowledge: Selected Interviews and Other Writings*. New York: Pantheon.

Frank, André G. (1968). *Development and Underdevelopment in Latin America*. New York: Monthly Review Press.

———— (1990). Revolution in Eastern Europe. *Third World Quarterly*.

Frasca, Tim (1988). New Bishops Take Chile's Catholic Church Rightward. *Latinamerica Press*, July 7.

Freire, Paulo (1970). *Pedagogy of the Oppressed*. New York: Seabury Press.

Freund, Bill (1984). *The Making of Contemporary Africa: The Development of African Society Since 1860*. Bloomington: Indiana University Press.

Friesen, Dorothy (1988). *Critical Choices: A Journey with the Filipino People*. Grand Rapids, Mich.: Eerdmans.

Fukuyama, Francis (1990). Are We at the End of History? *Fortune*, January 15.

Gabriel, Karl (1988). Power in the Contemporary Church in the Light of Sociological Theories: Max Weber, Michel Foucault and Hannah Arendt. *Concilium* 197.

Gallup, George, Jr., and Jim Castelli (1987). *The American Catholic People*. Garden City, N.Y.: Doubleday.

Gallup, George, Jr., and David Poling (1980). *The Search for America's Faith*. Nashville: Abingdon.

Galtung, Johan (1977). *Self-Reliance: Concept, Practice and Rationale*. Oslo: University of Oslo.

———— (1980). *The True Worlds*. New York: Free Press.

Gamoran, Adam (1990). Civil Religion in American Schools. *Sociological Analysis* 51.

Gannon, Thomas (ed.) (1987). *The Catholic Challenge to the American Economy: Reflections on the U.S. Bishops' Pastoral Letter on Catholic Social Teaching and the U.S. Economy*. New York: Macmillan.

———— (ed.) (1988). *World Catholicism in Transition*. New York: Macmillan.

Garcia, Samuel Ruiz (1988). Mexico: The Vocation of the Latin American Church Today. *LADOC* 18.

Garst, Daniel (1985). Wallerstein and His Critics. *Theory and Society* 14.

Gaventa, John (1980). *Power and Powerlessness*. Champaign: University of Illinois Press.

Geany, Dennis J. (1983). *The Prophetic Parish*. Minneapolis: Winston Press.

Geertz, Clifford (1973). *The Interpretation of Cultures*. New York: Basic Books.

Genovese, Eugene (1981). *From Rebellion to Revolution*. New York: Vintage Books.

George, Susan (1977). *How the Other Half Dies*. Montclair, N.J.: Allanheld, Osmun.

Georgescu-Roegen, Nicholas (1973). *The Entropy Law and the Economic Process*. Cambridge, Mass.: Harvard University Press.

Gerlach, L. P. and V. H. Hine (1970). *People, Power and Change*. Indianapolis: Bobbs-Merrill.

Gibellini, Rosino (ed.) (1979). *Frontiers of Theology in Latin America*. Maryknoll, N.Y.: Orbis Books.

Gibney, Mark (1984). Seeking Sanctuary: A Special Duty for the U.S.? *Commonweal*, May 18, p. 296.

Giddens, Anthony (1971). *Capitalism and Modern Social Theory*. Cambridge: Cambridge University Press.

———— (1987). *The Nation-State and Violence*. Berkeley: University of California Press.

Gilchrist, John (1969). *The Church and Economic Activity in the Middle Ages*. New York: Macmillan.

Gill, Robin (1975). *Social Context of Theology*. London: Mowbray.

—— (ed.) (1987). *Theology and Sociology: A Reader*. New York: Paulist Press.

Gillgannon, Michael J. (1988). Drugs, Debt and Dependency. *America*, October 29.

Gilson, Etienne (1956). *The Christian Philosophy of St. Thomas Aquinas*. New York: Random House.

Glazier, Michael (ed.) (1985). *Where We Are: American Catholics in the 1980s*. Wilmington, Del.: Michael Glazier.

Gleason, Philip (1973). Coming to Terms with American Catholic History. *Societas* 3(4).

Glock, Charles, and Robert Bellah (eds.) (1976). *The New Religious Consciousness*. Berkeley: University of California Press.

Goldsmit, Shulamit, and Ernest Sweeney (1988). The Church and Latin American Women in Their Struggle for Equality and Justice. *Thought* 63(249).

Goldthorpe, John H. (ed.) (1984). *Order and Conflict in Contemporary Capitalism: Studies in the Political Economy of Western European Nations*. Oxford: Clarendon Press.

Gonzales, Roberto, and Michael LaVelle (1985). *The Hispanic Catholic in the United States: A Socio-Cultural and Religious Profile*. New York: Northeast Catholic Pastoral Center for Hispanics.

Gorostiaga, Javier (1989). Colombia: Geopolitics and Liberation Theology. *LADOC New Keyhole Series* 4.

Gottwald, Norman K. (ed.) (1984). *The Bible and Liberation: Political and Social Hermeneutics*. Maryknoll, N.Y.: Orbis Books.

—— (1985). *The Hebrew Bible: A Socio-Literary Introduction*. Philadelphia: Fortress Press.

Goulet, Denis (1975). *The Cruel Choice: A New Concept in the Theory of Development*. New York: Atheneum.

Gourevitch, Peter (1986). *Politics in Hard Times: Comparative Responses to International Economic Crisis*. Ithaca, N.Y.: Cornell University Press.

Gowan, Donald E. (1986). *Eschatology in the Old Testament*. Philadelphia: Fortress Press.

Grace, Ed (1981). Italy: Disobedience as Witness. *Christianity and Crisis*, October 21.

Gramsci, Antonio (1983). *Selections from the Prison Notebooks*. New York: International Publishers.

Gran, Guy (1983). *Development by People*. New York: Praeger.

Granfield, Patrick (1987). *The Limits of the Papacy*. New York: Crossroad.

—— (1988). Legitimation and Bureaucratisation of Ecclesial Power. *Concilium* 197.

Grannis, Christopher, Arthur Laffin, and Elin Schade, 1981. *The Risk of the Cross: Christian Discipleship in the Nuclear Age*. New York: Seabury Press.

Gray, Francine duPlessix (1970). *Divine Disobedience: Profiles in Catholic Radicalism*. New York: Alfred A. Knopf.

Greeley, Andrew (1987). The Fall of an Archdiocese. *Chicago*, September.

—— (1988). Defection Among Hispanics. *America*, July 30.

—— (1989). On the Margins of the Church: A Sociological Note. *America*, March 4.

Greeley, Andrew, and Mary Durkin (1984). *Angry Catholic Women*. Chicago: Thomas More Press.

Greeley, Andrew, Mary Durkin, John Shea, David Tracy, and William McCready, (1981). *Parish, Priest and People: New Leadership for the Local Church*. Chicago: Thomas More Press.

Greeley, Andrew, and Michael Hout (1988). Musical Chairs: Patterns of Denominational Change. *Sociology and Social Research* 72(2).

Greeley, Andrew, and William McManus (1987). *Catholic Contributions: Sociology and Policy*. Chicago: Thomas More Press.

Green, James R. (1978). *Grass-Roots Socialism: Radical Movements in the Southwest, 1895–1943*. Baton Rouge: Louisiana State University Press.

——— (ed.) (1983). *Workers' Struggles, Past and Present*. Philadelphia: Temple University Press.

Greil, Arthur L., and David Kowalewski (1987). Church-State Relations in Russia and Nicaragua: Early Revolutionary Years. *Journal for the Scientific Study of Religion* 26(1).

Greinacher, Norbert, and Norbert Mette (eds.) (1988). Diakonia: Church for the Others. *Concilium* 198.

Gremillion, Joseph (1979). Puebla and Latin American Catholics. In John Eagleson and Philip Scharper (eds.), *Puebla and Beyond*. Maryknoll, N.Y.: Orbis Books.

——— (ed.) (1985). *The Church and Culture Since Vatican II: The Experience of North and Latin America*. Notre Dame, Ind.: University of Notre Dame Press.

Griffin, Keith, and Jeffrey James (1981). *The Transition to Egalitarian Development: Economic Policies for Structural Change in the Third World*. New York: St. Martin's Press.

Griffin, Leslie (1987). The Integration of Spiritual and Temporal: Contemporary Roman Catholic Church-State Theory. *Theological Studies* 48.

Guasti, Laura (1983). The Peruvian Military Government and the International Corporations. In Cynthia McClintock and Abraham Lowenthal (eds.), *The Peruvian Experiment Reconsidered*. Princeton, N.J.: Princeton University Press.

Guatemalan Bishops' Conference (1988). The Cry for Land. *LADOC* 19.

Gudorf, Christine (1983). Renewal or Repatriarchalization? Responses of the Roman Catholic Church to the Feminization of Religion. *Horizons* 10(2).

——— (1987). Indigenous Moral Problems in Peru. *America*, October 24.

Guillen, Arturo (1989). Crisis, the Burden of Foreign Debt, and Structural Dependence. *Latin American Perspectives* 16(1).

Gurr, Ted R. (1985). On the Political Consequences of Scarcity and Economic Decline. *International Studies Quarterly* 29.

——— (1988). War, Revolution and the Growth of the Coercive State. *Comparative Political Studies* 21.

Gutierrez, Gustavo (1973). *A Theology of Liberation: History, Politics and Salvation*. Maryknoll, N.Y.: Orbis Books.

——— (1984a). *The Power of the Poor in History*. Maryknoll, N.Y.: Orbis Books.

——— (1984b). *We Drink from Our Own Wells*. Maryknoll, N.Y.: Orbis Books.

——— (1988). *On Job*. Maryknoll, N.Y.: Orbis Books.

Gutierrez, Gustavo, and Richard Schaull (1977). *Liberation and Change*. Atlanta: John Knox Press.

Gutkind, Peter, and Immanuel Wallerstein (eds.) (1976). *The Political Economy of Contemporary Africa*. Beverly Hills: Sage Publications.

Haan, Norma, et al. (eds.) (1983). *Social Science as Moral Inquiry*. New York: Columbia University Press.

Habermas, Jurgen (1975). *Legitimation Crisis*. Boston: Beacon Press.

Hadden, Jeffrey K. (1987). Religious Broadcasting and the Mobilization of the New Christian Right. *Journal for the Scientific Study of Religion* 26(1).

Hadden, Jeffrey K., and Anson Shupe (eds.) (1986). *Prophetic Religions and Politics: Religion and the Political Order*. New York: Paragon House.

Hadjor, Kofi Buenor, and Brian Wren (eds.) (1985). Christian Faith and Third World Liberation. *Third World Book Review* 1(4–5).

Haight, Roger (1988). Poverty and Liberation Theology. *New Catholic World*, May/June.

Hammond, Philip E. (1980). The Conditions for Civil Religion: A Comparison of the

United States and Mexico. In Robert Bellah and Philip Hammond (eds.), *Varieties of Civil Religion*. New York: Harper and Row.

—— (1983). Power Changes and Civil Religion: The American Case. In Albert Besgeson (ed.), *Crises in the World-System*. Beverly Hills: Sage Publications.

—— (ed.) (1985). *The Sacred in a Secular Age: Toward Revision in the Scientific Study of Religion*. Berkeley: University of California Press.

—— (1988). Religion and the Persistence of Identity. *Journal for the Scientific Study of Religion* 27(1).

Hanna, Mary T. (1979). *Catholics and American Politics*. Cambridge, Mass.: Harvard University Press.

Hanratty, Dennis M. (1984). The Political Role of the Mexican Catholic Church: Contemporary Issues. *Thought* 59(233).

—— (1988). Church-State Relations in Mexico in the 1980s. *Thought* 63(250).

Hanson, Eric. O. (1980). *Catholic Politics in China and Korea*. Maryknoll, N.Y.: Orbis Press.

—— (1987). *The Catholic Church in World Politics*. Princeton, N.J.: Princeton University Press.

Harding, Vincent (1983). *There Is a River*. New York: Vintage Books.

Harmon, William (1985). Colour the Future Green? *Futures* 17(4).

Harrington, Michael (1983). *The Politics at God's Funeral*. New York: Holt, Rinehart and Winston.

Haskell, Gordon (1990). Democratic Stirrings in Bulgaria. *Dissent*.

Hastings, Adrian (1988). East, Central and Southern Africa. In Thomas Gannon (ed.), *World Catholicism in Transition*. New York: Macmillan.

Hauerwas, Stanley (1981). *A Community of Character*. Notre Dame, Ind.: University of Notre Dame Press.

—— (1985). *Against the Nations: War and Survival in a Liberal Society*. Minneapolis: Winston Press.

—— (1987). Will the Real Sectarian Stand Up? *Theology Today* 44(1).

—— (1988). The Sermon on the Mount, Just War and the Quest for Peace. *Concilium* (195).

—— (1989). *Christian Existence Today*. Durham, N.C.: Labyrinth Press.

Haughey, John C. (ed.) (1977). *The Faith That Does Justice: Examining the Christian Sources for Social Change*. New York: Paulist Press.

Healey, Joseph G. (1987). Four Africans Evaluate sccs in East Africa. *African Ecclesial Review* 29(5).

Hebblethwaite, Peter (1982). The Popes and Politics: Shifting Patterns in Catholic Social Doctrine. *Daedalus* 111(1).

—— (1986a). *Synod Extraordinary*. Garden City, N.Y.: Doubleday.

—— (1986b). *In the Vatican*. Bethesda, Md.: Adler and Adler.

—— (1988a). Changing Vatican Policies, 1965–85: Peter's Primacy and the Reality of Local Churches. In Thomas Gannon (ed.), *World Catholicism in Transition*. New York: Macmillan.

—— (1988b). Soundness, Docility Seem Criteria for Red Hat. *National Catholic Reporter*, June 17, p. 6.

Hegba, Meinrad (1988). The Evolution of Catholicism in West Africa: The Case of Cameroon. In Thomas Gannon (ed.), *World Catholicism in Transition*. New York: Macmillan.

Hehir, J. Bryan (1986). Church-State and Church-World: The Ecclesiological Implications. *CTSA Proceedings* 41.

—— (1989a). *Religion and Politics in the 1980s and 1990s: Evaluating the Catholic Position and Potential*. Lansing: Michigan Catholic Conference.

——— (1989b). Third World Debt and the Poor. *Origins* 18(36).

Heigh, John (1982). Basic Communities in Tanzania. *Pro Mundi Vita* 31.

Held, David (1987). *Models of Democracy*. Stanford, Calif.: Stanford University Press.

Hellwig, Monika (1983). Good News to the Poor: Do They Understand It Better? In James E. Hug (ed.), *Tracing the Spirit: Communities, Social Action, and Theological Reflection*. New York: Paulist Press.

Hempel, Carl (1965). *Aspects of Scientific Explanation*. New York: Free Press.

Hennelly, Alfred T. (1988). The Theology of Liberation's Origins, Content, and Impact. *Thought* 63(249).

Hennessey, James (1981). *American Catholics: A History of the Roman Catholic Community in the United States*. Oxford: Oxford University Press.

Herberg, Will (1955). *Protestant, Catholic, Jew*. New York: Harper and Row.

Herman, Edward (1987). Definitional Issues and the Law. *Crime and Social Justice*, nos. 27–28.

Herman, Edward, and Noam Chomsky (1988). *Manufacturing Consent: The Political Economy of the Mass Media*. New York: Pantheon Books.

Herrera, Marina (1987). Hispanic Catechesis: Teach All Peoples. *The Catechist* 21(4).

Heschel, Abraham J. (1962). *The Prophets*. New York: Harper and Row.

Hewett, W. E. (1988). Christian Base Communities (cebs): Structure, Orientation and Sociopolitical Thrust. *Thought* 63(249).

——— (1990). Religion and the Consolidation of Democracy in Brazil: The Role of the Communidades Eclesiais de Base (cebs). *Sociological Analysis* 50(2).

Higgins, George G. (1988). The Catholic Moment. *America*, July 2.

Higham, John (1981). *Strangers in the Land: Patterns of American Nativism, 1860–1925*. New York: Atheneum.

Hinchberger, Bill (1989). Brazil: The Left in City Hall. *NACLA* 23(1).

Hinkelammert, Franz (1986). *The Ideological Weapons of Death*. Maryknoll, N.Y.: Orbis.

Hirsch, Fred (1975). *Social Limits to Growth*. Cambridge, Mass.: Harvard University Press.

Hodgson, Marshall (1974). *The Venture of Islam: Conscience and History in a World Civilization*. Chicago: University of Chicago Press.

Hoffman, Stanley (1981). *Duties Beyond Borders*. Syracuse, N.Y.: Syracuse University Press.

Hoge, Dean (1979). A Test of Theories of Denominational Growth and Decline. In Dean Hoge and David Roozen (eds.), *Understanding Church Growth and Decline, 1950–1978*. New York: Pilgrim Press.

——— (1981). *Converts, Dropouts, Returnees: A Study of Religious Change Among Catholics*. New York: Pilgrim Press.

Hoge, Dean R., and David A. Roozen (eds.) (1979). *Understanding Church Growth and Decline, 1950–1978*. New York: Pilgrim Press.

Holland, Joe (1988). Beyond a Privatized Spirituality? *New Catholic World*, July/August.

Holland, Joe, and Anne Barsanti (eds.) (1988). *American and Catholic: The New Debate*. South Orange, N.J.: Pillar Books.

Holland, Joe, and Peter Henriot (1983). *Social Analysis*. Maryknoll, N.Y.: Orbis Books.

Hollenbach, David (1977). A Prophetic Church and the Catholic Sacramental Imagination. In John C. Haughey (ed.), *The Faith That Does Justice: Examining the Christian Sources for Social Change*. New York: Paulist Press.

——— (1987). War and Peace in American Catholic Thought: A Heritage Abandoned? *Theological Studies* 48.

——— (1988). Notes on Moral Theology: 1987. *Theological Studies* 49.

—— (1989). The Common Good Revisited. *Theological Studies* 50.

Holli, Melvin, and Peter d'A. Jones (1984). *Ethnic Chicago*. Grand Rapids, Mich.: Eerdmans.

Hood, Erin (1990). Will Hungary's Church Keep Up with Change? *Christian Century*, January 3–10.

Hopkins, Terence K. and Immanuel Wallerstein (eds.) (1982). *World-Systems Analysis: Theory and Methodology*. Beverly Hills: Sage Publications.

Horsley, Richard A., and John Hanson (1985). *Bandits, Prophets and Messiahs: Popular Movements at the Time of Jesus*. New York: Harper and Row.

Horvat, Branko (1983). *The Political Economy of Socialism*. Armonk, N.Y.: M. E. Sharpe.

Hoy, David C. (ed.) 1986. *Foucault: A Critical Reader*. Oxford: Basil Blackwell.

Hug, James E. (ed.) 1983. *Tracing the Spirit: Communities, Social Action, and Theological Reflection*. New York: Paulist Press.

Human Rights (entire issue) (1983). *Daedalus* 112(4).

Hundley, Tom (1988) Church Closings Stun Catholics in Detroit. *Chicago Tribune*, October 16, p. 3.

Hunthausen, Raymond (1988). "To Discover an Ethic That Is Social. *Origins* 18(5).

Hyett, Catherine (1987). Theories of Dependency. *The Ecumenist*, March/April.

Illich, Ivan (1977). *Toward a History of Needs*. New York: Bantam Books.

James, William (1958). *The Varieties of Religious Experience*. New York: New American Library.

Janz, Dennis (1990). Rooting Out Religion: The Albanian Experiment. *Christian Century*, July 25–August 1.

Jefferson, Gary, and Peter Petri (1990). From Marx to Markets. *Challenge*, September/October.

Jeffrey, Paul (1988). Nicaragua: Cardinal Obando Balks at Meeting Mothers of Disappeared. *Latinamerica Press*, October 20, p. 1.

Jennings, Theodore W. (ed.) (1985). *The Vocation of the Theologian*. Philadelphia: Fortress Press.

Jewett, Robert (1983). *The Captain America Complex*. Berkeley, Calif.: Bear.

John XXIII, Pope (1963). *Pacem in Terris*. Reprinted in David J. O'Brien and Thomas A. Shannon (eds.), *Renewing the Earth: Catholic Documents on Peace, Justice and Liberation* (1977). Garden City, N.Y.: Image Books.

John Paul II, Pope (1979a). Homily at Yankee Stadium. *Origins* 9(4).

—— (1979b). *Redemptor Hominis*. Washington, D.C.: U.S. Catholic Conference.

—— (1981). *Laborem Exercens*. Washington, D.C.: U.S. Catholic Conference.

—— (1983). Threats to the Church's Unity. *Origins* 12(40).

—— (1987). Message to the Brazilian Bishops. *LADOC* 17(10).

—— (1988a). Faith and Culture. *Origins* 18(3).

—— (1988b). Solidarity and Interdependence. *Origins* 18(15).

—— (1988c). The Virtue of Solidarity. *Origins* 18F.

—— (1988d). *Sollicitudo Rei Socialis. Origins* 17(38).

—— (1991). *Centesimus Annus. National Catholic Reporter*, May 24, 1991.

Jorstad, Eric (1984). Sanctuary for Refugees: A Statement on Public Policy. *Christian Century*, March 14, p. 275.

Judd, Stephen (1987). The Seamy Side of Charity Revisited: American Catholic Contributions to Renewal in the Latin-American Church. *Missiology* 15(2).

Kalilombe, Patrick (1987). A Cry of the Poor in Africa. *African Ecclesial Review* 29(4).

—— (1988). Diakonia in Universal Context: An African Point of View. *Concilium* (198).

Kantowitz, Edward (1983). *Corporation Sole: Cardinal Mundelein and Chicago Catholicism*. Notre Dame, Ind.: University of Notre Dame Press.

Katzenstein, Peter (1985). *Small States in World Markets*. Ithaca, N.Y.: Cornell University Press.

Kavanaugh, John F. (1986). *Following Christ in a Consumer Society*. Maryknoll, N.Y.: Orbis Books.

Keat, Russell, and John Urry (1982). *Social Theory as Science*, 2nd ed. London: Routledge and Kegan Paul.

Kellerman, Bill (1987). Apologist of Power: The Long Shadow of Reinhold Niebuhr's Christian Realism. *Sojourners* 16(3).

Kelley, Dean (1972). *Why Conservative Churches Are Growing*. New York: Harper and Row.

——— (1979). Commentary: Is Religion a Dependent Variable? In Dean Hoge and David Roozen (eds.), *Understanding Church Growth and Decline, 1950–1978*. New York: Pilgrim Press.

Kelly, George Armstrong (1979). *The Battle for the American Church*. Garden City, N.Y.: Doubleday.

Kelly, Gerard (1987). Ecclesiological Contours: The Vatican Perspective. *New Blackfriars* 68(804).

Kennedy, Paul (1987). *The Rise and Fall of the Great Powers*. New York: Vintage Books.

Kim, Anselm K. (1984–85). The Vatican, Marxism and Liberation Theology. *Cross Currents* 34.

King, Wayne (1985). Activists to Persist in Assisting People Fleeing Latin Lands. *New York Times*, January 16, p. 1.

Kinsler, F. Ross (1983). *Ministry by the People*. Geneva: WCC Publications.

Klare, Michael, and Peter Kornbluh (eds.) (1988). *Low Intensity Warfare*. New York: Pantheon.

Klarreigh, Kathie (1988). Battle Over Firebrand Priest Splits Catholic Church. *Latinamerica Press*, December 15, p. 3.

Komonchak, Joseph A. (1988). Not Catholic Enough? *Commonweal*, March 11.

Kowalewski, David (1976). The Protest Uses of Symbolic Politics in the USSR. *Journal of Politics* 42.

——— (1980a). Protest for Religious Rights in the USSR: Characteristics and Consequences. *Russian Review* 39(4).

——— (1980b). The Protest Uses of Symbolic Politics: The Mobilization Function of Protester Symbolic Resources. *Social Science Quarterly* 61(1).

Kowalewski, David, and Arthur Greil (1990). Religion as Opiate: Church and Revolution in Comparative Structural Perspective. *Journal of Church and State* 32.

Kselman, Thomas A. (1986). Ambivalence and Assumption in the Consent of Popular Religion. In Daniel H. Levine (ed.), *Religion and Political Conflict in Latin America*. Chapel Hill: University of North Carolina Press.

Kuhn, Thomas S. (1970). *The Structure of Scientific Revolutions*, 2nd ed., enlarged. Chicago: University of Chicago Press.

Küng, Hans (1967). *The Church*. New York: Sheed and Ward.

——— (1976). *On Being a Christian*. New York: Doubleday.

Küng, Hans, Yves Congar, and Daniel O'Hanlon (eds.) (1964). *Council Speeches of Vatican II*. Glen Rock, N.J.: Paulist Press.

Küng, Hans, and Jurgen Moltmann (eds.) (1988). A Council for Peace. *Concilium* 195.

Küng, Hans, and Leonard Swidler (eds.) (1987). *The Church in Anguish*. New York: Harper and Row.

Küng, Hans, Josef van Ess, Heinrich von Stietencron, and Heinz Bechert (1986). *Christianity and the World Religions: Paths to Dialogue with Islam, Hinduism and Buddhism*. Garden City, N.Y.: Doubleday.

Laffin, Arthur J. (1987). Convicted of Conscience. *Christianity and Crisis*, November 23.

Laffin, Arthur J., and Anne Montgomery (eds.) (1987). *Swords into Plowshares: Non-violent Direct Action for Disarmament.* San Francisco: Harper and Row.

Langguth, Gerd (1986). *The Green Factor in German Politics: From Protest Movement to Political Party.* Boulder, Colo.: Westview Press.

Langton, Kenneth P. (1986). The Church, Social Consciousness, and Protest? *Comparative Political Studies* 19(3).

Larson, Roy (1987). Cardinal Bernadin: The Pope's Man in the Middle. *Chicago,* September.

Lasch, Christopher (1979). *The Culture of Narcissism.* New York: W. W. Norton.

—— (1989a). The Obsolescence of Left and Right. *New Oxford Review,* April.

—— (1989b). Politics and Culture. *Salmagundi,* no. 81.

Latinamerica Press (1988, July 7), p. 2. Unsigned article on 10th General Assembly of Latin American Conference of Religious.

—— (1988, July 21), p. 2. Unsigned article on election of Bishop Ricardo Durand as president of Peruvian Catholic Bishops' Conference.

—— (1988, July 28). Two unsigned articles on death threats against Bishop Pedro Casaldáliga of Brazil, and campaign by Paraguayan dictator Alfredo Stroessner to discredit progressive Catholics.

—— (1988, October 20), p. 2. Unsigned article on remarks on economic austerity measures from Bishop Albano Quinn of Peru.

—— (1988, October 20), p. 3. Unsigned article, "Bishop's Account of Rome Inquiry."

—— (1988, December 15), p. 2. Unsigned article on episcopal appointments in Peru.

—— (1989, January 26). Unsigned article on Bishop Dario Castrillon Hoyos, president of CELAM.

—— (1989, February 3), p. 2. Unsigned article on Methodist bishops of Latin America on external debt.

—— (1989, March 9), p. 2. Unsigned article on BCCs in Santiago, Chile, asking for the resignation of Auxiliary Bishop Antonio Moreno.

—— (1989, March 23), p. 7. Unsigned article on new "Department for Special Operations in Low Intensity Conflict" at School of the Americas in Panama.

—— (1989, March 23). Unsigned article on kidnap and torture of Luis Tenderini, president of Justice and Peace Commission of the archdiocese of Olinda and Recife.

Lauritzen, Paul (1987). Is "Narrative" Really a Panacea? The Use of "Narrative" in the Work of Metz and Hauerwas. *Journal of Religion* 67(3).

Lazere, Donald (ed.) (1987). *American Media and Mass Culture.* Berkeley: University of California Press.

Lee, Bernard J., and Michael Cowan (1986). *Dangerous Memories.* Kansas City: Sheed and Ward.

Lee, Martin A., and Pia Gallegos (1987). Gustavo Gutiérrez: with the Poor. *Christianity and Crisis,* April 6.

Leege, David C., and Joseph Gremillion (eds.) (1984–86). *Notre Dame Study of Catholic Parish Life.* Notre Dame, Ind.: Institute for Pastoral and Social Ministry and Center for the Study of Contemporary Society.

Lekachman, Robert (1976). *A History of Economic Ideas.* New York: McGraw-Hill.

Leo XIII, Pope (1891). *Rerum Novarum.* Reprinted in *Five Great Encyclicals* (1939). New York: Paulist Press.

Lernoux, Penny (1979). The Long Path to Puebla. In John Eagleson and Philip Scharper (eds.), *Puebla and Beyond.* Maryknoll, N.Y.: Orbis Books.

—— (1980). *Cry of the People.* Middlesex: Penguin Books.

—— (1988). Shadow Darkening Church of Poor. *National Catholic Reporter,* June 17, p. 7.

—— (1989). *People of God.* New York: Viking.

Levine, Daniel H. (ed.) (1979a). *Churches and Politics in Latin America*. Beverly Hills: Sage Publications.

——— (1979b). Religion and Politics, Politics and Religion. In Daniel H. Levine (ed.), *Churches and Politics in Latin America*. Beverly Hills: Sage Publications.

——— (1981). *Religion and Politics in Latin America: The Catholic Church in Venezuela and Colombia*. Princeton, N.J.: Princeton University Press.

——— (1984a). Popular Organizations and the Church: Thoughts from Colombia. *Journal of Interamerican Studies and World Affairs* 26(1).

——— (1984b). Religion and Politics: Dimensions of Renewal. *Thought* 59(233).

——— (ed.) (1986a). *Religion and Political Conflict in Latin America*. Chapel Hill: University of North Carolina Press.

——— (1986b). Religion, the Poor and Politics in Latin America Today. In Daniel H. Levine (ed.), *Religion and Political Conflict in Latin America*. Chapel Hill: University of North Carolina Press.

——— (1986c). Colombia: The Institutional Church and the Popular. In Daniel H. Levine (ed.), *Religion and Political Conflict in Latin America*. Chapel Hill: University of North Carolina Press.

——— (1986d). Conflict and Renewal. In Daniel H. Levine (ed.), *Religion and Political Conflict in Latin America*. Chapel Hill: University of North Carolina Press.

——— (1987a). From Church and State to Religion and Politics and Back Again. *World Affairs* 150(2).

——— (1987b). Holiness, Faith, Power, Politics [review essay]. *Journal for the Scientific Study of Religion* 26(4).

——— (1988). Assessing the Impact of Liberation Theology in Latin America. *Review of Politics* 50(2).

——— (1990a). Popular Groups, Popular Culture, and Popular Religion. *Comparative Studies in Society and History* 32(4).

——— (1990b). How Not to Understand Liberation Theology, Nicaragua, or Both [review essay]. *Journal of Interamerican Studies and World Affairs* 32(3).

Lindblom, Charles (1977). *Politics and Markets*. New York: Basic Books.

Linkh, Richard M. (1975). *American Catholicism and European Immigration, 1900–1924*. New York: Center for Migration Studies.

Lipietz, Alain (1985). *The Enchanted World: Inflation, Credit and the World Crisis*. London: Verso.

Lipset, Seymour Martin, and Earl Raab (1978). *The Politics of Unreason*, 2nd ed. Chicago: University of Chicago Press.

Lipsky, Michael (1968). Protest as a Political Resource. *American Political Science Review* 62.

Lobinger, Fritz (1987). Christian Base Communities in Africa and in Brazil. *African Ecclesial Review* 29(3).

Lohfink, Norbert (1986). The Kingdom of God and the Economy in the Bible. *Communio* 13.

Lovin, Robin W. (ed.) (1986). *Religion and American Public Life*. Mahwah, N.J.: Paulist Press.

Lowe, Philip (1986). The Withered "Greening" of British Politics: A Study of the Ecology Party. *Political Studies* 34.

Lubeck, Paul (1979). Islam and Resistance in Northern Nigeria. In Walter L. Goldfrank (ed.), *The World-System of Capitalism: Past and Present*. Beverly Hills: Sage Publications.

Lucas, George R., Jr., and Thomas W. Ogletree (eds.) (1976). *Lifeboat Ethics: The Moral Dimensions of World Hunger*. New York: Harper and Row.

Luke, Tim (1989). *Screens of Power: Ideology, Domination and Resistance in Informational Society*. Champaign: University of Illinois Press.

McBrien, Richard (1970). *Church: The Continuing Quest.* New York: Newman/Paulist Press.

——— (1981). *Catholicism.* 2 vols. Minneapolis: Winston Press.

——— (1982). The Church of Tomorrow. In Regina Coll (ed.), *Women and Religion: A Reader for the Clergy.* New York: Paulist Press.

——— (1987). *Caesar's Coin: Religion and Politics in America.* New York: Macmillan.

——— (1988). Academic Freedom in Catholic Universities: The Emergence of a Party Line. *America,* December 3.

McCann, Dennis (1977). *Christian Realism and Liberation Theology: Practical Theologies in Conflict.* Maryknoll, N.Y.: Orbis Books.

——— (1987a). *New Experiment in Democracy: The Challenge for American Catholicism.* Kansas City: Sheed and Ward.

——— (1987b). There's Nobody Here But Us Post-Marxists. *Thought* 62(244).

McCann, Dennis P., and Charles Strain (1985). *Polity and Praxis: A Program for American Practical Theology.* Minneapolis: Winston Press.

McCarrick, Theodore (1987). The Integration of Catholics and American Political Life. *Origins* 17(5).

McCarthy, Thomas (1981). *The Critical Theory of Jurgen Habermas.* Cambridge, Mass.: MIT Press.

McClintock, Cynthia, and Abraham Lowenthal (eds.) (1983). *The Peruvian Experiment Reconsidered.* Princeton, N.J.: Princeton University Press.

McCloskey, Donald N. (1985). *The Rhetoric of Economics.* Madison: University of Wisconsin Press.

McCoy, Alfred (1984). *Priests on Trial.* Middlesex: Penguin Books.

McCoy, John A. (1987). The Catholic Church in Bolivia. *America,* October 24.

——— (1989). Liberation Theology and the Peruvian Church. *America,* June 6.

McDonagh, Enda (1980). *Church and Politics: From Theology to a Case Study of Zimbabwe.* Notre Dame, Ind.: University of Notre Dame Press.

——— (1988). Liberating Resistance and Kingdom Values. *Concilium* 195.

McElroy, Robert (1988). Revisiting John Courtney Murray: The Question of Method in Public Theology. *New Catholic World,* July/August.

MacEwan, Arthur, and William K. Tabb (eds.) (1989). *Instability and Change in the World Economy.* New York: Monthly Review Press.

McGovern, Arthur (1981). *Marxism: An American Christian Perspective.* Maryknoll, N.Y.: Orbis Books.

——— (1986). Latin America and Dependency Theory. *This World* 14.

MacIntyre, Alasdair (1984). *After Virtue,* 2nd ed. Notre Dame, Ind.: University of Notre Dame Press.

McKinney, William, and Dean Hoge (1983). Community and Congregational Factors in the Growth and Decline of Protestant Churches. *Journal for the Scientific Study of Religion* 22(1).

MacMullen, Ramsay (1984). *Christianizing the Roman Empire, A.D. 100–400.* New Haven, Conn.: Yale University Press.

Madelin, Henri (1988). The Paradoxical Evolution of the French Catholic Church. In Thomas Gannon (ed.), *World Catholicism in Transition.* New York: Macmillan.

Maduro, Otto (1987). Notes for a South-North Dialogue in Mission from a Latin-American Perspective. *Missiology* 15(2).

——— (1988a). The Desacralization of Marxism within Latin American Liberation Theology. *Social Compass* 35(2–3).

——— (1988b). North- and Latin American Catholicism: From Oppressive Solitude toward Liberating Solidarity. *Review of Latin American Studies* 1(1).

Mahan, Brian, and L. Dale Richesin (eds.) (1981). *The Challenge of Liberation Theology: A First World Response.* Maryknoll, N.Y.: Orbis Books.

Mahoney, Roger (1988). Perspectives for Viewing the Social Concerns Encyclical. *Origins* 18(5).

Maier, Charles S. (ed.) (1987). *Changing Boundaries of the Political.* Cambridge: Cambridge University Press.

Mainwaring, Scott (1984). The Catholic Church, Popular Education and Political Change in Brazil. *Journal of Interamerican Studies and World Affairs* 26(1).

—— (1986). *The Catholic Church and Politics in Brazil, 1916–1985.* Stanford, Calif.: Stanford University Press.

Mainwaring, Scott, and Alexander Wilde (eds.) (1989). *The Progressive Church in Latin America.* Notre Dame, Ind.: University of Notre Dame Press.

Malone, James (1986). Presidential Address to U.S. Bishops. *Origins* 16(23), p. 396.

Maloney, Thomas J. (1988). The Catholic Social Justice Tradition and Liberation Theology. *Thought* 63(249).

Mannheim, Karl (1936). *Ideology and Utopia.* San Diego: Harcourt Brace Jovanovich.

Marable, Manning (1980). *From the Grassroots: Social and Political Essays Toward Afro-American Liberation.* Boston: South End Press.

—— (1983). *How Capitalism Underdeveloped Black America.* Boston: South End Press.

Maradiaga, Oscar Rodriguez (1989). Medellin's Pastoral Implications. *Origins* 18(44).

Marer, Paul (1990). Hungary Joins the West. *Challenge*, September/October.

Marsden, George (ed.) (1984). *Evangelicalism and Modern America.* Grand Rapids, Mich.: Eerdmans.

Maritain, Jacques (1951). *Man and the State.* Chicago: University of Chicago Press.

Martin, David (1988). Catholicism in Transition. In Thomas Gannon (ed.), *World Catholicism in Transition.* New York: Macmillan.

Martin, T. R., and Gene Laczniak (1988). Executives' Scoreboard: CEOs Respond to the Economics Pastoral. *Commonweal*, June 3.

Martins, José Pedro (1988a). Brazil: Church Uneasy Over Recent Papal Appointments. *Latinamerica Press*, May 12.

—— (1988b). Brazil's Catholic Church, Vatican, Face Off on Media Control, Exercise of Power. *Latinamerica Press*, September 22, p. 5.

—— (1988c). Rome's Evangelization Drive Worries Brazilian Bishops. *Latinamerica Press*, July 14, p. 3.

—— (1989a). Brazil: Division of São Paulo Diocese Hits at Cardinal Arns. *Latinamerica Press*, April 6, p. 7.

—— (1989b). Brazilian Churches' Solution to Debt Problem: Don't Pay. *Latinamerica Press*, May 11, p. 3.

Marty, Martin (1976). *A Nation of Behavers.* Chicago: University of Chicago Press.

Marty, Martin, Dean Peerman (eds.) (1971). *New Theology No. 5.* New York: Macmillan.

May, Lary (ed.) (1989). *Recasting America: Culture and Politics in the Age of the Cold War.* Chicago: University of Chicago Press.

Mayer, Milton (1969). *On Liberty: Man v. the State.* Santa Barbara, Calif.: Center for the Study of Democratic Institutions.

Mazrui, Ali A. (1983). Exit Visa from the World System: Dilemmas of Economic and Cultural Disengagement. In Altaf Gauhar (ed.), *South-South Strategy.* London: Third World Foundation.

Mbiti, John (1972). Church and State: A Neglected Element of Christianity in Contemporary Africa. *African Theological Journal* 5.

Meconis, Charles A. (1979). *With Clumsy Grace: The American Catholic Left, 1961–1975.* New York: Seabury.

Meeks, Wayne A. (1983). *The First Urban Christians.* New Haven, Conn.: Yale University Press.

Melucci, Alberto (1980). The New Social Movements: A Theoretical Approach. *Social Science Information* 19.
———— (1985). The Symbolic Challenge of Contemporary Movements. *Social Research* 52.
Merton, Thomas (1966). *Raids on the Unspeakable.* New York: New Directions.
———— (1968a). *Conjectures of a Guilty Bystander.* Garden City, N.Y.: Doubleday.
———— (1968b). *Faith and Violence.* Notre Dame, Ind.: University of Notre Dame Press.
———— (1980). *The Nonviolent Alternative.* Notre Dame, Ind.: University of Notre Dame Press.
Mette, Norbert (1988). Solidarity with the Lowliest: Parish Growth Through the Witness of Practical Service. *Concilium* 198.
Metz, Johann (ed.) (1971). Perspectives of a Political Ecclesiology. *Concilium* 66.
———— (1981). *The Emergent Church.* New York: Crossroad.
Mexican Bishops of the Southern Pacific Region (1986). The Gospel and Temporal Goods. *LADOC* 16(4).
Mignone, Emilio F. (1988). *Witness to the Truth: The Complicity of Church and Dictatorship in Argentina.* Maryknoll, N.Y.: Orbis Books.
Militarization of Sub-Saharan Africa, The (1985). *Pro Mundi Vita,* Dossiers 34–35.
Miller, William D. (1982). *Dorothy Day: A Biography.* New York: Harper and Row.
Miscamble, Wilson D. (1987). Sectarian Passivism? *Theology Today* 44(1).
Mojes, Paul (1990). The Rehabilitation of Religion in the USSR and Eastern Europe. *Christian Century,* July 25–August 1.
Molineaux, David J. (1988). Peru: Bishops Turn Rightward but Grass-roots Church Thrives. *Latinamerica Press,* June 2, p. 3.
———— (1989). *LP* Interview with Brazil's Frei Betto. *Latinamerica Press,* January 26, p. 3.
Moltmann, Jurgen (1983). *The Power of the Powerless.* New York: Harper and Row.
Moore, Barrington (1966). *Social Origins of Dictatorship and Democracy.* Boston: Beacon Press.
Mott, Michael (1984). *The Seven Mountains of Thomas Merton.* Boston: Houghton-Mifflin.
Munoz, Heraldo (ed.) (1981). *From Dependency to Development.* Boulder, Colo.: Westview Press.
Murnion, Philip J. (1982). Strategies for Parish Renewal. In *The Parish Project Reader: Selected Articles from the Parish Ministry Newsletter, 1979–1982.* Washington, D.C.: National Conference of Catholic Bishops.
Murray, John Courtney (1960). *We Hold These Truths: Catholic Reflections on the American Proposition.* Kansas City: Sheed and Ward.
Mushaben, Joyce M. (1986). The Changing Structure and Function of Parties: The Case of the West German Left. *Polity* 18.
Musto, Ronald (1986). *The Catholic Peace Tradition.* Maryknoll, N.Y.: Orbis Books.
Mveng, Englebert (1988). African Liberation Theology. *Concilium* 199.
Myers, Ched (1988). *Binding the Strong Man.* Maryknoll, N.Y.: Orbis Books.
Narraro, Juan Carlos (1988). Too Weak for Change: Past and Present in the Venezuelan Church. In Thomas Gannon (ed.), *World Catholicism in Transition.* New York: Macmillan.
National Conference of Catholic Bishops (1983). *The Challenge of Peace: God's Promise and Our Response.* Washington, D.C.: U.S. Catholic Conference.
———— (1986). *Economic Justice for All: Catholic Social Teaching and the U.S. Economy.* Washington, D.C.: U.S. Catholic Conference.
———— (1987). National Pastoral Plan for Hispanic Ministry. *Origins* 17(26).
National Conference of Catholic Bishops, Committee on the Parish (1980). *The Parish: A People, A Mission, A Structure.* Washington, D.C.: U.S. Catholic Conference.

National Federation of Priests' Councils (n.d.). *Basic Christian Communities: The United States Experience*. Chicago.

——— (n.d.). *Developing Basic Christian Communities: A Handbook*. Chicago.

Neuhaus, Richard John (1984). *The Naked Public Square*, 2nd ed. Grand Rapids, Mich.: Eerdmans.

——— (1986). The Catholic Moment. *National Review*, November 7.

——— (1987). *The Catholic Moment: The Paradox of the Church in the Postmodern Era*. New York: Harper and Row.

——— (1991). The Pope Affirms the "New Capitalism." *Wall Street Journal*, May 3.

Neusner, Jacob (1985). *Israel in America*. Boston: Beacon Press.

New Catholic World (1984). The Economy (entire issue). *New Catholic World* 227(1360).

Niebuhr, H. Richard (1951). *Christ and Culture*. New York: Harper and Row.

——— (1959). *The Social Sources of Denominationalism*. New York: Meridian Books.

Niebuhr, Reinhold (1932). *Moral Man and Immoral Society*. New York: Charles Scribner's Sons.

——— (1943). *The Nature and Destiny of Man*, Vols. I and II. New York: Charles Scribner's Sons.

——— (1952). *The Irony of American History*. New York: Charles Scribner's Sons.

——— (ed.) (1971). *Marx and Engels on Religion*. New York: Schocken.

Njoroge, Lawrence (1987). African Christianity: A Portrait. *Chicago Studies* 26(2).

Noble, David F. (1984). *Forces of Production: A Social History of Industrial Automation*. New York: Alfred A. Knopf.

Nouwen, Henri (1983). *Gracias!: A Latin American Journal*. San Francisco: Harper and Row.

Novak, Michael (1981). *Toward a Theology of the Corporation*. Washington, D.C.: American Enterprise Institute.

——— (1982). *The Spirit of Democratic Capitalism*. New York: Simon and Schuster.

——— (ed.) (1983). Moral Clarity in the Nuclear Age. *National Review*, April 1.

——— (1984). Liberation Theology in Practice. *Thought* 59.

——— (1986). *Will It Liberate? Questions About Liberation Theology*. New York: Paulist Press.

O'Brien, David (1968). *American Catholics and Social Reform: The New Deal Years*. New York: Oxford University Press.

——— (1986). The Historical Context of North American Theology: The U.S. Story. *CTSA Proceedings* 41.

O'Brien, David, and Thomas Shannon (eds.) (1977). *Renewing the Earth: Catholic Documents on Peace, Justice and Liberation*. New York: Doubleday.

Oakes, Guy (1988–89). Farewell to *The Protestant Ethic? Telos* 78.

Obbo, Christine (1980). *African Women: Their Struggle for Economic Independence*. London: Zed Books.

Offe, Claus (1985a). *Contradictions of the Welfare State*. Cambridge, Mass.: MIT Press.

——— (1985b). *Disorganized Capitalism*. Cambridge, Mass.: MIT Press.

——— (1985c). New Social Movements: Challenging the Boundaries of Institutional Politics. *Social Research* 52.

Olson, Mancur, Jr. (1965). *The Logic of Collective Action*. Cambridge, Mass.: Harvard University Press.

Ophuls, William (1977). *Ecology and the Politics of Scarcity*. San Francisco: W. H. Freeman.

"Other" Model of Church in Latin America, The (1989). *LADOC New Keyhole Series* 4(3).

Ottenweller, Albert (1978). Parish Ministry: The Old and the New. In Evelyn Eaton

Whitehead (ed.), *The Parish in Community and Ministry*. New York: Paulist Press.

Packard, Jerrold M. (1985). *Peter's Kingdom: Inside the Papal City*. New York: Charles Scribner's Sons.

Paige, Jeffrey (1975). *Agrarian Revolution*. New York: Free Press.

Pals, Daniel (1986). Reduction and Belief: Recent Attacks on the Doctrine of Irreducible Religion. *Journal of Religion* 66.

Palumbo, Gene (1983). CELAM to Study "People's Church." *National Catholic Reporter*, March 25.

Pannikar, Raimundo (1973). *Worship and Secular Man*. Maryknoll, N.Y.: Orbis Books.

Pastor, Manuel (1989). Latin America, the Debt Crisis, and the International Monetary Fund. *Latin American Perspectives* 16(1).

Pastoral Team of Bambamarca (1985). *Vamos Caminando: A Peruvian Catechism*. Maryknoll, N.Y.: Orbis Books.

Paul VI, Pope (1967). *Progressio Populorum*. Washington, D.C.: U.S. Catholic Conference.

———— (1975). *Evangelii Nuntiandi*. Washington, D.C.: U.S. Catholic Conference.

Paus, Eva (1989). Direct Foreign Investment and Economic Development in Latin America: Perspectives for the Future. *Journal of Latin American Studies* 21.

Pawlikowski, John, and Donald Senior (eds.) (1984). *Biblical and Theological Reflections on the Challenge of Peace*. Wilmington, Del.: Michael Glazier.

Payer, Cheryl (1974). *The Debt Trap: The International Monetary Fund and the Third World*. New York: Monthly Review Press.

———— (1982). *The World Bank*. New York: Monthly Review Press.

Payment of the Foreign Debt (1986). *LADOC New Keyhole Series* 4.

Pelikan, Jaroslav (1985). *Jesus Through the Centuries*. New York: Harper and Row.

Perovick, Anthony N., Jr. (1985). Mysticism and the Philosophy of Science. *Journal of Religion* 65.

Perrin, Norman, and Dennis Duling (1982). *The New Testament: An Introduction*. San Diego: Harcourt Brace Jovanovich.

Persaud, Thakoor (1980). *Conflicts Between Multinational Corporations and Less Developed Countries: The Case of Bauxite Mining in the Caribbean with Special Reference to Guyana*. New York: Arno Press.

Peruvian Bishops' Conference (1988). Poverty, the Most Fundamental Violence. *LADOC* 18.

Philippine Bishops' Conference (1989). Philippine Bishops' Statement on Biblical Fundamentalism. *Origins* 18(37).

Piccone, Paul (1988). Reinterpreting 1968: Mythology on the Make. *Telos* 77.

———— (1988–89). Rethinking Protestantism, Capitalism and a Few Other Things. *Telos* 78.

Piehl, Mel (1982). *Breaking Bread: The Catholic Worker and the Origin of Catholic Radicalism in America*. Philadelphia: Temple University Press.

Pieris, Aloysius (1988). *An Asian Theology of Liberation*. Maryknoll, N.Y.: Orbis Books.

Pike, Fredrick B. (1988). Religion and Utopia in Peru: From Aprismo to Liberation Theology. *Thought* 63(250).

Pius XI, Pope (1931). *Quadragesimo Anno*. Reprinted in *Five Great Encyclicals* (1939). New York: Paulist Press.

Piven, Frances Fox, and Richard Cloward (1977). *Poor People's Movements*. New York: Vintage Press.

Pizzorno, Alessandro (1987). Politics Unbound. In Charles S. Maier (ed.), *Changing Boundaries of the Political*. Cambridge: Cambridge University Press.

Polanyi, Karl (1968). Aristotle Discovers the Economy. In George Dalton (ed.), *Primi-*

tive, *Archaic and Modern Economies: Essays of Karl Polanyi*. New York: Anchor Books.

Pontifical Justice and Peace Commission (1987). An Ethical Approach to the International Debt Question. *Origins* 16(34).

Popkin, Samuel (1979). *The Rational Peasant: The Political Economy of Rural Society in Vietnam*. Berkeley: University of California Press.

Pravera, Kate (1981). The United States: Realities and Responses. *Christianity and Crisis*, September 21.

Provost, James, and Knut Walf (eds.) (1988). Power in the Church. *Concilium* 197.

Quevedo, Orlando B. (1982). Pastoral Letter on the Small Christian Communities. *Pro Mundi Vita* 31.

Rahner, Karl (1979). Toward a Fundamental Theological Interpretation of Vatican II. *Theological Studies* 40.

Ratzinger, Joseph Cardinal (1985). *The Ratzinger Report*. San Francisco: Ignatius Press.

——— (1986). Church and Economy: Responsibility for the Future of the World Economy. *Communio* 13.

Rauff, Edward (1978). *Why People Join the Church*. New York: Pilgrim Press.

Rayan, Samuel (1988). Third World Theology: Where Do We Go from Here? *Concilium* 199.

Reese, Thomas (1988). Archbishop Lefebvre: Moving Toward Schism? *America*, June 4.

——— (1989). *Archbishop: Inside the Power Structure of the American Catholic Church*. San Francisco: Harper and Row.

Reichley, A. James (1985). *Religion in American Public Life*. Washington, D.C.: Brookings Institution.

Reilly, Charles (1986). Latin America's Religious Populists. In Daniel H. Levine (ed.), *Religion and Political Conflict in Latin America*. Chapel Hill: University of North Carolina Press.

Religion and Education (entire issue) (1988). *Daedalus* 117(2).

Religion and Socialism [cover story] (1988). *Social Change and Development* (Harare) 21.

Religion in Communist Dominated Areas (1988). Theses of Czechoslovak Catholics 27(1).

Religious Liberty and Eastern Europe (1990). *Church and State*, 43(8).

Religious Right, The (special issue) (1987). *Covert Action Information Bulletin* 27.

Religious Take Rights Office Diocese Drops (1989). *National Catholic Reporter*, May 19, p. 7.

Report of the Diocese of Nampula, Mozambique (1978). Church and Revolution. *Pro Mundi Vita* 17.

Richard, Pablo (1988). The Theological Literature of Latin America. *Concilium* 199.

Rifkin, Jeremy (1980). *Entropy*. New York: Viking.

Rifkin, Jeremy, and Ted Howard (1979). *The Emerging Order: God in the Age of Scarcity*. New York: Putnam.

Robbins, Thomas, and Dick Anthony (eds.) (1981). *In Gods We Trust: New Patterns of Religious Pluralism in America*. New Brunswick, N.J.: Transaction Books.

Robertson, Roland (1985). The Sacred and the World System. In Philip Hammond (ed.) *The Sacred in a Secular Age: Toward Revision in the Scientific Study of Religion*. Berkeley: University of California Press.

Robertson, Roland, and Joann Chirico (1985). Humanity, Globalization, and Worldwide Religious Resurgence: A Theoretical Explanation. *Sociological Analysis* 463.

Robichaud, Paul (1988). Catholic America Goes to War. *New Catholic World*, July/August.

Rodinson, Maxime (1974). *Islam and Capitalism*. London: Allen Lane.

Rodney, Walter (1982). *How Europe Underdeveloped Africa.* Washington, D.C.: Howard University Press.

Roelofs, H. Mark (1988). Liberation Theology: The Recovery of Biblical Radicalism. *American Political Science Review* 82(2).

Rojas, Jorge (1989). Chile: Catholic Church Debates Pardon for Rights Offenders. *Latinamerica Press*, February 3, p. 6.

Rome and the African Churches (1986). *Pro Mundi Vita*, Dossiers 37–38.

Romero, C. Gilbert (1985). Self-Affirmation of the Hispanic Church. *The Ecumenist* 23(3).

Romero, Oscar (1981). *A Martyr's Message of Hope* (sermons). Kansas City: Celebration Books.

Roof, Wade Clark, and William McKinney (1987). *American Mainline Religion.* New Brunswick, N.J.: Rutgers University Press.

Roozen, David (1984). What Hath the 1970s Wrought Religion in America? In Constant Jacquet (ed.), *Yearbook of American and Canadian Churches.* Nashville: Abingdon.

Roozen, David A., William McKinney, and Jackson Carroll (1984). *Varieties of Religious Presence: Mission in Public Life.* New York: Pilgrim Press.

Ross, John (1988). Mexico: Catholic Church Losing Flock to Evangelical Religions. *Latinamerica Press*, October 10, p. 1.

Rostow, W. W. (1960). *The Stages of Economic Growth.* London: Cambridge University Press.

——— (1980). *Why the Poor Get Richer and the Rich Slow Down.* Austin: University of Texas Press.

Rude, George (1980). *Ideology and Popular Protest.* New York: Pantheon.

Rudig, Wolfgang (1985). The Greens in Europe: Ecological Parties and the European Elections of 1984. *Parliamentary Affairs* 38.

Ruether, Rosemary (1970). *The Radical Kingdom: The Western Experience of Messianic Hope.* New York: Paulist Press.

——— (1972). *Liberation Theology.* New York: Paulist Press.

——— (1981). Basic Communities: Renewal at the Roots. *Christianity and Crisis*, October 21.

Rule, James (1990). Poland Today: Challenges, Problems, Doubts. *Dissent.*

Ryan, James L. (1989). *A Voice for Social Justice.* Lansing: Michigan Catholic Conference.

Sacred Congregation for the Doctrine of the Faith (1984). *Instruction Concerning Certain Aspects of Liberation Theology.* Vatican City.

——— (1986). Instruction on Christian Freedom and Liberation. Reprinted in *National Catholic Reporter*, April 25.

Said, Edward W. (1979). *Orientalism.* New York: Vintage Books.

Sanders, Thomas G. (1984). Catholicism and Authoritarianism in Chile. *Thought* 59(233).

——— (1988). Catholicism and Democracy: The Chilean Case. *Thought* 63(249).

Savage, John (1976). *The Apathetic and Bored Church Member.* Pittsfield, N.Y.: LEAD Consultants.

Sawyerr, Harry (1971). What is African Theology? *African Theological Journal* 4.

Schaar, John (1982). Review of *The Spirit of Democratic Capitalism. Nation* (234), March 24, p. 500.

Schacht, Joseph, and C. E. Bosworth (eds.) (1979). *The Legacy of Islam*, 2nd ed. Oxford: Oxford University Press.

Schillebeeckx, Edward (1981). *Ministry: Leadership in the Community of Jesus Christ.* New York: Crossroad.

Schmitter, Philippe, and Gerhard Lehmbruch (eds.) (1979). *Trends Toward Corporatist Intermediation*. Beverly Hills: Sage Publications.

Schreiter, Robert J. (1985). *Constructing Local Theologies*. Maryknoll, N.Y.: Orbis Books.

Schumpeter, Joseph A. (1950). *Capitalism, Socialism and Democracy*. New York: Harper and Row.

Schussler Fiorenza, Elisabeth (1984). *Bread Not Stone*. Boston: Beacon Press.

Scott, James (1976). *The Moral Economy of the Peasant*. New Haven, Conn.: Yale University Press.

―――― (1985). *Weapons of the Weak: Everyday Forms of Peasant Resistance*. New Haven, Conn.: Yale University Press.

Secret Military Document on Liberation Theology (1989). *LADOC New Keyhole Series* 4.

Segers, Mary C. (1988). Religious Convictions and Political Choice. *New Catholic World*, July/August.

Segundo, Juan Luis (1973). *The Community Called Church*. Maryknoll, N.Y.: Orbis Books.

―――― (1976). *The Liberation of Theology*. Maryknoll, N.Y.: Orbis Books.

―――― (1979). Capitalism versus Socialism: Crux Theologica. In Rosino Gibellini (ed.), *Frontiers of Theology in Latin America*. Maryknoll, N.Y.: Orbis Books.

―――― (1985). *Theology and the Church: A Response to Cardinal Ratzinger and a Warning to the Whole Church*. Minneapolis: Winston Press.

Seligson, Mitchell A., and Edward J. Williams (1981). *Maquiladoras and Migration Workers in the Mexico-United States Border Industrialization Program*. Austin: University of Texas Press.

Sen, Amartya (1983). Development: Which Way Now? *Economic Journal* 93.

Senghaas, Dieter (1985). *The European Experience: A Historical Critique of Development Theory*. Dover, Del.: Berg Publishers.

Setiloane, Gabriel M. (1975). Where Are We in African Theology? *African Theological Journal* 8(1).

17th Intelligence Conference of American Armies and Liberation Theology, The (1989). *LADOC New Keyhole Series* 4.

Sharpe, Eric J. (1986). *Comparative Religion: A History*. LaSalle: Open Court.

Shaull, Richard (1984). *Heralds of a New Reformation: The Poor of South and North America*. Maryknoll, N.Y.: Orbis Books.

Sheehan, Thomas (1986). *The First Coming: How the Kingdom of God Became Christianity*. New York: Vintage Books.

Sheridan, E. F. (ed.) (1987). *Do Justice! The Social Teaching of the Canadian Catholic Bishops (1945–1986)*. Sherbrooke: Editions Paulines.

Shinn, Roger L. (1987). Glimpses of Chinese Christianity. *Christianity and Crisis*, June 8.

Sibley, Mulford (1973). The Relevance of Classical Political Theory for Economy, Technology, and Ecology. *Alternatives* 2(2).

Sider, Ronald J. (1977). *Rich Christians in an Age of Hunger: A Biblical Study*. Downers Grove, Ill.: Inter-Varsity Press.

Siebel, Wigand (1988). The Exercise of Power in Today's Church. *Concilium* 197.

Simon, Michael A. (1982). *Understanding Human Action*. Albany: State University of New York Press.

Sin, Jaime (1987). Political Action: An Asian Viewpoint. *Origins* 17(20).

Skocpol, Theda (1977). Wallerstein's World System: A Theoretical and Historical Critique. *American Journal of Sociology* 82.

―――― (1979). *States and Social Revolutions*. Cambridge: Cambridge University Press.

Smart, Ninian (1973). *The Science of Religion and the Sociology of Knowledge.* Princeton, N.Y.: Princeton University Press.

—— (1976). *The Religious Experience of Mankind,* 2nd ed. New York: Charles Scribner's Sons.

—— (1985). Identity and Dynamic Phenomenology of Religion. *Journal of the Institute for the Study of Religion* 11(3).

Smith, Brian (1979). Churches and Human Rights in Latin America: Recent Trends on the Subcontinent. In Daniel H. Levine (ed.), *Churches and Politics in Latin America.* Beverly Hills: Sage Publications.

—— (1982). *The Church and Politics in Chile.* Princeton, N.J.: Princeton University Press.

—— (1986). Chile: Deepening the Allegiance of Working-Class Sectors to the Church in the 1970s. In Daniel H. Levine (ed.), *Religion and Political Conflict in Latin America.* Chapel Hill: University of North Carolina Press.

Smith, Michael P. (1983). *The Libertarians and Education.* London: George Allen and Unwin.

Smith, Wilfred Cantwell (1979). *Faith and Belief.* Princeton, N.J.: Princeton University Press.

—— (1981). *Towards a World Theology.* Philadelphia: Westminster Press.

—— (1982). *Religious Diversity.* New York: Crossroad.

Sobrino, Jon (1976). *Christology at the Crossroads.* Maryknoll, N.Y.: Orbis Books.

—— (1984). *The True Church and the Poor.* Maryknoll, N.Y.: Orbis Books.

—— (1987). *Jesus in Latin America.* Maryknoll, N.Y.: Orbis Books.

—— (1988). Unjust and Violent Poverty in Latin America. *Concilium* 195.

Sollicitudo Rei Socialis (special issue) (1988). *National Catholic Reporter,* May 27.

Song, C. S. (1986). *Theology from the Womb of Asia.* Maryknoll, N.Y.: Orbis Books.

Spretnak, Charlene (1986). *The Spiritual Dimensions of Green Politics.* Santa Fe, N. Mex.: Bear.

Spretnak, Charlene, and Fritjof Capra (1986). *Green Politics.* Santa Fe, N. Mex.: Bear.

Stafford, J. Francis (1987). This Home of Freedom. *Origins* 17(4).

Steinfels, Peter (1983). Michael Novak and His Ultrasuper Democraticapitalism. *Commonweal,* January 14.

Steinkamp, Hermann (1988). Diakonia in the Church of the Rich and the Church of the Poor: A Comparative Study in Empirical Ecclesiology. *Concilium* (198).

Stephens, John D. (1979). *The Transition from Capitalism to Socialism.* London: Macmillan.

Stinchcombe, Arthur L. (1983). *Economic Sociology.* New York: Academic Press.

Stockwell, John (1978). *In Search of Enemies.* New York: W. W. Norton.

Stringfellow, William (1966). *My People Is the Enemy.* Garden City, N.Y.: Doubleday.

—— (1973). *An Ethic for Christians and Other Aliens in a Strange Land.* Waco, Tex.: Word Books.

Stuhlmueller, Carroll. *Thirsting for the Lord.* Garden City, N.Y.: Doubleday.

Sullivan, William, and Richard Madsen (1988). The Bishops and Their Critics. *Commonweal,* February 26.

Suro, Roberto (1988). Pope Chooses 25 New Cardinals, Including Two American Prelates. *New York Times,* May 30, p. 1.

Sweeney, Ernest S. (1988). Conflict and Change in the Church in Latin America. *Thought* 63(249).

Tabb, William K. (ed.) (1986). *Churches in Struggle: Liberation Theologies and Social Change in North America.* New York: Monthly Review Press.

Talbot, John F. (1988). Religious Life in Solidarity. *America,* July 27.

Tawney, Roger H. (1947). *Religion and the Rise of Capitalism.* New York: Penguin Books.

Taylor, Mark Kline (1990). Whither Liberation Theology? [review essay]. *Christian Century*, December 12.

Theses of Czechoslovak Catholics (1988). *Religion in Communist Dominated Areas* 27(1).

Tilly, Charles (1978). *From Mobilization to Revolution*. Reading, Mass.: Addison-Wesley.

———— (1985). War Making and State Making as Organized Crime. In Peter Evans, Thede Skocpol, and Dietrich Rueschmeyer (eds.), *Bringing the State Back In*. Cambridge: Cambridge University Press.

Tipton, Steven M. (1982). *Getting Saved from the Sixties*. Berkeley: University of California Press.

Toolan, David (1988). Let the Bishops Take No Guff: An Interview with Eliot Janeway. *Commonweal*, June 3.

Torres, Sergio, and Virginia Fabella (eds.) (1978). *The Emergent Gospel: Theology for the Developing World*. Maryknoll, N.Y.: Orbis Books.

Tracy, David (1986). A Response to Gregory Baum. *CTSA Proceedings* 41.

Troeltsch, Ernst (1981). *The Social Teaching of the Christian Churches*, Vols. I and II. Chicago: University of Chicago Press.

Tucker, Robert (ed.) (1978). *The Marx-Engels Reader*. New York: W. W. Norton.

Ukpong, Justin (1988). Theological Literature from Africa. *Concilium* 199.

U.S. Catholic Conference Administrative Board (1987). Political Responsibility: Choices for the Future. *Origins* 17(21).

U.S. Catholic Conference Department of Social Development and World Peace (1974). Development-Dependency: The Role of Multinational Corporations. In Brian Benestad and Francis Butler (eds.) (1981), *Quest for Justice: A Compendium of Statements of the United States Catholic Bishops on the Political and Social Order, 1966–1980*. Washington, D.C.: United States Catholic Conference.

Vallier, Ivan (1970). *Catholicism, Social Control and Modernization in Latin America*. Englewood Cliffs, N.J.: Prentice-Hall.

VanDerLeeuw, G. (1986). *Religion in Essence and Manifestation*. Princeton, N.J.: Princeton University Press.

Van Dulmen, Richard (1988–89). Protestantism and Capitalism: Weber's Thesis in Light of Recent Social History. *Telos* 78.

Van Merrienboer, Edward (1988). The Poor as a Pastoral Option for Western Europe. *New Blackfriars* 69(813).

Vatican and Africa, The (cover story) (1985). *Africa Events* 1(8).

Viner, Jacob (1978). *Religious Thought and Economic Society*. Durham, N.C.: Duke University Press.

Waldmann, Irene (1988). *Education for Transformation*. Lansing: Michigan Catholic Conference.

Wallerstein, Immanuel (1974). *The Modern World-System, I: Capitalist Agriculture and the Origins of the European World-Economy in the Sixteenth Century*. New York: Academic Press.

———— (1979). *The Capitalist World-Economy*. London: Cambridge University Press.

———— (1980). *The Modern World-System, II: Mercantilism and the Consolidation of the European World-Economy, 1600–1750*. New York: Academic Press.

———— (1983). *Historical Capitalism*. London: Verso.

———— (1984). *The Politics of the World-Economy*. London: Cambridge University Press.

———— (1989). *The Modern World-System, III*. New York: Academic Press.

Wallerstein, Immanuel, William G. Martin, and Torry Dickinson (1982). Household Structures and Production Processes: Preliminary Theses and Findings. *Review* 3.

Wallis, Jim (1982). *The Call to Conversion*. San Francisco: Harper and Row.
────── (ed.) (1987). *The Rise of Christian Conscience*. San Francisco: Harper and Row.
Waltz, Kenneth (1979). *Theory of International Politics*. Reading, Mass.: Addison-Wesley.
Walzer, Michael (1965). *The Revolution of the Saints*. Cambridge, Mass.: Harvard University Press.
Wan-Tateh, Victor (1984). An Inquiry on the Relevance of Latin American Liberation Theology for West African Christianity Through a Cameroonian Case Study. Unpublished Th.D. thesis, Harvard University.
War in the Amazon (1989). *NACLA* 23(1).
Weakland, Rembert (1989). How Medellin and Puebla Influenced North America. *Origins* 18(44).
Weare, Kenneth M. (1984). The Church in Castro's Cuba. *Thought* 59.
Weber, Max (1964). *The Sociology of Religion*. Translated by Talcott Parsons. Boston: Beacon Press.
────── (1978). *Economy and Society*, Vol. I. Berkeley: University of California Press.
────── (1985). *The Protestant Ethic and the Spirit of Capitalism*. London: Unwin Paperbacks.
Weigand, William (1987). Third World Debt and U.S. Policy: Ethical Reflections. U.S. Catholic Conference, April.
Weigel, George (1986). John Courtney Murray and the Catholic Human Rights Revolution. *This World* 15.
────── (1987). *Tranquillitas Ordinis: The Present Failure and Future Promise of American Catholic Social Thought on War and Peace*. Oxford: Oxford University Press.
────── (1988). Reconceiving the Debate Over Religious Values in Public Life. *New Catholic World*, July/August.
────── (1989). *Catholicism and the Renewal of American Democracy*. New York: Paulist Press.
Weinstein, James (1984). *The Decline of Socialism in America: 1912–1925*. New Brunswick, N.J.: Rutgers University Press.
Wellisz, Stanislaw (1990). The Case of Poland. *Challenge*, September/October.
Weschler, Lawrence (1990). Poland Takes the Plunge. *Dissent*.
Whitehead, A. N. (1967). *Science and the Modern World*. New York: Free Press.
Whitehead, Evelyn Eaton (1978). *The Parish in Community and Ministry*. New York: Paulist Press.
Whitmore, Todd (ed.) (1989). *Ethics in the Nuclear Age: Strategy, Religious Studies, and the Churches*. Dallas: SMU Press.
Wiebe, Donald (1978). Is a Science of Religion Possible? *Social Science Review* 7(1).
────── (1985). A Positive Episteme for the Study of Religion. *Scottish Journal of Religious Studies*, Autumn.
Wilber, Charles (ed.) (1984). *The Political Economy of Development and Underdevelopment*, 3rd ed. New York: Random House.
Wilber, Charles (1991). Argument That the Pope "Baptized" Capitalism Holds No Water. *National Catholic Reporter*, June 7.
Wilber, Charles, and Kenneth P. Jameson (1983). *An Inquiry into the Poverty of Economics*. Notre Dame, Ind.: University of Notre Dame Press.
Wilber, Charles, and Kenneth P. Jameson (1984). Paradigms of Economic Development and Beyond. In Charles K. Wilber (ed.), *The Political Economy of Development and Underdevelopment*, 3rd ed. New York: Random House.
Williams, George Huntston (1981). *The Mind of John Paul II: Origins of His Thought and Action*. New York: Seabury.

Williams, William Appleman (1980). *Empire as a Way of Life*. Oxford: Oxford University Press.

Williams, William Appleman, Thomas McCormick, Lloyd Gardner, and Walter LeFeber (1989). *America in Vietnam: A Documentary History*. New York: W. W. Norton.

Wilmore, Gayraud S. (1984). *Black Religion and Black Radicalism*. Maryknoll, N.Y.: Orbis Books.

Wilson, Robert (1980). *Prophesy and Society in Ancient Israel*. Philadelphia: Fortress Press.

Windsor, Pat (1991). Neoconservatives Capitalize on Papal Encyclical. *National Catholic Reporter*, May 17.

Wink, Walter (1984). *Naming the Powers: The Language of Power in the New Testament*. Philadelphia: Fortress Press.

———— (1986). *Unmasking the Powers*. Philadelphia: Fortress Press.

Wirpsa, Leslie (1989). Colombia: Christians Organize to Protest Mounting Violence. *Latinamerica Press*, March 23, p. 7.

Witvliet, Theo (1985). *A Place in the Sun: An Introduction to Liberation Theology in the Third World*. Maryknoll, N.Y.: Orbis Books.

Wolf, Eric (1969). *Peasant Wars of the Twentieth Century*. New York: Harper and Row.

Wolfe, Alan (1981). *America's Impasse: The Rise and Fall of the Politics of Growth*. Boston: South End Press.

———— (1984). Toward a New Politics of the Left. *Nation*, September 22.

Wright, Erik Olin (1979). *Class, Crisis and the State*. London: Verso.

———— (1985). *Classes*. London: Verso.

Wright, Tennant C. (1987). Cuba: The Church Is Open. *America*, October 24.

Wuthnow, Robert (1980). World Order and Religious Movements. In Albert Bergeson (ed.), *Studies of the Modern World-System*. New York: Academic Press.

———— (1981). Comparative Ideology. *International Journal of Comparative Sociology* 22.

———— (1983). Cultural Crises. In Albert Bergeson (ed.), *Crises in the World-System*. Beverly Hills: Sage Publications.

Wuthnow, Robert, James D. Hunter, Albert Bergeson, and Edith Kurzweil (1984). *Cultural Analysis: The Work of Peter L. Berger, Mary Douglas, Michel Foucault and Jurgen Habermas*. London: Routledge and Kegan Paul.

Wynn, Wilton (1988). *Keepers of the Keys: John XXIII, Paul VI and John Paul II—Three Who Changed the Church*. New York: Random House.

Yoder, John Howard (1964). *The Christian Witness to the State*. Newton, Kan.: Faith and Life Press.

———— (1972). *The Politics of Jesus*. Grand Rapids, Mich.: Eerdmans.

———— (1984). *The Priestly Kingdom*. Notre Dame, Ind.: University of Notre Dame Press.

———— (1990). The Wider Setting of "Liberation Theology." *Review of Politics* 52(2).

Young, Henry J. (1977). *Major Black Religious Leaders, 1775–1940*. Nashville: Abingdon.

Zinn, Howard (1980). *A People's History of the United States*. New York: Harper and Row.

Zuesse, Evan M. (1985). *Ritual Cosmos: The Sanctification of Life in African Religions*. Athens: Ohio University Press.

INDEX

Michael L. Budde is Assistant Professor of
Political Science at Auburn University.

Library of Congress
Cataloging-in-Publication Data
Budde, Michael L.
The two churches : Catholicism and capitalism
in the World-System / Michael L. Budde.
Includes bibliographical references and index.
ISBN 0-8223-1229-8 (alk. paper)
1. Sociology, Christian (Catholic)
2. Capitalism—Religious aspects—Catholic
Church. 3. Catholic Church—Doctrines.
I. Title.
BX1753.B76 1992
261.8'5—dc20 91-42023CIP

DATE DUE
